CW01193033

KUWAIT, 1950–1965
Britain, the al-Sabah, and Oil

Shaikh Ahmad (r. 1921–50), January 1949. (From the BP Amoco Archive)

Kuwait, 1950–1965

Britain, the al-Sabah, and Oil

by
Simon C. Smith

*A British Academy
Postdoctoral Fellowship Monograph*

Published *for* THE BRITISH ACADEMY
by OXFORD UNIVERSITY PRESS

Oxford University Press, Great Clarendon Street, Oxford OX2 6DP

Oxford New York
Athens Auckland Bangkok Bogota Bombay
Buenos Aires Calcutta Cape Town Dar es Salaam
Delhi Florence Hong Kong Istanbul Karachi
Kuala Lumpur Madras Madrid Melbourne
Mexico City Nairobi Paris Singapore
Taipei Tokyo Toronto Warsaw

and associated companies in
Berlin Ibadan

Published in the United States by
Oxford University Press Inc., New York

© The British Academy, 1999

All rights reserved. No part of this publication may be reproduced,
stored in a retrieval system, or transmitted, in any form or by any means,
without prior permission in writing of the British Academy

British Library Cataloguing in Publication Data
Data available

ISBN 0-19-726197-3

Typeset by J&L Composition Ltd, Filey, North Yorkshire
Printed in Great Britain
on acid-free paper by
The Cromwell Press Limited
Trowbridge, Wilts

Contents

List of Illustrations	vi
Acknowledgements	vii
Map of Kuwait	viii
Introduction	1
1 Oil Expansion and its Consequences, 1950–1	15
2 Investment and Administrative Problems, 1952–5	36
3 Kuwait, Egypt, and the Suez Crisis, 1956	58
4 Kuwait and the Arab World, 1957–9	79
5 Kuwait's Progress towards Independence, 1959–61	100
6 Dependence and Independence, 1961–5	115
Conclusion	135
Appendices	
1 Oil Production and Revenue, 1946–65	143
2 Political Agents, Kuwait	144
3 Political Residents, Persian Gulf	145
4 British Politicians	146
5 Rulers of Kuwait	147
6 Al-Sabah Family Tree	148
Bibliography	149
Index	161

List of Illustrations

Frontispiece
Shaikh Ahmad (r. 1921–50), January 1949. (From the BP Amoco Archive)

Plates (between page 72 and page 73)
1. Shaikh Abdullah and C. J. Pelly at the former's investiture with the KCMG in February 1953. (St Antony's College, Oxford)
2. Shaikh Fahad (1906–1959). (Kuwait Ministry of Information)
3. Shaikh Abdullah, Sir William Fraser (Chairman, Anglo-Iranian Oil Company), Izzat Ja'far (Shaikh Abdullah's private secretary), June 1953. (From the BP Amoco Archive)
4. Shaikh Abdullah in the boardroom of the Kuwait Oil Company, June 1953. The seated figure fourth from the right is the managing director of the Kuwait Oil Company, C. A. P. Southwell. The seated figures sixth and seventh from the left are Shaikh Abdullah's representative in London, H. T. Kemp, and the State Secretary of Kuwait, Abdullah Mulla Saleh. (From the BP Amoco Archive)
5. C. A. P. Southwell and Shaikh Abdullah leaving Britannic House, June 1953. (From the BP Amoco Archive)
6. Shaikh Sa'ad and Shaikh Abdullah Mubarak at a review of Kuwait's police and public security forces, April 1961. (Kuwait Ministry of Information)
7. Discussions preceding Kuwait's achievement of full independence. From left to right: J. C. B. Richmond (Political Agent), Sir George Middleton (Political Resident), Edward Heath (Lord Privy Seal), Shaikh Abdullah. (Photograph Sir John Richmond)
8. Shaikh Sabah (Heir Apparent and Prime Minister) and Shaikh Abdullah arrive for the opening of the first session of Kuwait's National Assembly, 29 January 1963. (Kuwait Ministry of Information)

Endpapers
The oil terminal at Mina al Ahmadi in the late 1950s. (St Antony's College, Oxford)

Acknowledgements

In researching and preparing this book I have received generous assistance from a number of institutions and individuals. First, I should like to thank the British Academy for funding my research in the three years of my Postdoctoral Fellowship and publishing the resulting book through its PDF monograph scheme. I should also like to thank my host institution, Royal Holloway, University of London, and especially the members of the History Department for taking such a keen interest in my research and making me feel so at home during my time there. In particular I should like to record my gratitude to my 'mentor', Professor Tony Stockwell, and to the Head of Department during my Fellowship, Professor Francis Robinson. I also benefited greatly from discussions with Dr Matthew Jones, Dr Claudia Liebeskind, and Dr Catherine Schenk. My academic editor, Dr Vanessa Martin, made some helpful suggestions to improve the text. For reading the manuscript, I should like to thank Professor William Roger Louis and Professor Andrew Porter. My colleagues at the University of Hull, Simon Garrard and Richard Gorski, provided invaluable assistance in overcoming the innumerable technical problems which arose in producing the final manuscript. Thanks are also due to the staff of the Public Record Office, London; the Churchill Archives Centre, Cambridge; the BP Archive, Warwick; the Bodleian Library, Oxford; the Middle East Centre, St. Antony's College, Oxford; and the libraries of Royal Holloway, the School of Oriental and African Studies, the University of London, and the University of Hull. I am particularly grateful to the BP Archive for allowing the reproduction of photographs from the records of the Kuwait Oil Company. Furthermore, I must extend my thanks to the members of the academic seminars which I attended during my British Academy Fellowship, most notably the Commonwealth History/Decolonization Seminar at the Institute of Commonwealth Studies, the Imperial History Seminar at the Institute of Historical Research, and the Historians of Asia and the Middle East Seminar at Royal Holloway.

Finally, I should like to thank my mother and sister for supporting me through both good and bad times.

May 1998

Simon C. Smith
University of Hull

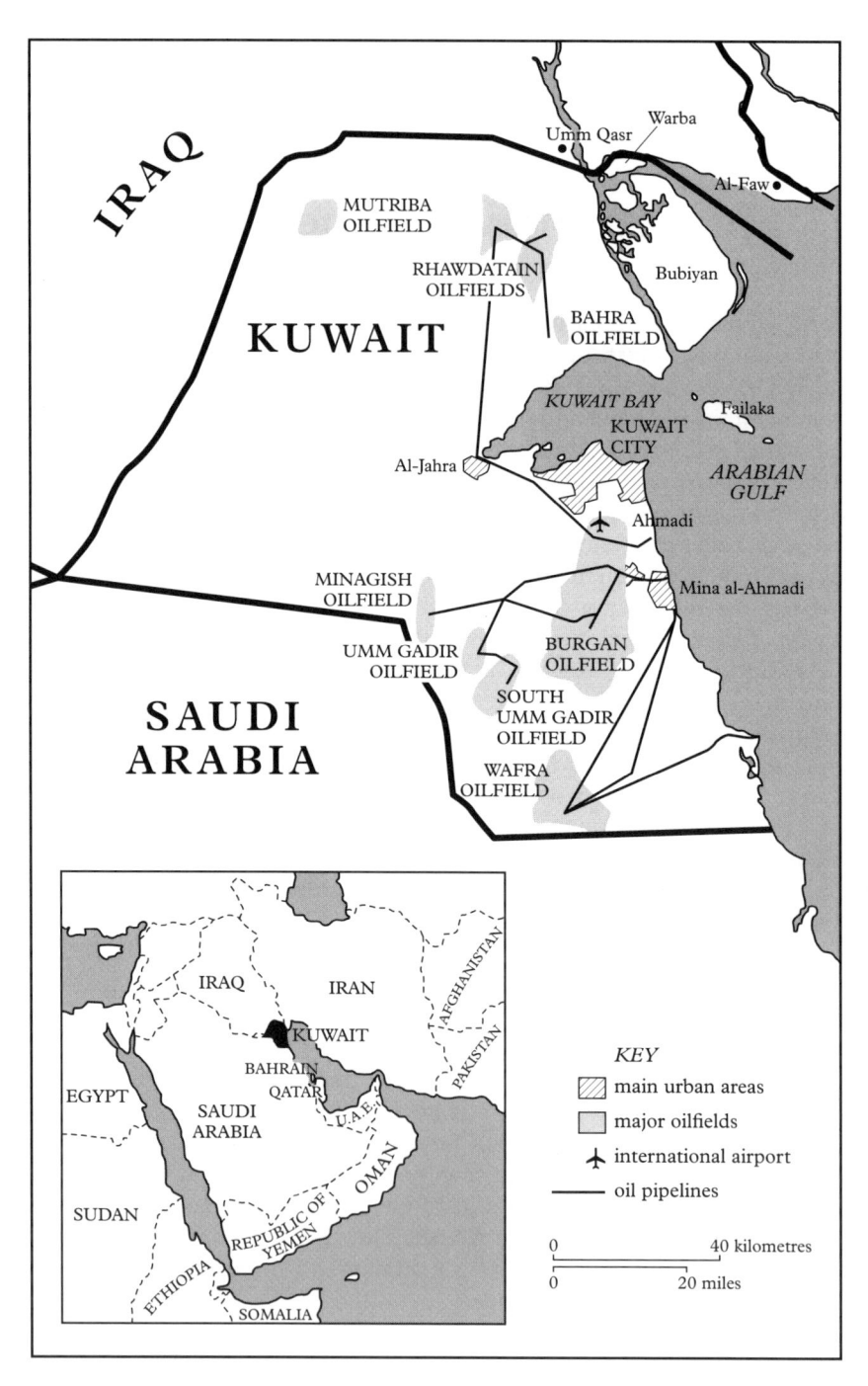

From Peter Mansfield, *Kuwait: Vanguard of the Gulf*, London: Hutchinson, 1990.

Introduction

This seems to me the chief problem of the Gulf—immense wealth suddenly poured into the hands of a few primitive Sheikhs whose territories consist of small areas of waterless desert which it is impossible to develop.[1]

'[B]oth the Shaikhs of the Persian Gulf and ourselves', noted the Political Resident in 1938, 'must realize, that the idea of popular movements ... have now permeated the Arab States, and must be taken account of.'[2] As these comments suggest, the growth of political consciousness in the Arab world posed a challenge not merely to the British but also to the traditional indigenous rulers. While many were displaced in either military coups or revolutions, the ruling family of Kuwait, the al-Sabah, survived the transition from dependent to independent status. Their survival is all the more noteworthy for the unprecedented strains placed on Kuwait, especially in the aftermath of the Second World War. Not only did the Shaikhdom face rapid economic growth as a result of the massive expansion in oil production, but it also confronted unparalleled pressure from other Arab countries jealous of Kuwait's new-found wealth. The ideological challenge presented by Arab nationalism was all the more dangerous to the al-Sabah for their semi-imperial relationship with Britain.

Despite the growing weight which Britain attached to the Gulf in general, and Kuwait in particular, the existing accounts of British imperial policy in the era of decolonization pay scant attention to the region.[3]

---

[1] Letter from John Troutbeck to B. A. B. Burrows, No. 104/25/2 (A), 8 April 1948, FO 371/68319.
[2] Letter from T. C. Fowle to R. T. Peel (India Office), No. 396-S, 18 July 1938, R/15/5/205.
[3] For example: R. F. Holland, *European Decolonization: An Introductory Survey*, Basingstoke: Macmillan, 1985; John Darwin, *Britain and Decolonisation: The Retreat from Empire in the Post-War World*, Basingstoke: Macmillan, 1988; A. N. Porter and A. J. Stockwell, *British Imperial Policy and Decolonization, 1938–1964*, 2 vols, Basingstoke: Macmillan, 1987 and 1989; John Darwin, *The End of the British Empire: The Historical Debate*, Oxford: Blackwell, 1991; P. J. Cain and A. G. Hopkins, *British Imperialism: Crisis and Deconstruction, 1914–1990*, London: Longman, 1993.

Nevertheless, Britain's presence in Kuwait and the Gulf increased after 1945, a development which stands in marked contrast with the great contraction of her imperial commitments elsewhere in the world. Although the loss of India in 1947 undermined Kuwait's traditional strategic importance to the imperial system, this was more than compensated for by the Shaikhdom's growing economic significance. Referring to Britain's defence budget early in 1962, an official of the Foreign Office emphasized that 'Kuwait is perhaps the only place where it can be shown to yield a positive dividend.'[4]

The rapid expansion in oil production from the late 1940s provided Britain with a strong new incentive to consolidate her position and maintain Kuwait's territorial integrity in the face of pressure from hostile Arab powers. In achieving these aims, Britain looked to the al-Sabah family. Indeed, the whole British presence came to rest on the fulcrum of indigenous monarchy. Unlike the Hashemite dynasty in Iraq, upon whom Britain also placed great reliance for the maintenance of her interests, the al-Sabah survived the upheavals of the post-war years.

The remarkable survival of the al-Sabah is ascribed by Jill Crystal to the new alliances which followed in the wake of large-scale oil production. On the one hand, the merchant class, which had traditionally challenged the ruling family for power, 'renounced their historical claim to participate in decision-making', in exchange for which the rulers 'guaranteed them a share of the oil revenues'.[5] In other words, the powerful economic elites traded power for wealth. On the other hand, oil revenues allowed the ruling family to pursue distributive policies designed to construct new political alliances. As Crystal states: 'Oil gave the rulers not only the freedom to turn away from their historical allies, but also the capacity to use the new oil-induced bureaucracies to develop new allies among state employees and recipients of the new state services.'[6]

This analysis possesses much explanatory power. In Kuwait, there was no flagrant distinction between self-indulgence by the ruling family and neglect of the ruled. Nevertheless, the subtle relationship which the al-Sabah wove with the British was also central to their ability to weather the persistent crises which rocked the Arab world. Although the ruling family ultimately relied on Britain for military protection from external threat, they avoided entering a stiflingly close relationship with the British. This was particularly important in the context of the growth of an Arab nationalism after 1945 which was rooted in anti-imperialism. The ability of the al-Sabah to subsume personal differences in the face of threats to the family

---

[4] Minute by J. G. S. Beith, 23 Jan 1962, FO 371/156670.
[5] Jill Crystal, *Oil and Politics in the Gulf: Rulers and Merchants in Kuwait and Qatar*, Cambridge: Cambridge University Press, 1995, p. 187.
[6] Ibid., p. 188.

as a whole was also crucial in their ability to survive. The dangers posed by family disunity were exposed in 1938 by the constitutional movement associated with the creation of a council or *Majlis*. Before analysing this episode, the political structure of Kuwait from the establishment of British protection in the late nineteenth century, through the upheavals of the First World War, to the development of oil production in the 1930s, will be examined.

I

Founded in the early eighteenth century, Kuwait town formed the focal point of a recognizable, though ill-defined, political entity.[7] In around 1716, the Bani Utub, a branch of the Aniza tribe, occupied Kuwait. The al-Sabah emerged as the leading political family, providing an unbroken line of rulers from the mid-eighteenth century.[8] With its strategic position at the head of the Gulf, Kuwait developed a vibrant economy based on pearling, shipbuilding, and long-distance commerce. Kuwait's international status, however, remained obscure. Referring to Kuwait in 1866, the former British Resident in the Persian Gulf, Arnold Kemball, observed: 'its Chief acknowledges fealty to the Sultan, and its numerous vessels carry the Ottoman flag, but its inhabitants, who are exclusively Arab pay neither tax nor tribute to the Turkish Treasury'.[9] In recognition of the help extended to the Turkish governor of Baghdad during a military expedition into the interior of the Arabian Peninsula in 1871, Shaikh Abdullah II was appointed as Ottoman *qaimmaqam*, or district governor.[10] This title, however, entailed no administrative duties and should be seen as an honour conferred on an individual for special services.[11] Four years later the Ottoman authorities included Kuwait in the new *vilayet*, or province, of Basra.[12] Nevertheless, no Ottoman administration was extended to the Shaikhdom, and the local population continued to pay no taxes to the Ottoman authorities. Writing in 1896, the Legal Adviser to the British Embassy in Constantinople noted

---

[7] For an account of origins of modern Kuwait, see Ahmad Mustafa Abu-Hakima, *History of Eastern Arabia, 1750–1800: The Rise and Development of Bahrain and Kuwait*, Beirut: Khayats, 1965.
[8] See Alan Rush, *Al-Sabah: History and Genealogy of Kuwait's Ruling Family, 1752–1987*, London: Ithaca Press, 1987. The first Ruler of Kuwait, Shaikh Sabah I, ruled from c. 1752–64.
[9] Richard Schofield, *Kuwait and Iraq: Historical Claims and Territorial Disputes*, second edition, London: Royal Institute of International Affairs, 1993, p. 11.
[10] Maurice Mendelson and Susan Hulton, 'Iraq's Claim to Sovereignty over Kuwait', in Richard Schofield (ed.), *Territorial Foundations of the Gulf States*, London: UCL Press, 1994, p. 119.
[11] Ahmad Mustafa Abu-Hakima, *The Modern History of Kuwait, 1750–1965*, London: Luzac and Company, 1983, p. 90.
[12] David Finnie, *Shifting Lines in the Sand: Kuwait's Elusive Frontier with Iraq*, London: I. B. Tauris, 1992, p. 7.

that 'The country of Koweit, although entirely independent, figures in the maps as being a part of the Ottoman Empire.'[13] In a similar vein, the Ambassador himself, Sir Philip Currie, opined that the Ruler of Kuwait was 'in reality an independent potentate and only nominally subject to the Sultan [of Turkey]'.[14]

In 1896, Shaikh Mubarak seized power from his brother, Shaikh Muhammad, in a violent coup. Although Mubarak initially sought recognition from the Ottoman empire, Ottoman proposals to place a quarantine officer in Kuwait persuaded him of the advantages of drawing closer to Britain to maintain his independence.[15] Despite initial procrastination, concern about the extension of German and Russian influence in the region in the late 1890s prompted the British to draw Kuwait firmly within their sphere.[16] '[W]e don't want Koweit', remarked the Permanent Under-Secretary at the India Office, Sir Arthur Godley, 'but we don't want anyone else to have it.'[17] Accordingly, Britain concluded a secret agreement with Shaikh Mubarak on 23 January 1899, by which he pledged himself 'not to receive the agent or representative of any other Power or Government at Kuwait, or at any other place within the limits of his territory, without the previous sanction of the British Government'.[18] Mubarak also bound himself and his successors 'not to cede, sell, lease, mortgage, or give for occupation or for any other purpose, any portion of his territory to the Government or subjects of any other power without the previous consent of Her Majesty's Government'. Five years later, the Government of India, which had assumed responsibility for British interests in the Persian Gulf in 1873, despatched Captain S. G. Knox to Kuwait as Britain's first Political Agent. Following Turkish protests, Knox was withdrawn in May 1905, only to be reinstated five months later. Although the Political Agent became a permanent feature of the British establishment in Kuwait, he 'remained a background figure, setting the limits to political disputes, but playing only

---

[13] Schofield, *Kuwait and Iraq*, p. 14.

[14] H. Rahman, *The Making of the Gulf War: Origins of Kuwait's Long-Standing Territorial Dispute with Iraq*, Reading: Ithaca Press, 1997, p. 10.

[15] Salwa Alghanim, *The Reign of Mubarak al-Sabah: Shaikh of Kuwait 1896–1915*, London: I. B. Tauris, 1998, pp. 38, 199. See also Malcolm Yapp, 'The Nineteenth and Twentieth Centuries', in Alvin J. Cottrell (ed.), *The Persian Gulf States: A General Survey*, Baltimore: Johns Hopkins University Press, 1980, p. 57.

[16] Majid Khadduri, 'Iraq's Claim to the Sovereignty of Kuwayt', *New York University Journal of International Law and Politics*, 23 (1990): 10; Rahman, *Making of the Gulf War*, pp. 13–14; Alghanim, *The Reign of Mubarak al-Sabah*, pp. 59–73.

[17] Briton Cooper Busch, 'Britain and the Status of Kuwayt, 1896–1899', *Middle East Journal*, 21, 2 (1967): 196.

[18] J. G. Lorimer, *Gazetteer of the Persian Gulf, Oman and Central Arabia*, Vol. 1, Part 1B, Westmead, Farnborough: Gregg International Publishers Limited, 1970 (first published Calcutta, 1915), pp. 1048–9.

a small domestic role'.[19] Indeed, neither the Political Agent, nor the Political Resident in the Persian Gulf based at Bushire in southern Persia, possessed any formal powers in Kuwait's internal administration. Their advice might on occasion be sought, but the Ruler of Kuwait was under no obligation to accept it.

Despite the 1899 agreement, Kuwait's status continued to defy precise definition, a situation compounded by Britain's recognition of Ottoman suzerainty over the Shaikhdom in September 1901. 'It seems to me', recorded the Viceroy of India, Lord Curzon, 'that we are now in the quaint situation of having admitted and denied the suzerainty of the Sultan, both accepted and repudiated his sovereignty, and both asserted and given away the independence of the Sheikh.'[20] In a similar vein, the Foreign Secretary, Lord Lansdowne, declared: 'no one knows where his [Mubarak's] possessions begin and end, and our obligations towards him are as ill-defined as the boundaries of his Principality'.[21] Clarification was provided by the Anglo-Ottoman Convention of 29 July 1913, under which the Ottomans recognized the validity of the 1899 agreement while the British acknowledged Kuwait as an autonomous *qada*, or sub-district, of the Ottoman empire. The outbreak of the First World War, however, prevented the ratification of the convention. During the war, Mubarak supported Britain against the Ottomans in return for which the Shaikhdom of Kuwait was recognized as 'an independent Government under British protection'.[22]

In spite of the increased international prestige which Kuwait derived from allying herself with the victorious British, the inter-war years brought new challenges to the Shaikhdom. The rise of strong neighbouring powers, principally Saudi Arabia and Iraq, from the ashes of the Ottoman empire provided Kuwait with threats to its independence. At the Uqair Conference towards the end of 1922, Britain attempted to settle the borders between Iraq, Najd (the precursor to Saudi Arabia), and Kuwait. In an effort to placate the ruler of Najd, Abdul Aziz Ibn Saud, who was obliged to relinquish large areas to Iraq, the conference coordinator, Sir Percy Cox, gave two-thirds of the territory claimed by Kuwait to Najd.[23] A diamond-shaped Neutral Zone between Najd and Kuwait was also created. Although the loss of territory to Najd was a bitter blow, some solace could be taken

---

[19] Crystal, *Oil and Politics in the Gulf*, p. 66.
[20] Briton Cooper Busch, *Britain and the Persian Gulf, 1894–1914*, Berkeley and Los Angeles: University of California Press, 1967, p. 210.
[21] Alghanim, *The Reign of Mubarak al-Sabah*, p. 165.
[22] Cited in Hassan A. al-Ebraheem, *Kuwait: A Political Study*, Kuwait: Kuwait University Press, 1975, p. 168.
[23] Malcolm Yapp, 'British Policy in the Persian Gulf', in Cottrell, *The Persian Gulf States*, pp. 88-9; Ewan W. Anderson and Khalil H. Rashidian, *Iraq and the Continuing Middle East Crisis*, London: Pinter Publishers, 1991, pp. 101–2; John C. Wilkinson, *Arabia's Frontiers: The Story of Britain's Boundary Drawing in the Desert*, London: I. B. Tauris, 1991, p. 145.

in April 1923 from Cox's recognition of Kuwaiti ownership of the strategic islands of Warba and Bubiyan in the north-western reaches of the Gulf.[24] Iraq's tendency to turn covetous eyes to the two islands, however, presented Kuwait with an ongoing threat from her northern neighbour. Between 1928 and 1937, moreover, Ibn Saud imposed trade sanctions against Kuwait in retaliation for its refusal to collect customs and transit duties on his behalf on goods bound for Najd.[25] The instability caused by disputes with neighbouring states was compounded by the incursion of oil companies into Kuwait.

As early as 1911, the oil prospects of Kuwait attracted the interest of major companies. In that year, the managing director of the Anglo-Persian Oil Company,[26] Charles Greenway, entered into correspondence with the Political Resident with a view to acquiring an oil concession in Kuwait.[27] Unable to reach satisfactory terms, and discouraged by the unfavourable result of a geological survey in 1926, Anglo-Persian withdrew from negotiations. Encouraging tests elsewhere in the Persian Gulf, however, persuaded the Company to renew its interest in Kuwait in 1931. By this time, an American organization, the Gulf Oil Corporation, had also entered the fray. By the end of 1933, the two competitors agreed to form a joint enterprise, the Kuwait Oil Company (KOC). On 23 December 1934, the KOC secured a seventy-five-year concession.[28] Four years later, oil was discovered in commercial quantities at Burgan, south of Kuwait Bay.[29]

In facing the new challenges of the inter-war years, the al-Sabah by no means presented a united front. Dynastic competition within the family following the two short reigns of Shaikh Jabir (1915–17) and Shaikh Salim (1917–21) was intense. Primogeniture was not an established principle, and when Jabir's son, Ahmad, succeeded in 1921, Salim's thwarted sons entered a prolonged period of opposition. The principal rivalry was played out between Shaikh Ahmad and Salim's eldest son, Shaikh Abdullah.

Even before Ahmad's accession, the British privately supported his candidature, the Political Agent, James Carmichael More, declaring: 'Ahmad

---

[24] Richard Schofield, 'The Kuwaiti Islands of Warbah and Bubiyan, and Iraqi Access to the Gulf', in Schofield, *Territorial Foundations*, p. 161; Habibur Rahman, 'Kuwaiti Ownership of Warba and Bubiyan Islands', *Middle Eastern Studies*, 29, 2 (1993): 304–5.

[25] Abdul-Reda Assiri, *Kuwait's Foreign Policy: City-State in World Politics*, Boulder, Colorado: Westview Press, 1990, p. 5.

[26] The Anglo-Persian Oil Company was renamed the Anglo-Iranian Oil Company in 1935.

[27] J. H. Bamberg, *The History of the British Petroleum Company: Volume 2: The Anglo-Iranian Years, 1928–1954*, Cambridge: Cambridge University Press, 1994, p. 147.

[28] A. H. T. Chisholm, *The First Kuwait Oil Concession Agreement: A Record of the Negotiations, 1911-1934*, London: Frank Cass, 1975, pp. 37–80; Peter Mansfield, *Kuwait: Vanguard of the Gulf*, London: Hutchinson, 1990, pp. 30–2; M. W. Khouja and P. G. Sadler, *The Economy of Kuwait: Development and Role in International Finance*, London: Macmillan, 1979, pp. 21–3.

[29] Foreign Office note on petroleum developments in the Arabian Peninsula, 11 June 1938, R/15/5/249.

would be a great improvement on Salim as shaikh.'[30] Indeed, Salim was described as 'unstable and ignorant of any view or mode of life beyond that of the bedouin'.[31] While more accessible and cosmopolitan than his predecessor, Ahmad proved to be independently minded and jealous of his authority. Reporting on his 1937 tour of the Persian Gulf and Saudi Arabia, the head of the Eastern Department at the Foreign Office, G. W. Rendel, remarked: 'Shaikh Ahmad is a youngish man with a strong personality, considerable charm, and a determination to have his own way.'[32] Rendel also described Britain's position in Kuwait as 'anomalous and ill-defined' and her attempts to influence Shaikh Ahmad as being met with 'bland obstruction'. A few months later Rendel suggested: 'His Excellency's present policy seems to be to play off the British, the Iraqis and the Saudis against each other, and to maintain his independence and prosperity by a precarious equilibrium of the three.'[33] The attendant dangers of this strategy soon became apparent.

The prospects for harmonious relations between Kuwait and Iraq seemed good in the months leading up to the latter's admission to the League of Nations as an independent state on 3 October 1932. Correspondence between the Iraqi Prime Minister and Shaikh Ahmad in July and August confirmed the existing frontier between the two countries, including Kuwaiti ownership of Warba and Bubiyan.[34] Yet within a short time relations between Iraq and Kuwait soured. The Iraqis were particularly indignant about Shaikh Ahmad's inability to curb the thriving trade in smuggled goods between the two territories, a practice which was undermining Iraqi customs revenues. In order to resolve this problem, Iraqi newspapers began calling for the absorption of the Shaikhdom.[35] Not surprisingly, Britain was keen to resist Iraqi pressure. In May 1937, Rendel remarked: 'it is of the utmost importance to us from the imperial strategic point of view — and incidentally also in view of the new oil resources which appear to exist in Koweit — that no other Power should establish itself in

---

[30] Telegram from Political Agent (Kuwait) to the Civil Commissioner (Baghdad), No. 87/C, 28 Aug 1920, R/15/5/94.
[31] Letter from the Political Agent (Kuwait) to the Civil Commissioner (Baghdad), No. 130 C, 19 Sept 1918, R/15/5/102.
[32] Report by G.W. Rendel on his tour of the Persian Gulf and Saudi Arabia, Feb–March 1937, p. 10, R/15/1/540.
[33] 'Kuwait', Memorandum by Rendel, 10 May 1937, R/15/1/540.
[34] Schofield, *Kuwait and Iraq*, pp. 63–4; Finnie, *Shifting Lines*, pp. 78–9; Rahman, 'Kuwaiti Ownership of Warba and Bubiyan', p. 305. The text of the letters is reproduced in *The GCC Border Disputes Seminar: With Special Reference to Iraq and Kuwait*, London: Gulf Centre for Strategic Studies, 1992, pp. 81–2.
[35] Saeed Khalil Hashim, 'The Influence of Iraq on the Nationalist Movements of Kuwait and Bahrain, 1920–1961', PhD. thesis, University of Exeter, 1984, p. 36. See also Rahman, *Making of the Gulf War*, pp. 100–4.

Koweit, and that Koweit should remain definitely under British control.'[36] Substance to Iraqi claims was provided in the course of 1938.

In April, the Iraqi Foreign Minister, Taufiq al-Suwaidi, argued that Kuwait, as a former part of the *vilayet* of Basra, should belong to Iraq.[37] In response, the British Ambassador in Baghdad, Sir Maurice Patterson, argued that under article 16 of the treaty of Lausanne (1923) Turkey had renounced all rights over Kuwait and that as such these rights could not be inherited by another power.[38] Patterson's carefully considered arguments did not deter the Iraqis from pursuing their claim. In September, al-Suwaidi handed the Parliamentary Under-Secretary of State for Foreign Affairs, R. A. Butler, an *aide-mémoire* stating: 'The Iraqi Government, as the successor to the Ottoman Government in the Wilayets [*vilayets*] of Mosul, Baghdad and Basra, considers that Kuwait should properly be incorporated in Iraq.'[39]

In an attempt to facilitate their territorial ambitions, the Iraqis began conducting a systematic propaganda campaign designed to destabilize the Shaikhdom and undermine the legitimacy of Shaikh Ahmad.[40] One notable article, which was published in the Baghdad newspaper *Al-Kifah* in February 1938, berated the Ruler for the backwardness of his administration and the lack of government-sponsored reforms.[41] A constant stream of invective also cascaded from King Ghazi of Iraq's private radio station.[42] Ahmad's authority was challenged not only by external pressure, but also by internal strife.

By the late 1930s, discontent with Ahmad's rule began to surface. In March 1938, the Political Agent, G. S. de Gaury, noted the appearance of graffiti calling for reform on the street walls of Kuwait town.[43] Members of the al-Sabah family had been uneasy about Ahmad's conduct for some time.'[T]he Subah family', reported de Gaury,

> are intensely dissatisfied with the tiny allowances which the Shaikh gives them ... and they have in this the sympathy of the notables, since the Shaikh allocates to the State or municipality for public services very little of his

[36] Memorandum by Rendel, 10 May 1937, R/15/1/540.

[37] Schofield, *Kuwait and Iraq*, p. 75.

[38] Letter from Sir Maurice Patterson (British Ambassador, Iraq) to Lord Halifax, No. 162, 19 April 1938, R/15/5/207.

[39] Finnie, *Shifting Lines*, p. 114.

[40] Letter from H. R. P. Dickson (Political Agent, Kuwait) to the Political Resident (Bushire), No. C-269, 5 Sept 1935, R/15/5/126; Schofield, *Kuwait and Iraq*, pp. 72–4; Daniel Silverfarb, *Britain's Informal Empire in the Middle East: A Case Study of Iraq, 1929–1941*, New York: Oxford University Press, 1986, p. 68.

[41] Translation of an article in *Al-Kifah*, 12 Feb 1938, R/15/5/205.

[42] Hashim, 'The Influence of Iraq', p. 81; Matthew Elliot, 'The Death of King Ghazi: Iraqi Politics, Britain and Kuwait in 1939', *Contemporary British History*, 10, 3 (1996): 69.

[43] Telegram from Political Agent (Kuwait) to Political Resident (Bushire), No. C-98, 4 March 1938, R/15/5/205.

income, which is identical with that of the State. He has saved a very large sum and bought estates abroad, and his parsimony is a by-word in Kuwait.[44]

Indeed three leading members of the al-Sabah family, including the Ruler's cousin, Shaikh Abdullah, approached de Gaury, pleading with him to intercede with Shaikh Ahmad for an increase in their allowances.[45] 'The prospect of Oil royalties', mused de Gaury, 'may have turned their thoughts this way'.

Opposition to the Ruler developed not only within the al-Sabah family, but also among 'an influential group inclined towards progressives as represented in Iraq'.[46] Iraqi newspapers, furthermore, fomented opposition to Shaikh Ahmad by conducting a ceaseless campaign of vilification.[47] The spectre of renewed Iraqi intervention in Kuwait caused the British considerable anxiety. 'There is a risk', noted an official of the India Office, 'that if we do nothing to remove existing grievances some of the malcontents will look increasingly to Iraq for sympathy and encouragement to the detriment of our position in Koweit.'[48] Dislike of the Ruler and his administration crystallized in March 1938 as a result of the arrest and brutal beating of a dissident, Muhammad al-Barrak, who stood accused of disseminating anti-government propaganda and intriguing against the Shaikh.[49] In an effort to calm the increasingly fraught atmosphere in Kuwait, de Gaury interviewed the Ruler, expressing His Majesty's Government's abhorrence at the treatment of Muhammad al-Barrak. De Gaury reported that Ahmad's only response to these admonishments was to screw up his face 'like a child about to cry'.[50] 'The suggestion that any new democratic movement should be drawn by him into useful channels', expatiated de Gaury, 'seemed to be beyond his comprehension . . . . Such understanding as he has acquired of political forms, has, I fear, long ago ranged him on the side of dictators.'[51]

Initially, the British were keen to see reform within the Ruler's administration. 'If the Shaikh were a sound, level-headed ruler', expostulated the Political Resident, T. C. Fowle, 'the fact that his rule is a "one man show" would matter very little. As, however, he is far from being either sound or level-headed I feel it is essential to try to put some check on his actions.'[52]

---

[44] Ibid.
[45] Letter from the Political Agent (Kuwait) to the Political Resident (Bushire), No. C/130, 19 March 1938, R/15/5/205.
[46] Letter from G. S. de Gaury to Fowle, No. C/129, 19 March 1938, FO 371/21832.
[47] Hashim, 'The Influence of Iraq', pp. 89–91.
[48] Letter from Peel to L. Baggally (Foreign Office), 11 May 1938, R 15/5/205, cited in Falah Al-Mdairis, 'The Arab Nationalist Movement in Kuwait from its Origins to 1970', PhD. thesis, University of Oxford, 1987, p. 97.
[49] Crystal, *Oil and Politics*, p. 47.
[50] Letter from de Gaury to Fowle, No. C-212, 13 June 1938, R/15/5/205.
[51] Ibid.
[52] Letter from Fowle to the Secretary of State for India, No. C/334, 18 June 1938, R/15/5/205.

Fowle went so far as to write to Ahmad imploring him to associate himself with his family and people, suggesting that this requirement would be fulfilled by the formation of a Council consisting of members of the al-Sabah family and some heads of the leading families in Kuwait.[53]

Shaikh Ahmad was unable to resist the inexorable pressure for political reform, and at the end of June 1938 reluctantly gave his assent to the election of a Council, or *Majlis*.[54] As a result, the heads of the 150 leading families of Kuwait gathered and elected a Council of fourteen, with Shaikh Abdullah as President. In an effort to divide the opposition, the Ruler's clique, led by his secretaries, the director of the municipality, and a merchant named Khalid Zaid, offered large sums of money and various privileges to anyone who would defect from the Council. The Council responded angrily to such crude tactics, and charged Ahmad with acting against the interests of both the majority of Kuwaitis and the al-Sabah family. In a final attempt to regain the initiative, Ahmad released Muhammad al-Barrak from prison, while his supporters sought to undermine the Council by claiming that it was the product of foreign intrigue, as well as being anti-religious. These actions found little support, however, and on 6 July Ahmad gave his assent to the Council. When a declaration of the functions of the new Council was presented to him on 9 July, Ahmad was reported to have 'broken down so completely' in the face of this document, which took away from him control of the state's income, that he deferred signature for a few hours.[55] Fowle described the political changes as having turned the Ruler into a 'cypher',[56] ascribing the acquisition of such extensive powers by the Council to the 'crass stupidity' of Shaikh Ahmad who had 'persevered in futile intrigues to undermine the Council, which merely served to exacerbate both them, and public opinion generally'.[57] Referring to British policy in the Persian Gulf, Fowle went on to urge that 'as the chief exponents of democracy His Majesty's Government cannot ally themselves with the Shaikhs to stamp these movements out, even if this were practicable'.

The creation of representative government in Kuwait did pose problems for the British, nevertheless. On the one hand, Shaikh Ahmad perceived the

---

[53] Letter from Fowle to Shaikh Ahmad, No. C/333, 18 June 1938, R/15/5/205. Following the death of Shaikh Salim in 1921, a twelve-man council was established. Although it elicited from the new Shaikh, Ahmad, a commitment to ongoing consultation, internal disagreements brought about its swift demise. See Jill Crystal, *Kuwait: The Transformation of an Oil State*, Boulder, Colorado: Westview, 1992, p. 18.

[54] The following is based on a letter from the Political Agent (Kuwait) to the Political Resident (Bushire), No. C-235, 6 July 1938, R/15/5/205.

[55] Letter from de Gaury to Fowle, No. C-246, 12 July 1938, R/15/5/205.

[56] Letter from the Political Resident (Bushire) to the Secretary of State for India, No. 275, 16 July 1938, R/15/5/205.

[57] Letter from Fowle to Peel, No. 396-S, 18 July 1938, FO 371/21832.

Council as 'the enemy' and sought to 'enlist the aid and support of His Majesty's Government against them'.[58] Indeed, Fowle recorded that he had been chided by Ahmad for being too conciliatory towards the Council. 'The Shaikh', explained Fowle, 'has all a weak man's urge for table thumping tactics, especially if these tactics are employed by somebody else on his behalf.'[59] Furthermore, Ahmad's temporary conversion to the idea of the appointment of a British Adviser for Kuwait was interpreted as 'an attempt to use the power of the British Government to break the Council'.[60] On the other hand, the Council began to claim powers which conflicted with British interests. Article 3 of the inaugural law, which delineated the functions of the Council, claimed authority in the conduct of foreign affairs.[61] Moreover, the Council began to address communications to the Kuwait Oil Company direct, by-passing both the Ruler and the Political Agent.[62] In an attempt to overcome the problems inherent in divided authority in Kuwait, the Acting Political Resident, Hugh Weightman, emphasized that Britain should seek to

> disabuse both parties — and in particular the Shaikh — of any idea that we regard them as alternative and mutually repugnant manifestations of authority in Kuwait, or that we are likely to take sides in their disagreements. No progress can be made until the Shaikh realises that the His Majesty's Government recognise the Council as an essential feature of the administration of Kuwait and, by implication, that they are not prepared to assist in any manoeuvres designed to destroy it. On the other side the Council must understand that in spite of their 'Inaugural Law' we regard the Shaikh as the symbol of authority in Kuwait.[63]

In the second half of 1938, the Council clearly held the upper hand in the power struggle with Shaikh Ahmad. For example, the former succeeded in securing the dismissal of the latter's State Secretary, Khan Bahadur Mulla Saleh, as well as his Egyptian social secretary, Izzat Ja'far.[64] Moreover, Shaikh Abdullah assumed control of the administration of Ahmad's estates in Iraq, while the revenues from the Kuwait Oil Company were handed to the Council.[65] Members of the al-Sabah family had already taken responsibility for the allocation of funds from the family estates, a function formerly performed by Shaikh Ahmad, or his secretary.[66] Towards

---

[58] Letter from H. Weightman to Peel, No. C/554, 22 Aug 1938, R/15/5/205.
[59] Letter from Fowle to J. P. Gibson (India Office), No. C/804, 19 Oct 1938, R/15/1/548.
[60] Letter from Weightman to Peel, No. C/554, 22 Aug 1938, R/15/5/205.
[61] Letter from Gibson to Fowle, 30 Sept 1938, R/15/1/548.
[62] Letter from Fowle to Gibson, No. C/804, 19 Oct 1938, R/15/1/548.
[63] Letter from Weightman to Peel, No. C/554, 22 Aug 1938, R/15/5/205.
[64] Ibid.
[65] Note by the Political Agent (Kuwait) on a conversation between His Highness the Shaikh of Kuwait and the Political Resident, 19 Oct 1938, R/15/1/548.
[66] Letter from de Gaury to Fowle, No. C-246, 12 July 1938, R/15/5/205.

the end of the year, however, the political tide began to turn against the Council.

The large Shi'ah community, which formed over a quarter of the total population of Kuwait town, was bitterly opposed to the all-Sunni Council.[67] Indeed, the Shi'ahs favoured the Ruler since his State Secretary, Khan Bahadur Mulla Saleh, a Persian Shi'ah by origin, had protected their interests and given them access to the head of state. In addition to the alienated Shi'ahs, an opposition grouping, which included not only conservative members of the al-Sabah family, but also merchants who had lost monopolies as a result of council legislation, began to coalesce. Encouraged by this development, the Ruler sought to dismiss the Council, an objective articulated to de Gaury on 15 December.[68]

Aware of the Ruler's intentions, the Council members withdrew to the fortified Citadel in Kuwait town.[69] As tension grew, Shaikh Abdullah, with the encouragement of de Gaury, set about drawing up an arbitration plan. The deadlock was broken by the intervention of the semi-nomadic farmers of the fortified villages along the south coast of Kuwait, known as the Qusour. In their enthusiasm for reforms, the Council had threatened them with punishment should they persist in concealing, in their baskets of tomatoes, pitted, bad, or unripe ones. So incensed were the people of the Qusour, whose tomatoes were reputed always to have been in such a condition, that they answered the Ruler's call to arms and, supported by his bedouin followers, entered Kuwait town. Seizing the moment, Ahmad issued an ultimatum that the Citadel must surrender.

On 17 December frantic negotiations ensued. Four representatives from each side were selected to argue their case before an arbitration panel. As an essential preliminary to discussions, Ahmad insisted that the arbitrators should occupy the Citadel. Once this had occurred, the Council was informed that further negotiations would be abortive, but that the Ruler had agreed to fresh elections, provided that he retained the right of veto on the Council's decisions. The Ruler also took control of the arms reserve. Commenting on this revival in Shaikh Ahmad's fortunes, Fowle suggested that 'It might well be commemorated by the Ruling Family of Kuwait adding to their Coat of Arms: "a Shaikh rampant upon a field of pitted tomatoes".'[70]

A new Council of twenty was chosen by an electorate numbering 400. Twelve of the original members were re-elected, while Shaikh Abdullah was re-appointed as president. Having refused to accept a purely advisory role, rather than an executive one, the second Kuwait Council was dissolved on

[67] Letter from Fowle to Gibson, No. C/806, 19 Oct 1938, R/15/5/205.
[68] Telegram from Political Agent (Kuwait) to Political Resident (Bushire), No. 404, 17 Dec 1938, R/15/5/205.
[69] The following is based on Kamal Osman Salih, 'The 1938 Kuwait Legislative Council', *Middle Eastern Studies*, 28, 1 (1992): 91–2.
[70] Letter from Fowle to Peel, No. 785-S, 29 Dec 1938, R/15/5/206.

7 March 1939.[71] Three days later a Kuwaiti dissident, Muhammad al-Munayyis, arrived in Kuwait town, exhorting members of the late Council to resist the Ruler until the Iraqi army arrived.[72] Turning these events to his advantage, Shaikh Ahmad arrested those Council members who had intrigued against him. On 12 March, Ahmad established an advisory council, consisting of nine notables and four members of the al-Sabah family, with Shaikh Abdullah once again as president.[73] While the Shaikh had succeeded in suppressing the extremist minority who looked to Iraq for support, the events of 1938–9 had the effect of permanently undermining his authority. The most tangible evidence of this is provided by the growth in the power and influence of Shaikh Abdullah and his followers, the so-called *Aulad Salim*.

Abdullah had proved to be a politician of sagacity during the controversies which attended the *Majlis* movement. Fearing that agitation in 1938 might turn against not only the Ruler, but also the whole al-Sabah family, he successfully associated himself with the rising tide in favour of representative government.[74] By so doing he also ensured that al-Sabah family members who had been excluded by Shaikh Ahmad would occupy a central position within the administration. Writing in 1949, the Political Agent noted that 'The *Aulad Salim* are immensely powerful in their sphere, since their authority is closely supported by the merchants whose interests are allied to theirs. They control the details of finance, customs, supplies and police.'[75] Drawing a parallel with British constitutional arrangements, the Political Agent proceeded to liken the Ruler's department to Whitehall, and Abdullah's to the city of London. 'In their respective spheres', he concluded, 'each party is all powerful and jealous of its authority. They give nothing away and only co-operate when their common interests and authority is threatened.'[76]

A number of conclusions can be drawn from the *Majlis* movement. Often characterized as an attempt by merchants to reassert their influence,[77] the *Majlis* movement can be represented more accurately as an alliance of those who had been marginalized by the authoritarian rule of Shaikh Ahmad. This alliance was lent powerful support by leading

---

[71] Salih, 'Kuwait Legislative Council', p. 93; J. E. Peterson, *The Arab Gulf States: Steps Toward Political Participation*, New York: Praeger, 1988, p. 32.

[72] Crystal, *Oil and Politics*, p. 49. Although wiser counsel eventually prevailed, on 19 February 1939 King Ghazi of Iraq had ordered the army Chief of Staff, Husain Fawzi, to 'occupy Kuwait immediately' (Elliot, 'The Death of King Ghazii, pp. 69–70).

[73] Salih, 'Kuwait Legislative Council', p. 94.

[74] Letter from Fowle to Peel, No. 396-S, 18 July 1938, FO 371/21832.

[75] Letter from the Political Agent (Kuwait) to Sir Rupert Hay (Political Resident, Bahrain), No. R (4/25), 2 Jan 1949, R/15/5/213.

[76] Ibid.

[77] Salih, 'Kuwait Legislative Council', p. 70; Crystal, *Transformation of an Oil State*, p. 19.

members of the al-Sabah family who had been excluded from the administration. Writing in early 1939, de Gaury had recalled that 'the Ruling family here, unlike those of other Arab States, were allowed to take no part whatever in Administrative affairs, and were kept in the background socially'.[78] Although Ahmad eventually succeeded in suppressing the *Majlis* movement, his weakened position obliged him to permit Shaikh Abdullah and his followers to assume key positions within the state.

While the *Majlis* movement reflected internal rivalries within the Kuwait polity, it can in no real sense be represented as a reaction to intrusive British imperialism. Although the KOC provided a future source of instability, its activities were still on a fairly small scale. In July 1942, the KOC suspended drilling operations altogether and plugged all wells in view of the precarious war situation.[79] As regards the representatives of the British government in the Gulf, they had traditionally eschewed involvement in internal administrative matters in Kuwait, and throughout the dispute in 1938–9 studiously avoided becoming identified too closely with either side. As Fowle recalled: 'Various attempts were made by the popular party to enlist the open support of de Gaury, who, however, acted with tact and discretion in refusing to be drawn into the struggle'.[80] The growth of Britain's economic interest in Kuwait in the aftermath of the Second World War, nevertheless, convinced Britain of the necessity of taking a more active role in Kuwait's internal affairs. In 1946, the Political Residency was transferred from Bushire to Bahrain. Although this measure was taken primarily in the interests of removing an obvious target for Iranian anti-imperialism,[81] the move did symbolize Britain's growing interest in the Arab side of the Gulf. Two years later, the Foreign Office assumed responsibility for the Gulf Shaikhdoms.[82] This change facilitated the more intrusive policies which Britain pursued with respect to Kuwait in the post-war years. As the retiring Political Resident, Sir Rupert Hay, remarked in 1953:

> I have found that the Foreign Office takes a closer interest in matters of detail and is more concerned to ensure that the Shaikhdoms are properly administered than the Government of India, who were always most reluctant to interfere in their internal affairs.[83]

Britain's attempts to expand her role in the internal affairs of Kuwait, and the extent to which the al-Sabah were prepared to acquiesce in this, will be the subject of the next chapter.

---

[78] Letter from de Gaury to Fowle, No. C-4, 6 Jan 1939, R/15/5/206.
[79] Letter from Peel to M. R. Bridgeman, 14 Aug 1943, FO 371/34908.
[80] Letter from Fowle to Peel, No. 396/S, 18 July 1938, FO 371/21832.
[81] 'Location of the Headquarters of the Political Resident in the Persian Gulf', Memorandum by the Secretary of State for Foreign Affairs, 8 March 1946, CP (46) 101, CAB 129/8.
[82] Cabinet Conclusions, 8 Jan 1947, CM (47) 4, CAB 128/9.
[83] Letter from Hay to Sir Winston Churchill, No. 56, 25 June 1953, FO 371/104270.

1: Oil Expansion and its Consequences 1950–1

> The situation which is developing in Kuwait is not healthy. There is a great deal of money, no real financial control and too much power in the hands of Abdulla Mulla over whose activities Col. Crichton has no control.[1]

Writing in 1931, Britain's representative in Kuwait, H. R. P. Dickson, remarked: 'The policy of the Political Agent has been, and is, to interfere as little as he possibly can with the internal administration of the State.'[2] On the eve of the Second World War, some frustration with the policy of non-intervention can be detected among British officers in the Gulf. In April 1939, the Political Agent in Bahrain, Hugh Weightman, expressed his regret that 'we seem reluctant to use the means we possess to deter a crew of feeble and ill-conditioned shaikhs from treating the wishes of His Majesty's Government with quite such persistent disrespect'.[3] Referring to the rulers of the Gulf Shaikhdoms, nevertheless, Weightman conceded: 'We certainly do not want to administer their disgusting territories and people.'[4] By the early 1950s Britain's traditional policy of respecting Kuwait's autonomy in local affairs was challenged by the dramatic growth in oil revenues which threatened not only to destabilize the Shaikhdom's internal equilibrium, but also to inflict damage on Britain and the sterling area. Britain's response to these twin problems was to increase pressure for the appointment of British personnel to the Kuwait administration. Although successful in securing the engagement of 'experts', Britain soon discovered that

---

[1] Minute by R. F. G. Sarell, 25 Sept 1951, FO 371/91283.
[2] *Kuwait Administrative Report for the Year 1931*, Papers of H. R. P. Dickson, Box 3 File 5.
[3] Cited in Rosemarie Said Zahlan, 'Hegemony, Dependence and Development in the Gulf', in Tim Niblock (ed.), *Social and Economic Development in the Arab Gulf*, London: Croom Helm, 1980, p. 67.
[4] Ibid.

they provided no panacea for the problems facing Kuwait. Indeed, in the discussions over the revision of the Kuwait Oil Company's Concession in 1951, Britain had to rely on more informal methods of influencing the Ruler. Before addressing these questions, the background to the employment of British advisers will be discussed.

I

In June 1938, as opposition to the Ruler mounted in advance of the *Majlis* movement, Shaikh Abdullah had suggested the appointment of a British adviser with a position equivalent to that of Charles Belgrave who, since his appointment to the Bahrain government in 1926, had enjoyed wide-ranging powers.[5] In analysing the reasons for this sudden conversion to the idea of an adviser, the Political Agent, G. S. de Gaury, suggested: 'Sheikh Abdullah . . . possibly foresees that the present agitation may turn not only against Sheikh Ahmad but also against the whole Ruling family, and knowing that in Bahrain we have supported the Ruling family, views that form of administration favourably.'[6] By August, Shaikh Ahmad was expressing his willingness to accept an adviser, although it is clear that this merely represented an attempt to enlist the support of the British in his political battles with the Council. As de Gaury observed:

> It seems to me that whoever is politically on the underside for the moment here is in favour of a British Adviser. It was not so long ago since the present members of the Council were sending me messages to say that they needed an Adviser to control the Sheikh. Now that they are in office I do not think they would favour one for a moment.[7]

This impression was confirmed by the Political Resident, C. G. Prior, who recorded: 'so far as I can make out . . . neither the Shaikh nor the Council were really in favour of the proposal and merely played with it in the hope of restricting the other's powers when their own stars were temporarily in eclipse'.[8]

Towards the end of the Second World War, Shaikh Ahmad, in conversation with the Political Agent, opined that state finances would never be properly run until he had a British financial adviser.[9] Although Ahmad justified his comments with reference to the projected growth in oil revenues, it is clear that his support for an adviser resulted from antipathy

---

[5] See Mahdi Abdulla al-Tajir, *Bahrain 1920–1945: Britain, the Shaikh and the Administration*, London: Croom Helm, 1987.
[6] Letter from G. S. de Gaury to Sir Trenchard Fowle, No. C/220, 24 June 1938, R/15/5/205.
[7] Letter from de Gaury to H. Weightman, No. C/268, 17 Aug 1937, R/15/5/205.
[8] Letter from C. G. Prior to Hay, No. C/693, 9 Nov 1939, R/15/5/213.
[9] Telegram from the Political Agent to the Political Resident, No. 683, 16 Sept 1944, R/15/5/213.

towards the *Aulad Salim* which dominated the finance department (see introduction). The Political Agent reported that 'His Highness was convinced that the "Aulad Salim" habitually misappropriated State funds, and that he would be only too glad to have someone independent of them, and whom he could trust, in charge of the finances'.[10] Fear of alienating the Abdullah clique, coupled with a reluctance to face criticism from other Arab countries, discouraged the Ruler from pursuing the appointment of an adviser.[11] Indeed, Ahmad pleaded for time to prepare the ground before any appointment, quoting an Arab proverb to the effect that 'if you lean on a stick too suddenly it will break, whereas with gentle pressure it will hold'.[12]

The Ruler's procrastination caused mounting concern. Referring to the prospect of growing oil revenues, R. J. Hallows of the Commonwealth Relations Office commented: 'there would appear to be a serious risk that disastrous consequences might flow from this sudden acquisition of wealth, should the Sheikh remain without the help and guidance of a capable administrator possessing a good knowledge of finance'.[13] Seizing upon reports that large quantities of sugar had been stolen or sold from warehouses for smuggling out of Kuwait, the Political Agent pointed out to Ahmad the desirability of appointing a British adviser in order to eradicate such malpractices. The Ruler, however, resisted this pressure with the comment that he was not a traitor to his state.[14]

In analysing Ahmad's reaction, the new Political Resident, Sir Rupert Hay, noted: 'It has to be remembered that Kuwait is much more truly Arab than either Bahrain or Muscat and in much closer touch with modern Arab movements and the appointment of a British Adviser there at the present moment would almost certainly be the subject of much criticism both within and without the State.'[15] The head of the Middle East Office in Cairo, John Troutbeck, also voiced concerns about the appointment of an adviser:

> In our empire all our efforts are extended towards giving the natives more and more independence. I cannot see how we can hope to move successfully in an opposite direction in the Arab world. Whatever may be the feelings of one or two petty chiefs, the urge for independence from western rule is surely bound to grow even in these little Arab states in the Gulf. Of course the immediate result where western authority is discarded is a lowering of the standard of

---

[10] Letter from Political Agent to Hay, 3 Aug 1946, R/15/5/213.
[11] Letter from Hay to the Secretary of State for India, No. C/420, 7 July 1946, R/15/5/213; Letter from F. A. K. Harrison (India Office) to D. A. Greenhill (Foreign Office), 30 April, 1947, FO 371/61423.
[12] Letter from Hay to J. P. Gibson (Commonwealth Relations Office), No. 600-S, 20 March 1948, R/15/5/213.
[13] Letter from R. J. Hallows to L. F. L. Pyman (Foreign Office), 13 Oct 1947, FO 371/61424.
[14] Letter from Hay to E. P. Donaldson (India Office), No. C/3, 20 Jan 1947, FO 371/61446.
[15] Ibid.

administration as is only too evident in Egypt. But I do not believe we can stop this by trying to put the clock back and force upon these countries British advisers with clearly defined executive authority. They just won't stand for it. All we can safely do is to offer advisers and trust that they will in fact exercise authority by the sheer force of their personality and experience.[16]

With specific reference to Kuwait, Troutbeck continued: 'Both the Sheikh and the population attach great importance to their independence and, if an adviser were forced upon them, and if in addition they were forced to give him executive authority, the result would be that he would get no co-operation and would therefore do no good.' The Foreign Office, however, was adamant that an adviser was necessary. 'There is no doubt', maintained the head of the Eastern Department, B. A. B. Burrows, 'that with the expansion of oil interests the deficiencies of the State administration will become both more apparent and more the object of criticism both inside and outside the State. That criticism will fall not only upon the Shaikh but also upon us, and neither we nor the Shaikh will have any adequate defence to offer.'[17]

Despite the Sultan of Muscat's appointment in October 1948 of a British officer, B. Woods-Ballard, to assist in the running of the state's internal administration,[18] the Ruler of Kuwait continued to resist pressure for an adviser, citing both internal and external disapprobation of such an appointment. While the British were prepared to accept the Ruler's concerns as genuine, they feared that criticism was 'likely to grow more rather than less formidable the longer we delay'.[19] Reviewing the whole question at the beginning of 1949, the Political Agent remarked:

> I do not know why the Shaikh broached the subject of an adviser in the first place, though at a venture I suggest he wanted, with H.M.G.'s backing, to frighten the *Aulad Salim* whose mismanagement at that time was probably bringing the State into public obloquy. It is clear today that, for whatever the reason may have been, the Shaikh has changed his mind and is only prepared to employ an adviser under the strongest pressure from H.M.G.[20]

Hay was opposed to such pressure being applied. 'I still feel', he remarked, 'that it would be a mistake to force the Shaikh to appoint such advisers against his will and that advisers so appointed would find it extremely difficult if not impossible to function in the face of opposition which they would encounter.'[21] In April 1949, however, Ahmad unexpectedly asked his

---

[16] Letter from John Troutbeck to B. A. B. Burrows (Foreign Office), No. 104/25/2 (A), 8 April 1948, FO 371/618319.
[17] Letter from Burrows to Hay, No. E 15065/848/91, 9 Dec 1948, R/15/5/213.
[18] Letter from Hay to Burrows, 31 Oct 1948, FO 371/68319.
[19] Minute by A. C. Stewart, 25 Nov 1948, FO 371/68347.
[20] Letter from the Political Agent to Sir Rupert Hay, 2 Jan 1949, R/15/5/213.
[21] Letter from Hay to Burrows, No. 57/2/49, 14 Jan 1949, FO 371/74959.

London representative, H. T. Kemp,[22] to obtain the services of a British doctor to act as his chief medical officer. 'This matter', noted Hay, 'has some bearing on the whole question of British advisers for Kuwait as if we can find them a doctor who proves a success, the Shaikh is more likely to turn to us for assistance in running the other departments of his Government.'[23] Dr E. Parry, along with a British matron and a British anaesthetist, were duly engaged by Kemp on behalf of the Ruler.[24] In June 1950, moreover, Ahmad asked Kemp to find three British police officers to help in the policing of British and American employees of the oil companies in Ahmadi.[25] Nevertheless, Ahmad remained equivocal on the question of the appointment of a financial adviser, obliging the British increasingly to rely on advice tendered through traditional channels, principally the Political Agent.[26] Developments in Qatar in 1949, however, appeared initially to enhance the prospect of the appointment of advisers for Kuwait.

In July 1949, the Ruler of Qatar, Shaikh Abdalla, began receiving payments from the Qatar Petroleum Company. This stimulated envy among disaffected members of his family, who demanded an increase in their allowances. Under the weight of this opposition, Abdalla abdicated in favour of his eldest son, Ali, on 20 August.[27] In return for British recognition, the new Ruler agreed to request a British adviser.[28] British officials in the Gulf were unanimous in their support for the appointment of such an officer. As time went on, however, Ali's enthusiasm for an adviser appeared to wane, prompting Hay to remark: 'it may be necessary to threaten him with withdrawal of our favour and even appoint another ruler in his place

---

[22] Although Kemp was initially employed as the Ruler's representative in London with the Kuwait Oil Company, his remit expanded with the growth of the Kuwaiti state, becoming the Ruler's adviser on a whole range of subjects outside his original terms of reference ('Mr Kemp and the Kuwait London Office', Minute by Greenhill, 15 May 1953, FO 371/104269).

[23] Letter from Hay to Burrows, 30 April 1949, R/15/5/227.

[24] Kuwait Annual Report for 1949, FO 371/82003. Hay subsequently described Parry as 'an excellent man' and predicted that the new chief medical officer would prove 'a great success' (Letter from Hay to Burrows, No. 220/4/49, 25 Oct 1949, R/15/5/231).

[25] Letter from the Political Agency (Kuwait) to Hay, No. C/149 (4/25), 12 June 1949, R/15/5/231.

[26] Minute by Alan Leavett, 2 Feb 1950, FO 371/82009.

[27] Letter from Hay to Ernest Bevin, No. 66, 1 Sept 1949, FO 371/74944. Commenting on the impact of events in Qatar on Kuwait, the Political Agent, H. G. Jakins, recorded: 'I gather that the Sheikh himself — but no one else — was a little shaken over events in Qatar which were popularly interpreted as having arisen out of the Ruler's meanness and his reluctance to meet demands for a more equitable distribution of revenue. The Sheikh here is mean but the purse strings are held by Abdulla Salim not the Sheikh and the minor Sheikhs are not badly treated as they were in Qatar' (Letter from H. G. Jakins to Hay, No. C/279 (5/16), 1 Dec 1949, R/15/5/268).

[28] Jill Crystal, *Oil and Politics in the Gulf: Rulers and Merchants in Kuwait and Qatar*, Cambridge: Cambridge University Press, 1995, p. 120.

if he tries to go back on his request for a British adviser'.[29] The Acting Political Resident, H. G. Jakins, was particularly concerned about the impact on the rest of the Gulf if Ali succeeded in defying the British. 'There is little purpose in taking decisions at a high level on the future development of Arab States', he intoned, 'if an entirely unbaked ruler of one of the smallest of them successfully snaps his fingers at us. As I see it Qatar is the key position to the future of the whole Gulf. Everything depends on whether Qatar follows Bahrain or the Saudi Arabian example.'[30] Much to the relief of the British, Ali consented to receive an adviser at the beginning of November.[31]

The man selected for the post, Group Captain Phillip Plant,[32] failed to provide the role model which Britain had intended. By June 1950, Hay felt compelled to inform the Foreign Office that 'Plant is floundering a good deal in Qatar largely on account of his inexperience.'[33] Plant's first budget, a copy of which he failed to keep, was described by an official of the Foreign Office as betraying 'lamentable incompetence',[34] while local criticism focused on his perceived extravagance.[35] In November, C. J. Pelly (Political Agent, Bahrain) was calling for Plant's replacement by a younger man.[36] According to Pelly, the trouble with Plant was 'not so much that he does too well out of the State, but that what he does do, he does in such a blatant and ham-handed fashion'.[37] Despite the disappointing results of Plant's first few months in office, the British did not abandon the hope of securing the appointment of a British adviser for Kuwait. The death of Shaikh Ahmad in January 1950 gave Britain an opportunity to pursue this objective.

As Ahmad's health deteriorated, the British began to speculate about who would succeed. Shaikh Abdullah was generally regarded as the heir-apparent, referring to himself in conversation as 'the Prince of Wales'.[38] His principal rival for the throne was his uncle, Shaikh Abdullah Mubarak, who enjoyed considerable prestige as the last surviving son of Mubarak the Great (r. 1896–1915). When Ahmad fell seriously ill in 1942, Abdullah Mubarak was described as having 'behaved in a manner rather reminiscent of Henry V',

---

[29] Telegram from Hay to the Foreign Office, No. 510, 27 Oct 1949, FO 371/74946.
[30] Letter from Jakins to J. A. F. Gethin, No. C/R–485, 19 Oct 1949, FO 1016/62.
[31] Telegram from Hay to the Foreign Office, No. 525, 8 Nov 1949, FO 371/74946.
[32] Plant, who was fifty-three at the time of his appointment, was seconded from the Air Ministry's Middle East Intelligence.
[33] Letter from Hay to G. W. Furlonge, No. 126/37/50, 14 June 1950, FO 1016/62.
[34] Minute by C. M. Rose, 25 Sept 1950, FO 371/82157. See also Letter from C. J. Pelly to Hay, No. C/R–559, 1 Nov 1950, FO 1016/62.
[35] Letter from Pelly to R. M. Andrew, No. 126/42/50, 19 Sept 1950, FO 1016/62.
[36] Letter from Pelly to Hay, No. C/R–569, 11 Nov 1950, FO 1016/62.
[37] Letter from Pelly to Andrew, No. 126/42/50, 19 Sept 1950, FO 1016/62.
[38] Letter from Hay to Thomas Hickinbotham (Political Agent, Kuwait), No. C/462, 24 April 1942, R/15/5/194.

while Abdullah 'controlled himself and did not behave objectionably'.[39] In assessing the claims of the two rival candidates, Hay suggested that 'Abdullah Salim might make the better ruler while Abdullah Mubarak is more likely to be friendly towards us'.[40] Nevertheless, Hay felt that the prospect of an undisputed and peaceful succession was not very bright. Jakins, who became Political Agent for Kuwait at the end of 1949, was equally pessimistic, predicting that Abdullah Mubarak would make an attempt to seize the throne.[41] Moreover, Shaikh Abdullah's chances of succeeding appeared to be threatened by the fact that he was absent from the Shaikhdom at the time of Ahmad's death. Nevertheless, shortly before Ahmad's demise Abdullah told Hay that all the members of the al-Sabah family were united in regarding him as the next Ruler.[42] Abdullah's confidence was soon justified. On his return to Kuwait on 31 January, Abdullah was acclaimed by all the members of the ruling family. With the accession of a new Ruler, the British renewed their efforts to secure the appointment of a British adviser to Kuwait.

Even before Ahmad's death, Jakins had suggested that British recognition of his successor should be conditional upon the acceptance of an adviser.[43] Jakins went so far as to suggest that if Abdullah Mubarak agreed to receive an adviser, Britain should be prepared to accept him as Ruler.[44] At the beginning of February, Jakins pressed Abdullah to accept a financial adviser, pointing out that it would be inappropriate for him to continue to head the finance department now that he had ascended the throne.[45] Jakins also indicated that if the term 'adviser' was unacceptable it could be replaced with that of 'expert'. Moreover, Jakins urged Abdullah to expel the late Ruler's private secretary, Izzat Ja'far, from the palace. Abdullah's only response to these admonishments was to promise to consult members of his family. In keeping with the views of the Political Agent, the Foreign Office was of the opinion that formal recognition should be delayed until Britain had received satisfaction on the question of the appointment of an adviser.[46] Hay, nevertheless, deprecated this idea, arguing:

> it will be fatal to allow Abdulla Salim to gain [the] impression that we are withholding recognition in order to force him to accept an adviser. We do not want to start off on the wrong foot with him and if an adviser is appointed

---

[39] Letter from A. C. Galloway (Political Agent, Kuwait) to Hay, No. R/1 (4/2), 19 Jan 1949, R/15/5/180.
[40] Letter from Hay to Bevin, No. 9, 27 Jan 1949, R/15/5/180.
[41] Telegram from Jakins to the Foreign Office, No. 25, 18 Jan 1950, FO 371/82162.
[42] Telegram from Hay to the Foreign Office, No. 7, 20 Jan 1950, FO 371/82162.
[43] Telegram from Jakins to the Foreign Office, No. 37, 22 Jan 1950, FO 371/82162.
[44] Telegram from Jakins to the Foreign Office, No. 26, 18 Jan 1950, FO 371/82162.
[45] Telegram from the Political Agent to the Political Resident, No. 62, 5 Feb 1950, FO 1016/119.
[46] Telegram from the Foreign Office to the Political Agent, No. 40, 7 Feb 1950, FO 1016/119.

with his unwilling consent and he refuses on this account to cooperate with him we shall be worse off than we are now.[47]

Before Abdullah's return to Kuwait at the end of January, Hay had taken the opportunity to raise the question of a British adviser. Abdullah responded by commenting that he required no other adviser than the Political Agent.[48] At a social function, the late Ruler's wife, Lady Ahmad, told Hay's wife that the whole al-Sabah family were opposed to the appointment of an adviser. Moreover, Hay himself reported that a group of merchants had told one of his informers that had there been an immediate engagement of an adviser, the ruling family would at once have been split by dissension and Abdullah would very likely have been assassinated.[49] Moreover, in conversations with the Political Agent, Abdullah expressed fear of criticism from neighbouring states if he suddenly introduced Britons into Kuwait's internal administration.[50]

Such was the consternation in Kuwait caused by Britain's delay in recognizing Abdullah that the Foreign Office reluctantly agreed to desist from linking recognition with the engagement of an adviser. However, the Foreign Office was concerned that Abdullah should at least receive a formal expression of the great importance which the British government attached to this question.[51] Enclosed in the letter of recognition, therefore, was a note from Jakins which conveyed His Majesty's Government's hope that the Ruler would appoint suitably trained experts.[52] In his reply, Abdullah emphasized the 'great progressive steps' which Kuwait had made in the last five years, but made no formal commitment to receive British advice.[53] During discussions with Hay in March, Abdullah stated that he would be strongly criticized in Iraq and elsewhere if he agreed immediately on his accession to an appointment which his predecessor had resisted for so long, and asked to be given six or seven months' grace. Hay supported this request in view of Abdullah's need to reconcile his family to the idea, justifying this approach with the comment: 'the appointment of an Adviser will serve no useful purpose if it results in serious dissension in the ruling family or arouses such opposition that the Adviser is unable to function'.[54]

An opportunity to apply pressure for the appointment of an adviser presented itself in July 1950. In that month, Abdullah had approached the KOC for an increase in his royalties (see below). The Assistant Political

---

[47] Telegram from the Political Resident to the Agent, No. 56, 9 Feb 1950, FO 1016/119.
[48] Letter from Hay to Jakins, 31 Jan 1950, FO 1016/119.
[49] Letter from Hay to Furlonge, 30 March 1950, FO 371/82009.
[50] Telegram from the Political Agent to the Political Resident, No. 71, 12 Feb 1950, FO 1016/119.
[51] Telegram from the Foreign Office to the Political Agent, No. 45, 11 Feb 1950, FO 1016/119.
[52] Letter from Jakins to Shaikh Abdullah, No. 42 (92/33/50), 21 Feb 1950, FO 371/82029.
[53] Letter from Abdullah to Jakins, No. R 6 3966, 21 Feb 1950, FO 371/82029.
[54] Letter from Hay to Furlonge, 30 March 1950, FO 371/82009.

Agent, J. A. F. Gethin, suggested that the Company should be persuaded to reply to the Ruler that they would only consider his request following the engagement of British personnel in the Kuwait administration.[55] Although C. J. Pelly sympathized with Gethin's idea, he expressed concern, referring to oil companies generally, that 'once one allows them to mix politics with business they continue to interfere in politics'.[56] The Foreign Office also had marked doubts about using the KOC to promote the policies of the British government. In particular, it was feared that the Company might try to present Britain's demands for the employment of advisers as the chief stumbling block in the negotiations over an increase in oil royalties.[57] The Foreign Office also felt that it would be counter-productive to pressure the Ruler at a time when he was establishing his position within the al-Sabah family.

In the months following his accession, Abdullah had embarked upon enhancing his popularity within the al-Sabah. One of his first acts on taking office was to repay all the debts owed by the family.[58] Reviewing Abdullah's first few weeks in power, Hay noted that he was more popular with the ruling family and the general public than Ahmad had been, and he was 'genuinely anxious for His Majesty's Government's friendship and support'.[59] Nevertheless, Hay also noted that Abdullah would carry out reforms slowly and do his best to carry his people with him. Hay concluded with guarded optimism:

> There is ... good reason to hope that he will steadily improve the general administration of the state and that he will spend its enormous income wisely, but whether he will employ British experts to assist him in this will depend on the extent to which he will be able to persuade not only himself, but other members of his family and the public that this is desirable.[60]

During discussions with Hay at the end of September 1950, the Foreign Office suggested a further approach to the Ruler on the engagement of an adviser. Hay, nevertheless, disparaged any attempt to give the Ruler an order, once again stressing the problems confronting the Ruler in reconciling his family to the idea of outside advice.[61] However, both the British authorities in the Gulf and the Foreign Office were at one in their opinion that advisers should be selected through the Ruler's London representative, Kemp. This procedure would have the advantage, as one official put it, of

---

[55] Letter from Gethin to Pelly, 24 July 1950, FO 371/82117.
[56] Letter from Pelly to T. E. Rogers, No. 689/11/50, 10 Aug 1950, FO 371/82117.
[57] Minute by Rogers, 4 Sept 1950, FO 371/82117.
[58] Letter from Jakins to Hay, No. 122/1/50, 21 Feb 1950, FO 371/82163.
[59] Letter from Hay to the Secretary of State for Foreign Affairs, No. 23 (170/170/50), 11 March 1950, FO 371/82029.
[60] Ibid.
[61] Minute by Rose, 29 Sept 1950, FO 371/82009.

avoiding 'being blamed for producing another Plant'.[62] Indeed, the example of Qatar convinced the British that they should not take an active part in the selection procedure. In mid-October 1950, much to their relief, the Ruler instructed Kemp to engage two experts, one for the finance department and another for the customs department.[63] Jakins, however, sounded a note of caution. '[I]t is not completely desirable', he argued,

> that we should rely on the financial experts taking our chestnuts out of the fire for us. Experts engaged by local government tend to show a sturdy independence of His Majesty's Government and we must ... expect that they consider their first loyalty is to the local government.[64]

What had finally influenced Abdullah to engage British personnel is difficult to establish. Jill Crystal argues that Abdullah had one aim in accepting British advisers: countering domestic pressure from his relatives, especially Abdullah Mubarak and Fahad Salim.[65] In particular, Crystal argues that in the early 1950s two conflicting forces were at work in the Kuwait polity. On the one hand, as the ruling family began to assume more government positions it became more powerful relative to the rest of society. On the other, the Ruler became less powerful in comparison with his own relatives. 'It was this family trouble', contends Crystal, 'that compelled him to allow in the British advisors that Ahmad had for years refused.'[66] It seems unlikely, however, that Abdullah's acceptance of British advisers represented an attempt to control his relations. His initial delay, and subsequent acceptance of advisers, can be ascribed to his need to reconcile the al-Sabah to the presence of British personnel in the internal administration of Kuwait. Abdullah would not have been able to persuade family members of the necessity of advisers if there had been any suspicion that this measure was designed to curtail their powers. Moreover, in disputes between the advisers and the Shaikhs, the Ruler rarely sided with the former against the latter.

Crystal's argument is more convincing when applied to the late 1930s and 1940s. It was during this period that the ruling family was at its most divided. Shaikh Ahmad sporadically supported the idea of a British adviser in the hope that this official would act as a counterweight to his opponents within the family, the *Aulad Salim*. Not surprisingly, the Salim branch of the family took the lead in opposing the appointment.[67] However, the accession of Abdullah in 1950 meant that the Salim faction was dominant, and consequently had less to fear from the engagement of British advisers.

---

[62] Minute by Rose, 13 Oct 1950, FO 371/82010.
[63] Telegram from Gethin to the Foreign Office, No. 210, 15 Oct 1950, FO 371/82010.
[64] Letter from Jakins to Hay, 28 Nov 1950, FO 371/82010.
[65] Crystal, *Oil and Politics in the Gulf*, p. 68.
[66] Ibid.
[67] Letter from the Political Agent to the Political Resident, No. C/33, 13 Jan 1947, R/15/5/213.

Moreover, if Abdullah's intention had been to use these officials to control recalcitrant members of his family, it is surprising that he did not seek to engage experts for Abdullah Mubarak's security department. If any member of the ruling family needed the restraining hand of a British adviser, it was Abdullah Mubarak. Described by the Foreign Office as 'impulsive, arbitrary and spendthrift', Abdullah Mubarak managed to turn his security forces into a small army under his direct command. His freedom of action remained unchecked until 1961 when concerted action by the al-Sabah forced his resignation and exile. Abdullah's decision to accept British advisers did not derive from a desire to use them to control his family. Indeed, such a policy would have been dangerous to his own position. It would seem likely that Abdullah agreed to the engagement of advisers in the belief that they were necessary for the development of the state in the context of the huge expansion in oil revenues following the end of the Second World War.

At the end of 1950, Kemp met officials of the Foreign Office to discuss developments in Kuwait.[68] Kemp informed his hosts that during a recent visit to Kuwait he had heard many rumours that the British government was trying to impose advisers in order to secure direct control of the Ruler and his administration. L. A. C. Fry (Eastern Department, Foreign Office) assured Kemp that Britain's only concern was to ensure a sound administration in Kuwait and to train a new generation of people who would eventually replace British personnel. For his part, Kemp emphasized that experts appointed to the Kuwait government would require a good deal of patience and tact in order to win the Ruler's confidence. He also warned that reforms could only be introduced slowly, and that great changes could not be expected at the outset.

The man selected by Kemp to become the Ruler's 'financial expert' was Colonel G. C. L. Crichton, a former secretary to the Government of India in the Foreign Department. Although he had no Arabic, the Foreign Office welcomed the appointment since it considered that he had sufficient 'standing' for the post.[69] The position of customs expert went to H. L. Roper who had been director of customs in the Sudan from 1943 to 1949 and, unlike Crichton, spoke Arabic. Both Crichton and Roper took up their new posts in early 1951.

One of Crichton's first acts on taking office was to submit a report to the Ruler on the financial administration of Kuwait.[70] Crichton began by asserting that 'the existing system of financial administration, though

---

[68] The following is based on a record of a meeting on 29 December 1950 to discuss experts for Kuwait, FO 371/91270.
[69] Minute by Rose, 11 Dec 1950, FO 371/82010.
[70] The following is based on a report on the financial administration of Kuwait and suggestions for re-organization by G. C. L. Crichton (undated), FO 1016/129.

suitable in former times, is . . . quite inadequate to deal with the present considerable financial resources of the State'. He proceeded to note that the finance department had no responsibility for the allocation of revenue among the other departments and no means of supervising or controlling their expenditure. As Crichton observed, the finance department had become 'the servant of the other Departments and not, as it should be, the controlling authority'. To remedy this situation, Crichton advocated that responsibility for the management and allocation of the state's revenues should be vested in the finance department. In addition, he urged that steps needed to be taken to coordinate the planning and execution of development projects, suggesting the employment of an engineering expert for this task. 'Unless this is done', he cautioned, 'it will not be possible to estimate or to control expenditure'.

Writing in January 1951, Jakins had observed:

> One difference between Bahrain and Kuwait is that at Bahrain the administration was more or less there before the wealth came while in Kuwait the reverse is the case. What Kuwait requires is experts who are absolute masters of their subject, who can make order out of chaos, build up an administration almost from scratch and set the country firmly on its feet.[71]

Crichton's first few months in office, however, belied these early hopes. Although the Ruler accepted the broad principles of Crichton's report, including the selection of a state engineer to oversee all development, he was soon reputed to be 'overwhelmed by his responsibilities'.[72] Reviewing the financial expert's character, Jakins remarked:

> Crichton is a very pleasant person but he is clearly no pioneer. He gives the impression of having worked where the files were presented to him profusely tabbed by efficient clerks who stood by to respond to calls for papers. Here there are no files, no clerks and no precedents and Crichton is completely at sea.[73]

The Treasury also expressed disquiet about Crichton's appointment, arguing that he possessed 'neither the personality nor the knowledge to be able to advise the right courses of action and to put them across to the Ruler'.[74] The Foreign Office was equally perturbed by Crichton's early performance. '[P]artly no doubt through his lack of Arabic', mused an official, 'Col. Crichton is not in a position to influence affairs in Kuwait to the extent which is desirable'.[75] The language barrier forced Crichton to rely on the State Secretary, Abdullah Mulla Saleh,[76] to act as interpreter.[77]

---

[71] Letter from Jakins to Hay, No. 11/13/51, 29 Jan 1951, FO 371/91270.
[72] Letter from Hay to Furlonge, 18 July 1951, FO 371/91271.
[73] Letter from Jakins to Pelly, 5 Sept 1951, FO 371/91271.
[74] Minute by D. R. Serpell, 3 March 1952, T 236/4287.
[75] Minute by Sarell, 25 Sept 1951, FO 371/91283.

This proved to be unfortunate since Crichton was reported to regard the State Secretary as 'public enemy No. 1'.[78] Moreover, Abdullah Mulla was ill-disposed to Crichton since the latter's appointment appeared to threaten his position of influence over the Ruler. Indeed, the State Secretary sought to establish a parallel administration to the one which Crichton was aiming to create.[79]

Such was Crichton's disenchantment that he spoke of resigning, only to be dissuaded from doing so by Kemp.[80] Jakins' response to this news was far from euphoric. 'Crichton', he recorded, '... will never be good in Kuwait but one can only hope that if he stays he will prove to be adequate.'[81] Crichton's principal recommendation to overcome the initial problems which he faced was to advocate the constitution of a development board to control all state spending. Although Jakins welcomed this, he argued that 'the need for a Development Board would not be so pressing if Crichton were of a calibre adequate for the post to which he has been appointed'.[82]

The fairness of Jakins' condemnation of Crichton's performance is, perhaps, questionable. Although Crichton clearly arrived in Kuwait both ill-prepared and poorly briefed, the magnitude of the task confronting him, coupled with the lack of administrative infrastructure, would have taxed the most able administrator. Moreover, Crichton did achieve some tangible successes in his first few months in office. For example, he secured the Ruler's consent for the appointment of more British experts, including General W. F. Hasted,[83] a former president of Loughborough Engineering College, to act as the Kuwait government's controller of development. Moreover, the Ruler agreed in principle to the establishment of a development board, with Crichton as chairman, to oversee state expenditure.[84] Although this was applauded by the Foreign Office, concern was expressed

---

[76] Abdullah Mulla Saleh had succeeded his father as State Secretary in 1938, managing to retain his post under Shaikh Abdullah. In addition to his official position, Abdullah Mulla was a businessman, possessing a large number of commercial interests in Kuwait.
[77] 'Abdullah Mullah Saleh', Note by Rose, 19 Sept 1951, FO 371/91260.
[78] Ibid.
[79] Letter from Jakins to Pelly, 5 Sept 1951, FO 371/91271.
[80] Ibid.
[81] Ibid.
[82] Ibid.
[83] William F. Hasted (1897–1977); MC (1916); commissioned Royal Engineers, 1915; Deputy Chief Engineer, British Forces, Iraq and Persia, 1941–2; Chief Engineer, Royal Air Force, India, 1942–4; Chief Engineer, 14th Army Burma, 1944–5; Chief Engineer, Allied Land Forces, South-East Asia, 1945; Engineer-in-Chief, India, 1946–7; Controller of Aerodromes, Ministry of Civil Aviation, 1947–8; President, Loughborough College, 1950–1; Controller of Development, Kuwait, 1952–4.
[84] Letter from Hay to Sarell, 10 Nov 1951, FO 371/91271.

over Crichton's proposed chairmanship of this new body. As one official commented:

> The object of having a Kuwaiti as chairman was to ensure the necessary local authority for schemes for improvement which might run counter to the machinations of Abdullah Mullah and others. With Col. Crichton as chairman it is likely to prove more difficult to bring within the scope of the board the Security and Education Departments of the government and the administration may well develop on . . . lopsided lines.[85]

The Foreign Office was particularly keen to see Abdullah Mubarak become chairman of the board, since, as one official put it,

> it would be a mistake to risk the opposition of so powerful a figure by leaving him out, especially if, as we still hope, it is possible to broaden the basis of the Board's work. . . . It also seems to us that in view of the likelihood that [Abdullah] Mubarak will succeed the present Ruler, it might endanger the future of any general Board or Council which is formed if he were to be excluded now from membership.[86]

'Thanks to his visit to this country early this year,' noted another official, 'Mubarak is a good friend of ours and it is important that we should retain his support.'[87]

Shaikh Abdullah Mubarak found himself in an awkward position within the al-Sabah hierarchy. Although he enjoyed enormous prestige as the last surviving son of Mubarak the Great, he was viewed with suspicion by both the Jabir and the Salim factions of the family. His relative isolation within the al-Sabah encouraged him to seek support elsewhere, particularly from the British government. Indeed, the principal object of Abdullah Mubarak's visit to London in June 1951 was widely believed to be to present himself as the leading candidate for the succession. As Jakins noted: 'his restrained behaviour in London — on which there have been many approving comments from various sources — was intended to impress his suitability on His Majesty's Government'.[88] During his stay, Abdullah Mubarak was every bit the dignified statesman, visiting Scotland Yard, the Police Training School at Hendon, the Old Bailey, the Houses of Parliament, Hampton Court, the Royal Academy, and Windsor Castle. During the evenings he tended to stay in his hotel room, being under the impression that His Majesty's Government would be watching and judging his every movement.[89] The only time he ventured out was to take a

---

[85] Minute by Rose, 26 Nov 1951, FO 371/91271.
[86] Letter from Furlonge to Hay, 6 Dec 1951, FO 371/91271.
[87] Minute by Rose, 4 Dec 1951, FO 371/91271.
[88] Memorandum by Jakins, enclosed in his letter to Pelly, 2 Sept 1951, FO 371/91355.
[89] 'Visit of Shaikh Abdullah Mubarak to the United Kingdom', Note by Gethin, 29 June 1951, FO 371/91355.

ride on the top of a London bus. On another occasion, J. A. F. Gethin found Abdullah Mubarak seated on the floor of his hotel room, playing cards with his servants. Despite Abdullah Mubarak's ambitions to succeed his nephew as Ruler, the British were wary about according him any kind of recognition as heir-apparent. '[S]uch action', warned Hay, 'might well offend the Ruler and lead to strained relations between him and Abdullah Mubarak.'[90]

The Foreign Office hoped not only that Crichton's proposed development board would provide a powerful body, chaired by a leading Shaikh, but also that it might develop into an embryonic executive council, or cabinet. However, the new Political Agent, C. J. Pelly, disavowed this idea, noting that it was 'too ambitious for Kuwait'.[91] The Foreign Office reluctantly accepted this assessment, along with Crichton's chairmanship of the board. Nevertheless, C. M. Rose (Eastern Department, Foreign Office) cautioned that, 'He [Crichton] will have to move carefully . . . since the example of Mr. Belgrave in Bahrain was one of the chief factors contributing to the reluctance of the Kuwaitis to appoint a British adviser.'[92] The apparent need for a strong British presence in the Kuwait administration, however, was emphasized by the prospect of increased oil revenues in the early 1950s.

II

Reviewing the repercussions of Britain's diplomatic reverse at the hands of Egypt during the 1956 Suez crisis (see Chapter 3), Ritchie Ovendale has argued that 'The "wind of change" associated with Africa, was evident elsewhere. In the Middle East the British interest shifted increasingly to securing the oil supplies from Kuwait in particular, and the Gulf in more general terms.'[93] In Nigel John Ashton's estimation, the switch in Britain's Middle Eastern priorities came even later. The overthrow in 1958 of Britain's allies in Iraq, he argues, prompted a re-evaluation of her regional interests 'leading to a concentration of effort more directly on the protection of the economically vital oil-supplying Gulf states'.[94] In contrast with the interpretations of Ovendale and Ashton, however, it can be suggested that a shift in emphasis towards the Gulf was already in evidence

---

[90] Letter from Hay to Jakins, 28 Sept 1951, FO 371/91355.
[91] Letter from Pelly to Hay, 12 Dec 1951, FO 371/91271.
[92] Minute by Rose, 8 Jan 1952, FO 371/91271.
[93] Ritchie Ovendale, *Britain, the United States, and the Transfer of Power in the Middle East, 1945–1962*, London: Leicester University Press, 1996, p. 178.
[94] Nigel John Ashton, *Eisenhower, Macmillan and the Problem of Nasser: Anglo-American Relations and Arab Nationalism, 1955–59*, Basingstoke: Macmillan, 1996, p. 193.

by the early 1950s as Kuwait's oil production and revenues began to expand rapidly.

Using figures supplied by the Ministry of Fuel and Power, the Foreign Office estimated that oil royalties for the period 1945 to 1950 would rise from virtually nothing to £3.5 million per annum.[95] This spectacular increase was described as being 'out of all proportion to the domestic requirements of the territory'. Shaikh Ahmad's growing surplus was soon causing concern to the British. Commenting on the build-up of Kuwaiti savings deposited in the Imperial Bank of Iran, Hay noted that 'The money is lying in the Bank without paying any interest and is becoming an embarrassment to the Manager.'[96] Hay concluded that Kuwait required outside assistance in the management of its finances. The Political Agent, however, suggested that Ahmad had 'not the courage to incur the odium of appointing a foreign adviser on his own initiative'.[97] It is not surprising, therefore, that when Shaikh Ahmad met officials of the Foreign Office in 1949 he expressed the hope that Britain would not change her policy of non-interference in Kuwait's internal affairs.[98] Britain, however, was increasingly reluctant to agree to such an undertaking. 'The Financial Administration of Kuwait', remarked an official of the Foreign Office, 'is too important to allow us to divest ourselves of responsibilities for its future.'[99] Indeed, during the discussions in 1951 between the Kuwait Oil Company and Shaikh Abdullah over an increase in oil royalties, the British were keen to encourage the conclusion of an agreement which would not damage the sterling area. This was particularly important in the context of the strains to which sterling was subjected in 1950–1 owing to the ending of Marshall Aid from the United States and the outbreak of the Korean War.[100]

To a certain extent, the post-war sterling area system had its origins in the sterling bloc which involved member countries linking their exchange rates to the floating pound following Britain's abandonment of the gold standard in 1931. The sterling area which emerged after 1945, however, witnessed some distinct innovations. In particular, most members observed common exchange controls against the rest of the world, while maintaining national reserves in sterling and pooling foreign exchange earnings, the main purpose of the sterling area being 'to restrict convertibility of sterling into dollars in the context of the post-war dollar shortage and generally to

---

[95] Letter from Greenhill to W. F. Crawford (British Middle East Office), 6 May 1947, POWE 33/250.
[96] Letter from Hay to the Secretary of State for India, No. C/420, 7 July 1946, R/15/5/213.
[97] Letter from Political Agent to Hay, No. C/367, 4 June 1946, R/15/5/213.
[98] Note of Mr Burrows' interview with His Highness, 20 May 1949, R/15/5/213.
[99] Minute by Rose, 28 Oct 1950, FO 371/82010.
[100] See Alec Cairncross, *The British Economy since 1945*, Oxford: Blackwell, 1992, pp. 55–6.

conserve foreign exchange'.[101] Kuwait, however, was not a full member of the sterling area. While tending to keep reserves in sterling, it neither pooled foreign exchange,[102] nor coordinated exchange control policy. Indeed, exchange control was limited to an administrative measure whereby Kuwaiti residents requiring foreign exchange were obliged, in certain cases, to apply to the Political Agent whose approval was signified by the issue of letters of recommendation.[103] Kuwait's special position within the sterling area, coupled with the Shaikhdom's tradition of internal autonomy, presented Britain with great difficulties in the management of the Kuwait economy. This was revealed during the negotiations which ushered in a new agreement between Shaikh Abdullah and the Kuwait Oil Company in 1951.

Under the 1934 concession, the Kuwait Oil Company agreed to provide an initial payment of 475 000 rupees, an annual rental of 95 000 rupees, and royalty payments of three rupees per ton, a rate considerably lower than that secured by the governments of Iran, Iraq, and Saudi Arabia.[104] In July 1950, Abdullah approached the Kuwait Oil Company with a view to increasing his oil royalties. This request, however, became entangled in a separate dispute over the islands of Kubr, Qaru, and Umm al Maradim.[105] A concession for the three islands had been granted to the American Independent Oil Company by Shaikh Ahmad, a decision which his successor was determined to honour.[106] The Kuwait Oil Company, however, contended that it held the rights to these islands and attempted to take the matter to arbitration under article 18 of the 1934 concession agreement.[107] Acting on the advice of his legal representative, H. R. Bal-

---

[101] Catherine R. Schenk, *Britain and the Sterling Area: From Devaluation to Convertibility in the 1950s*, London: Routledge, 1994, p. 8. Under the terms of the American loan which had been secured at the end of 1946, Britain agreed to allow sterling to be freely converted into dollars by mid-1947. The flight from sterling, which followed the return to convertibility on 15 July, threatened both to exhaust Britain's dollar reserves and to undermine the value of sterling as a trading currency. Consequently, convertibility was suspended on 20 August. Before this suspension, the monthly dollar drain had reached the figure of $650 million (C. C. S. Newton, 'Sterling Crisis of 1947 and the British Response to the Marshall Plan', *The Economic History Review*, 37, 3 (1984): 398).

[102] In 1948, a Treasury official conceded: 'It is ludicrous to suggest that the Sheikh should be asked to surrender to the sterling area pool any dollars he may receive from oil companies' (Minute by F. M. Loughnane, 31 March 1948, T 236/5196).

[103] 'Kuwait: Exchange Control', Bank of England note, Sept 1963, OV 72/14.

[104] Peter Mansfield, *Kuwait: Vanguard of the Gulf*, London: Hutchinson, 1990, p. 32; Y. S. F. al-Sabah, *The Oil Economy of Kuwait*, London: Kegan Paul International, 1980, p. 39.

[105] Under article 5 of the Anglo-Ottoman Convention of 1913, the islands of Qaru and Umm al Maradim were recognized as belonging to Kuwait (Richard Schofield (ed.), *Territorial Foundations of the Gulf States*, London: UCL Press, 1994, p. 43).

[106] Notes for meeting with C. A. P. Southwell by H. T. Kemp, 7 Nov 1951, BP 107364.

[107] Minute by Alan Leavett, 3 July 1950, FO 371/82117.

lantyre, Abdullah argued that Islamic law prevented him, as a sovereign ruler, from submitting to arbitration.

The Foreign Office viewed the Ruler's claim with scepticism. For one thing, Islamic law was seen as having no application to the 1934 concession, and for another, Ahmad's signature of the agreement was deemed to have bound him and his successors to observe its terms, including the right to seek arbitration.[108] The KOC's response to the Ruler's procrastination was to postpone consideration of an increase in oil royalties until the islands dispute had been settled.[109] Although it is difficult to establish precise cause and effect, soon after this announcement Ballantyre abandoned the idea of appealing to Islamic law in the Ruler's dispute with the KOC.[110] Developments in Saudi Arabia, moreover, acted as a spur to the settlement of the royalty question in Kuwait.

In December 1950, the government of Saudi Arabia had secured a 50/50 profit-sharing agreement with the Arabian-American Oil Company,[111] an arrangement to which other Middle East oil producers aspired. On 1 April 1951, the Iraqi premier, Nuri al-Said, publicly committed himself to achieving as favourable a result as Saudi Arabia.[112] During the resulting negotiations, the Anglo-Iranian Oil Company, which owned half of the KOC and nearly one quarter of the Iraq Petroleum Company, found itself in a weak position. In particular, the loss of oil following the Iranian government's abrogation of its concession in March 1951 left the Company short of oil and consequently more dependent on other producers.[113] By 13 August, accord was reached on the basis of the 50/50 profit-sharing principle, the agreement in its final form being signed on 3 February 1952.[114] In April 1951, Abdullah made a further request to the Kuwait Oil Company for an increase in royalties.[115] As early as July the

---

[108] Minute by J. A. C. Gutteridge, 24 July 1950; Note of Mr Ballantyre's call on the Foreign Office, 27 July 1950, FO 371/82117.

[109] Letter from Southwell to Kemp, 13 Oct 1950, FO 371/82117.

[110] Telegram from Jakins to the Foreign Office, No. 225, 31 Oct 1951, FO 371/82117.

[111] Irvine H. Anderson, *Aramco, the United States and Saudi Arabia: A Study of the Dynamics of Foreign Oil Policy, 1933–1950*, Princeton, NJ: Princeton University Press, 1981, p. 194; Stephen Hemsley Longrigg, *Oil in the Middle East: Its Discovery and Development*, second edition, London: Oxford University Press, 1961, p. 210; Irvine H. Anderson, 'The American Oil Industry and the Fifty-Fifty Agreement of 1950', in James A. Bill and William Roger Louis (eds), *Musaddiq, Iranian Nationalism and Oil*, London: I. B. Tauris, 1988, pp. 143–63.

[112] Daniel Silverfarb, 'The Revision of Iraq's Oil Concession, 1949–52', *Middle Eastern Studies*, 32, 1 (1996): 78.

[113] Ibid., pp. 77–8.

[114] J. H. Bamberg, *The History of the British Petroleum Company: Volume 2: The Anglo-Iranian Years, 1928–1954*, Cambridge: Cambridge University Press, 1994, p. 339; Majid Khadduri, *Independent Iraq, 1932–1958: A Study in Iraqi Politics*, London: Oxford University Press, 1960, p. 354.

[115] Crystal, *Oil and Politics in the Gulf*, p. 64.

Company agreed in principle to a 50/50 profit-sharing formula.[116] The prospect of a sharp rise in Kuwait's oil wealth, however, created some misapprehension in Whitehall.

'Since the Kuwait Oil Company's concession provides for payments to the Ruler in Indian rupees,' explained the Foreign Office, 'we are concerned over the effect on India's sterling balances of any similar provision in the new agreement when much bigger sums will be involved.'[117] Indeed, the Foreign Office was worried lest the purchase of rupees for sterling by the Company from the Reserve Bank of India should increase the sub-continent's sterling balances at a time when Britain was negotiating a long-term financial agreement for their reduction.[118] Thus the Foreign Office was keen for the wording of the new concession agreement with the Ruler of Kuwait to provide for payment entirely in sterling. Although the Ruler readily agreed to receive sterling from Anglo-Iranian, he requested dollars from Gulf Oil, the American partner of the Kuwait Oil Company.[119]

The Ruler was already receiving dollars from the American Independent Oil Company (AMINOIL), which since 1948 had held the concession in the Neutral Zone between Saudi Arabia and Kuwait.[120] In contrast with normal sterling area practice, the Ruler did not pool these dollar revenues in London.[121] Britain was prepared to acquiesce in the terms of the AMINOIL concession since the annual payment amounted to only $625 000. Nevertheless, the sums involved in the case of the Kuwait Oil Company were so large that, as the Foreign Office put it, 'the proposed further breach in Sterling Area practice would involve the United Kingdom in great difficulty and embarrassment. A precedent would be set and this would endanger the whole basis of the Sterling Area itself which is of vital importance to the United Kingdom and Commonwealth.'[122]

A number of specific concerns were voiced by the British. First, they were reluctant to forego the dollars earned from Gulf Oil's purchases of sterling from London in order to make their share of payments to the Ruler.[123] Furthermore, the Treasury was worried about the possible effect

---

[116] Telegram from Southwell to L. T. Jordan (General Manager, Kuwait Oil Company), 12 July 1951, BP 106876.

[117] Telegram from the Foreign Office to the Bahrain Residency, No. 534, 10 Oct 1951, FO 371/91337.

[118] For a discussion of India's sterling balances, see B. R. Tomlinson, 'Indo-British Relations in the Post-Colonial Era: The Sterling Balances Negotiations, 1947–49', *Journal of Imperial and Commonwealth History*, 13, 3 (1985): 142–62.

[119] Telegram from Pelly to the Foreign Office, No. 235, 11 Nov 1951, FO 371/91338.

[120] Letter from Hay to Bevin, No. 122, 23 July 1948, POWE 33/1957.

[121] Letter from L. A. C. Fry to Pelly, 28 April 1954, POWE 33/2082.

[122] Telegram from the Foreign Office to the Bahrain Residency, No. 619, 17 Nov 1951, FO 371/91338.

[123] 'Payments under the Kuwait Oil Agreement', Note by Rose, 13 Nov 1951, FO 371/91338.

of the Ruler's proposal on other oil-producing members of the sterling area such as Iraq.[124] Underpinning Britain's position was a determination to conserve scarce dollar reserves by obtaining the bulk of her oil for sterling, a principle which would be undermined if oil companies began making payments to Middle East oil producers in dollars.[125]

The final discussions between Abdullah and the KOC over the new concession were held in Kuwait in November. 'The main difficulty ... in the negotiations', recorded Pelly,

> was that on the one side was the Shaikh of Kuwait, ignorant, obscurantist and hypersensitive to any reflection on his 'honour' (which in this case he identified with doing as well for Kuwait out of his oil company as other countries, notably Iraq, do for theirs); on the other, advising the negotiators, were American lawyers, quite incapable of giving their support to a plain, unqualified statement — the only sort the Shaikh understands.[126]

In their final stages, the negotiations were led by the managing director of the KOC, C. A. P. Southwell, a man described by Pelly as 'obtuse, verbose and imprecise'. '[I]t seems a pity', concluded Pelly, 'that with such interests at stake the A.I.O.C. cannot produce a negotiator of higher calibre'. On the Kuwaiti side, Kemp, in whom Abdullah placed implicit trust, proved the most influential figure. Crichton, by contrast, was a marginal figure. Indeed, far from being consulted over discussions with the KOC in 1951, he was denied even a sight of the new oil agreement.[127]

Despite the evident difficulties and misunderstandings which characterized the talks between the KOC and the Ruler, the new concession agreement was ready for signature at the end of November. Under this agreement, profits were to be split equally between the Company and the Ruler, the latter's share coming in the form of a royalty at the rate provided by the 1934 concession agreement, and a local income tax.[128] The payment provisions were framed in this way in order to allow Gulf Oil to claim income tax relief in the United States on account of tax paid in Kuwait.[129] Although Anglo-Iranian claimed similar relief in the United Kingdom, their claim was rejected on the grounds that the proposed tax did not represent a genuine income tax which could be regarded as a tax corresponding to those imposed on the Company in the UK.[130] As regards

---

[124] Ibid.
[125] As an indication of the importance of this concern, by December 1951 the cost to Britain of replacing Iranian oil, which had been paid for in sterling, with dollar oil was running at an annual figure of $300 million (Silverfarb, 'Revision of Iraq's Oil Concession', p. 89).
[126] Letter from Pelly to Hay, 12 Dec 1951, FO 371/91340.
[127] Minute by Serpell, 3 March 1952, T 236/4287.
[128] Memorandum signed by C. A. P. Southwell for the companies and H. T. Kemp for His Highness, 26 Nov 1951, FO 371/91339.
[129] 'Kuwait income tax law', Note by Rose, 15 Dec 1951, FO 371/91340.
[130] Ibid.

Oil Expansion, 1950–1

the disputed islands of Kubr, Qaru, and Umm al Maradim, the KOC was prepared to compromise in the interests of securing a wider settlement. On 9 November 1951, Southwell was authorized to relinquish the Company's claims to the three islands,[131] a decision which was enshrined in the new concession agreement.[132]

Much to the relief of the British, the Ruler consented to receive all his payments from the Kuwait Oil Company in sterling following assurances that Britain recognized his right to convert sterling into rupees in any amounts required for current needs, and that Britain would supply dollars for any goods essential for the benefit of the state and not available for sterling.[133] The British also promised neither to require the surrender of the Ruler's AMINOIL dollars to the central reserves in London, nor to suggest that he should use them to finance his dollar expenditure on development.[134] Furthermore, the British authorities in Kuwait were prepared to treat requests from the al-Sabah ruling family for foreign exchange, either for overseas travel or the purchase of property abroad, with considerable latitude. As the Political Agent, J. C. B. Richmond, explained in 1960: 'this exception in favour of the Ruler and his family and the few seniormost Shaikhs, is the price we pay for securing the Ruler's agreement to accept the whole of his royalties from the Kuwait Oil Company in sterling and not to insist on a dollar element'.[135] Writing three years earlier, the Economic Counsellor to the Political Resident, N. M. P. Reilly, noted: 'It is the fact that he [the Ruler] can salt away his Aminoil dollars which, to a large extent, permits him to rest content with the Kuwait Oil Company sterling payment arrangement.'[136] Having secured the Ruler's agreement to the acceptance of payments in sterling, the British were confronted with the problem of ensuring that he employed his revenue in ways which would not harm the sterling area. This will be the subject of the next chapter.

---

[131] Telegram from Neville A. Gass (Managing Director, Anglo-Iranian Oil Company) to Southwell, 9 Nov 1951, BP 107579.

[132] Memorandum signed by C. A. P. Southwell for the companies and H. T. Kemp for His Highness, 26 Nov 1951, FO 371/91339.

[133] 'Payments under the Kuwait Oil Agreement', Note by Rose, 13 Nov 1951, FO 371/91338; Note of a meeting in S. Goldman's room at the Treasury, 6 Feb 1952, T 236/4287; 'Kuwait: Seabed Concession', Minute by A. Duke, 29 Feb 1956, T 236/5197.

[134] 'Persian Gulf Exchange Control', Note by P. T. Sloman, 2 April 1954, T 231/705.

[135] Letter from J. C. B. Richmond to R. A. Beaumont, No. 1119/60, 26 April, 1960, FO 371/148988.

[136] Letter from N. M. P. Reilly to M. E. Johnston (Treasury), No. 10814/18/57, 25 July 1957, T 236/5199.

2: Investment and Administrative Problems, 1952–5

> The problem of adapting the administration in Kuwait to the increasing strains which are imposed upon it as a result of the increasing revenues and expanding economy is a vast one.[1]

> H.M.G. have no right to intervene directly in internal affairs and can exert influence only through guidance and advice.... A further unfortunate but inescapable fact is that in internal matters, and especially in the problem of development, our advice is far from welcome. The Ruler and particularly his family (true to Arab tradition) regard the disposal of the oil revenues as their private concern and are deeply suspicious of attempts to interfere.[2]

Having secured the Ruler's acceptance of his payment from the Kuwait Oil Company in sterling, the British were left with the problem of ensuring that his surplus revenues were used in a manner which would bring maximum benefit to Britain and the sterling area, while causing as little disruption to Kuwait as possible. As the Foreign Office warned:

> In Kuwait there are the risks of inflation, over-expenditure and the effect of a possible decline in revenues in the future. For the sterling area there is the danger to the United Kingdom balance of payments which could result from indiscriminate spending or lending abroad.[3]

In *Arabia Without Sultans*, Fred Halliday characterizes the al-Sabah as compliant custodians of imperial interests.[4] By contrast with this interpretation,

---

[1] Minute by C. M. Rose, 6 May 1952, FO 371/98325.
[2] 'Kuwait', Minute by L. A. C. Fry, 26 Oct 1954, FO 371/109822.
[3] Draft Foreign Office paper on Her Majesty's Government's position in and policy towards Kuwait, 15 April 1953, POWE 33/1927.
[4] Fred Halliday, *Arabia Without Sultans*, Harmondsworth: Penguin Books, 1979, pp. 432–3.

the ruling family's rapid awakening to its new status and wealth created conditions unfavourable for the exertion of British influence over Kuwait and the internal administration. Nevertheless, such was the value which was placed on the Shaikhdom, and such were the fears about the possible damage to British interests that economic and administrative mismanagement could cause, that Britain sought, through a combination of informal advice and formal pressure, to intervene in Kuwaiti affairs. This can be seen with respect to the investment of the Ruler's surplus sterling.

I

In an attempt to off-set the loss of oil from Iran following the nationalization of the Anglo-Iranian Oil Company by the Iranian premier, Muhammad Musaddiq, in March 1951,[5] the Kuwait Oil Company, half-owned by Anglo-Iranian, began to increase production in Kuwait.[6] In December 1950, for example, daily oil production in Kuwait stood at 500 000 barrels; by October of the following year, this figure had increased to over 700 000, with the prospect of reaching 900 000 barrels per day by the spring of 1952.[7] This rise in production, coupled with the 50/50 profit-sharing agreement of 1951, witnessed a sudden and dramatic growth in Kuwait revenues from £6 million in 1951 to a projected figure of £50 to £60 million for the following year.[8] The question of the investment of the Ruler's sterling balances was one which caused particular concern. With the continuing dollar shortage in mind, an official of the Treasury commented: 'It is not going to be easy to persuade the Sheikh to put his money into sterling at a time when dollars must seem to him to be more attractive than ever.'[9] Moreover, the Bank of England noted: 'The fact that so much sterling will be going to this primitive but vital area makes the problem one

---

[5] For accounts of the nationalization crisis, see William Roger Louis, *The British Empire in the Middle East, 1945–1951: Arab Nationalism, the United States, and Postwar Imperialism*, Oxford: Clarendon, 1984, pp. 632–89; J. H. Bamberg, *The History of the British Petroleum Company: Volume 2: The Anglo-Iranian Years, 1928–1954*, Cambridge: Cambridge University Press, 1994, pp. 410–511; James Cable, *Intervention at Abadan: Plan Buccaneer*, Basingstoke: Macmillan, 1991; Mostafa Elm, *Oil, Power and Principle: Iran's Oil Nationalization and its Aftermath*, Syracuse, NY: Syracuse University Press, 1992.
[6] Susan Strange, *Sterling and British Policy: A Political Study of an International Currency in Decline*, Oxford: Oxford University Press, 1971, p. 107; Homa Katouzian, 'Oil Boycott and the Political Economy: Musaddiq and the Strategy of Non-oil Economics', in James A. Bill and William Roger Louis (eds), *Musaddiq, Iranian Nationalism and Oil*, London: I. B. Tauris, 1988, p. 207.
[7] Letter from H. G. Jakins to Sir Rupert Hay, 16 Oct 1951, FO 371/91260.
[8] *Persian Gulf: Annual Review for 1951*, FO 371/98323; Telegram from the Commonwealth Relations Office to the UK High Commissioner in India, No. 1876, 4 Oct 1951, T 236/4286.
[9] 'Persian Gulf', Minute by M. T. Flett, 21 Jan 1952, T 236/4286.

of considerable importance.'[10] The Political Resident in the Persian Gulf, Sir Rupert Hay, described the situation as 'frightening', and emphasized that 'It is fully time that we started to guide the Ruler on the right lines regarding the disposal of his surplus revenue'.[11]

The Foreign Office was also mindful of the challenges facing both Britain and Kuwait in the light of rapidly increasing oil revenues. Its position was typified by the Head of the Eastern Department, G. W. Furlonge, who minuted: 'the great increase of production foreshadowed in Kuwait and Qatar, combined with the higher rates of royalty which the Rulers are likely to receive, can only result in the revenues, particularly in Kuwait, soon growing out of all proportion to the capacity of these small States to absorb them'.[12] 'On the other hand', continued Furlonge, 'the existing policy of guiding the individual States towards eventual independence precludes us from assuming direct responsibility for their administration, and the capacity of the Rulers and their populations to evolve administrations able to cope with these swollen revenues is strictly limited.' The Foreign Secretary, Anthony Eden, also entered the debate, declaring: 'This wants watching. I know most of these Sheikhdoms fairly well, and we must follow a well laid policy or we may run into troubles.'[13]

During a meeting of officials held at the Foreign Office at the beginning of 1952, the conclusion was reached that 'His Majesty's Government have a dual interest in the uses to which Kuwait's vast sterling revenues are put by virtue of their obligation towards the Ruler as protecting power and through their own interest in safeguarding the position of sterling'.[14] Towards the end of 1951, Sir Rupert Hay had advocated the despatch of an official to Kuwait to make recommendations to the Ruler with respect to the disposal of his surplus revenue.[15] The Permanent-Under Secretary at the Foreign Office, Sir William Strang, had already suggested that his deputy, Sir Roger Makins, embark on a study visit to the Persian Gulf.[16] Makins accepted the task, travelling to Kuwait in February 1952.

Makins was accompanied by C. E. Loombe[17] of the Bank of England

---

[10] 'Middle East Oil: Iraq and the Persian Gulf', Note by the Bank of England, 23 Nov 1951, POWE 33/1969.
[11] Letter from Hay to G. W. Furlonge, No. 111.12/16, 13 Nov 1951, FO 371/91300.
[12] 'The Persian Gulf', Minute by Furlonge, 5 Nov 1951, FO 371/91283.
[13] Minute by Anthony Eden, 1 Dec 1951, FO 371/91283.
[14] Note of a meeting held in the Foreign Office to discuss the administration of Persian Gulf oil revenues, 15 Jan 1952, POWE 33/1969.
[15] Letter from Hay to Furlonge, No. 111.12/16, 13 Nov 1951, FO 371/91300.
[16] Minute by Sir William Strang, 10 Sept 1951, FO 371/91341.
[17] Claude Evan Loombe (1905–78); CMG; Chartered Bank, 1924–41; Ministry of Finance, Iraq Government, 1941–5; entered the Bank of England, 1945; Adviser, 1945–64; Adviser to the Governors, 1964–5; Director, British Bank of the Middle East, 1965–77; Chairman, 1967–74; member, Kuwait Currency Board, 1960–9; Jordan Currency Board, 1956–60; Libyan Currency Board, 1952–6.

and D. R. Serpell of the Treasury, the three meeting the Ruler on 20 February 1952. In reporting the results of these discussions, Makins remarked: 'It was hard enough to explain to Nuri [the Iraqi premier] the working of the sterling area, but I cannot adequately describe to you the difficulty of doing so to Abdullah'.[18] During the meeting, Makins attempted to impress upon the Ruler the fact that such was the size of his income from the KOC that only part of it could be absorbed by current expenditure and development projects. The specific proposals which Makins made fell into two categories: the selection of advisers to allocate funds for normal expenses of government and development; and the establishment of a small committee in London which would make investments in sterling securities on behalf of the Ruler. When Abdullah pressed for an explanation of the danger to sterling posed by his unused balances, Makins focused on the potential loss of confidence in sterling. '[I]f such great sums remained uninvested', he argued, 'they might prove a weakening influence on sterling in which Kuwait and other countries in the sterling area had a strong mutual interest'.[19] The Shaikh, however, temporized, promising only to consult with his London representative, Kemp. When Kemp met with Foreign Office officials, he expressed the view that there was a good chance of the Ruler accepting Britain's investment proposals.[20] Nevertheless, Kemp subsequently warned against pressuring the Ruler, suggesting a further approach to him in the autumn. The investment proposals were also delayed by acute administrative problems which afflicted Kuwait in the course of 1952.

In April and May both the Political Agent, C. J. Pelly, and the General Manager of the Kuwait Oil Company, L. T. Jordan, reported rumours of Shaikh Abdullah's impending abdication.[21] The veracity of this rumour was confirmed by the State Secretary, Abdullah Mullah Salleh, who informed Pelly that the Ruler had been experiencing great trouble with the disobedience and extravagance of the other Shaikhs and, in an attempt to bring them into line, had threatened abdication.[22] One of the Shaikhs' principal crimes involved the marking out of large areas of desert with the object of claiming huge sums in compensation when the land was reclaimed for development projects. Commenting upon this malpractice, Pelly opined: 'the Al Sabah are without peers, even in the Gulf, in the exercise of rapacity and selfishness'.[23] The Kuwait administrative report for 1951, moreover, reported that the Shaikhs were guilty of 'behaving often as

---

[18] Telegram from Sir Roger Makins to the Foreign Office, No. 24, 21 Feb 1952, T 236/4287.
[19] Ibid.
[20] 'Kuwait', Minute by E. A. Berthoud, 26 Feb 1952, T 236/4287.
[21] Telegram from C. J. Pelly to the Foreign Office, No. 91, 28 April 1952, FO 371/98325; Letter from L. T. Jordan to C. A. P. Southwell, No. 190, 6 May 1952, BP 106876.
[22] Telegram from Pelly to the Foreign Office, No. 93, 29 April 1952, FO 371/98325.
[23] Letter from Pelly to Hay, 27 May 1952, FO 371/98325.

independently of the central authority of the Ruler as did the barons of pre-Tudor times'.[24] '[T]he struggle at present' agreed Hay, 'is more between the King and his unruly barons than between the people at large and the aristocracy'.[25] The Foreign Office's response to the mounting sense of crisis in Kuwait was to revive the idea of an executive council consisting of leading Shaikhs which, while having authority to make decisions and issue instructions in all spheres, would be responsible directly to the Ruler.[26] More controversially, the Foreign Office advocated the appointment of a senior British adviser who would supervise all administrative, economic, and financial matters, as well as being a member of the prospective executive council. Referring to the proposed appointment, however, Sir Rupert Hay noted: 'It would ... be very unpopular in Kuwait and the Ruler might well become even more disposed to abdication if he thought we were insisting on it.'[27] Moreover, while accepting that the existing adviser, Colonel Crichton, was 'not quite the man for the job', Hay was prepared to give him a few more months before seeking to supersede or replace him.[28]

Crichton, himself, not unnaturally, expressed initial doubt about the appointment of a senior adviser. 'The use of the word "Senior" ... ', remarked Crichton,

> suggests the existence of a belief, somewhere, that the difficulties attending our task here would yield to more mature and skilled advice than His Highness is now receiving. If this is so ... it reveals a misconception of the root causes of these difficulties. These causes are (1) the lack of a basic administration adequate to cope with the very large scheme of development to which the State is committed and (2) the inability or reluctance of the Ruler to enforce measures which he has been advised, and has agreed, to adopt for the improvement of his administration.[29]

Crichton was, however, in favour of the selection of an Arab-speaking personal assistant to the Ruler, as well as the engagement of British 'experts' to head each department of government.[30] Hay provided support for Crichton's suggestion, arguing that 'both the Ruler and the general public in Kuwait would more readily accept two or three more British experts at low level than a senior adviser of the Belgrave type'.[31] While Britain debated what palliative measures to take, the administrative

---

[24] *Kuwait Administrative Report for 1951*, FO 371/98323.
[25] Letter from Hay to Eden, No. 64, 11 June 1952, FO 371/98333.
[26] Telegram from the Foreign Office to Bahrain, No. 311, 30 April 1952, FO 371/98325.
[27] Telegram from Hay to the Foreign Office, No. 242, 30 April 1952, FO 371/98325.
[28] Letter from Hay to R. F. G. Sarell, 21 April 1952, FO 371/98349.
[29] Letter from G. C. L. Crichton to Pelly, 13 May 1952, FO 371/98349.
[30] Telegram from Hay to the Foreign Office, No. 310, 6 June 1952; Letter from Hay to A. D. M. Ross, 7 June 1952, FO 371/93350.
[31] Telegram from Hay to the Foreign Office, No. 26, 31 May 1952, FO 371/93350.

problems grew ever more serious. It was the activities of the Ruler's half-brother, Shaikh Fahad, which caused the most concern.

As a prominent member of the *Aulad Salim*, Fahad had taken a leading role in the finance department, where he soon acquired a reputation for malfeasance. In 1940, the advisory council took the opportunity afforded by Fahad's absence in Bahrain to inspect his accounts. On his return he was confronted with certain discrepancies leading to heated exchanges during which Fahad is alleged to have spat at two council members.[32] The British also questioned his scrupulousness, the Political Agent describing his financial administration as doing 'neither him nor the state credit'.[33] Fahad was also viewed with suspicion by Britain on account of his political affiliations. During a visit to Alexandria in August 1944, for example, he caused some consternation by discussing Arab unity with the Egyptian premier, Nahas Pasha.[34] Britain's misgivings about Fahad were exemplified by Hay who described him as 'thoroughly dishonest'.[35] Moreover, in advising the Foreign Office on how the wayward Shaikh should be treated during his visit to London in December 1950, Hay suggested: 'he should be treated with consideration as the brother of the Ruler but not too effusively in view of his past reputation for embezzling state funds'.[36] Britain's suspicions of Fahad were heightened following the appointment in June 1951 of Enoch Sevier Duncan as America's first consul in Kuwait.[37] Fahad was reported to have taken Duncan 'under his wing', placing a house belonging to one of his wives at the new consul's disposal.[38] Duncan also hired Salim Garabet, an Iraqi friend of Fahad, to act as his interpreter.[39]

Fahad's administrative empire in Kuwait provided him with considerable scope to frustrate British wishes. In addition to being head of the health department, he took control of the department of public works, as well of the municipality, in April 1952. Clearly concerned about this accumulation of offices, Pelly spoke to the Ruler advising him to banish Fahad.[40] Abdullah, however, merely temporized. Fahad's obstructive potential was soon demonstrated over development projects.

---

[32] *Administration Report of the Kuwait Political Agency for the Year 1940*, by A. C. Galloway, 26 Jan 1941, R/15/5/364.
[33] Telegram from the Political Agent to C. G. Prior, No. 642, 23 Aug 1944, R/15/5/217.
[34] Ibid.
[35] Telegram from Hay to the Foreign Office, No. 410, 1 Dec 1950, FO 371/82163.
[36] Ibid.
[37] Britain had initially resisted the appointment of an American consul, fearing that it would inevitably lead to demands from Egypt and Iraq for similar representation in Kuwait (Letter from B. A. B. Burrows to J. Palmer (US Embassy, London), 16 Aug 1949, FO 371/75038).
[38] Letter from Jakins to the Acting Political Resident, No. 6 (90/33/51), 17 Sept 1951, FO 371/91354.
[39] Miriam Joyce, *Kuwait, 1945–1996: An Anglo-American Perspective*, London: Frank Cass, 1998, p. 16.
[40] 'Kuwait administration and advisers', Minute by Rose, 23 June 1952, FO 371/98351.

In July 1952, Fahad informed the controller of development, W. F. Hasted, that the decisions of the development board could only be implemented if they were subsequently approved by both the municipality and himself.[41] Hasted was particularly concerned that contracts with British firms would be cancelled, a fear that was realized when Fahad refused to confirm an order for accommodation for government supervisory staff. Matters came to a head when the Ruler proposed to embark on a three-week cruise without first making adequate arrangements with respect to the exercise of authority while he was away. On 10 July, both Hasted and Crichton urged Abdullah to concede limited authority to the development board during his absence, prompting the harassed Ruler to declare his intention to abdicate.[42]

Abdullah's renewed threat to relinquish power did not cause the Foreign Office undue alarm. 'If Fahad is to be prevented from impeding the sound development of Kuwait and administrative chaos is to be avoided', remarked C. M. Rose (Eastern Department), 'we may have to risk the Ruler carrying out his threat to abdicate.'[43] Rose proceeded to describe Abdullah as 'an irresolute and rather broken reed from whom it is virtually impossible to get any decision on a matter of importance'. Indeed, the Foreign Office was prepared to countenance the accession of Abdullah Mubarak provided that he enjoyed the support of the al-Sabah and that a personal assistant to the Ruler had already been installed.[44] Pelly, nevertheless, expressed doubt about whether Abdullah would be prepared to stand down in favour of Abdullah Mubarak, describing the latter's 'increasing extravagance, flamboyance and impulsiveness' as 'hateful' to the Ruler.[45] Referring in his memoirs to Abdullah Mubarak's epicurean ways, Pelly's successor, G. W. Bell, recalled: 'The number of his palaces, the wealth he had accumulated and his occasional indiscretions in the cabarets of Beirut and Paris caused his nephew the Ruler frequent embarrassment.'[46]

In an attempt to resolve the growing sense of crisis, Hay wrote to the Ruler urging him not only to employ a British personal assistant, but also to delegate authority to the development board and the finance department. Although Abdullah thanked Her Majesty's Government for their advice, he gave Delphic replies to the specific recommendations.[47] In discussions with Pelly, however, the Ruler was more blunt, expressing his

---

[41] Telegram from J. A. F. Gethin to the Foreign Office, No. 175, 9 July 1952, FO 371/98351.
[42] Telegram from Gethin to the Foreign Office, unnumbered, 10 July 1952, FO 371/98351.
[43] Minute by Rose, 14 July 1952, FO 371/98351.
[44] Telegram from the Foreign Office to the Bahrain Residency, No. 459, 14 July 1952, FO 371/98351.
[45] Telegram from Pelly to the Foreign Office, No. 49, 17 July 1952, FO 371/998341.
[46] Sir Gawain Bell, *Shadows on the Sand*, London: C. Hurst and Company, 1983, p. 231.
[47] Telegram from Pelly to the Foreign Office, No. 192, 5 Aug 1952, FO 371/98351.

annoyance at these attempts to interfere in Kuwait's internal affairs.[48] The limits on Britain's influence in Kuwait were emphasized by her inability to displace Shaikh Fahad. Indeed, it was increasingly accepted that cooperation, rather than confrontation, was the best way to deal with him, Hay recording that 'As Fahad cannot be got rid of, Crichton is doing his best to placate him. Parry is already on good terms with him and Crichton has now induced Hasted to try and make friends with him.'[49] Fahad's promotion to the presidency of the development board in December 1952 merely emphasized the need to maintain tolerable working relationships with him. With the abatement of the immediate administrative crisis, British attention once more focused on the investment of the Ruler's surplus revenue.

II

When the Political Agent, C. J. Pelly, interviewed the Ruler in October, Abdullah admitted that he had not understood what Makins had said to him eight months earlier with respect to either sterling or the sterling area.[50] The Foreign Office was forced to concede that 'the Ruler may not like our ideas about how he should spend his sterling, especially when it is pretty clear that our immediate aim is to "sterilize" his money or direct it into channels which will place as little strain as possible on sterling and the U.K.'s resources.'[51] The Colonial Office suggested that part of the Ruler's surplus should be used to promote Muslim education along the East Coast of Africa.[52] The Treasury was sceptical about such schemes, nevertheless. 'Our first concern as regards the Sheikh's oil royalties', remarked an official, 'must be to secure his agreement to our investment proposals and we must be most careful not to do anything which might prejudice this object.'[53] On 21 October, however, the Ruler expressed willingness broadly to comply with Britain's recommendations for the investment of his sterling surplus.[54] What swayed him is unclear, but it would seem likely that Kemp's support for the British proposals proved decisive. The knowledge that a healthy rate of interest could be realized from sterling securities no doubt also influenced the Ruler's decision. However, the First Secretary at the Bahrain Residency, C. M. Pirie-Gordon, expressed concern about the long-term prospects for Kuwait's support of sterling. 'In considering this problem', he observed,

---

[48] Telegram from Pelly to the Foreign Office, No. 186, 2 Aug 1952, FO 371/98351.
[49] Letter from Hay to D. A. Greenhill, 28 Nov 1952, FO 371/98352.
[50] Telegram from Pelly to the Foreign Office, No. 243, 20 Oct 1952, FO 371/98399.
[51] Letter from Berthoud to Sir L. Rowan, 16 Oct 1952, FO 371/98399.
[52] Letter from W. L. Gorell Barnes to Sir James Bowker, 23 Sept 1952, FO 371/98458.
[53] Letter from Flett to Bowker, 20 Oct 1952, FO 371/98458.
[54] Telegram from Pelly to the Foreign Office, No. 245, 21 Oct 1952, FO 371/98399.

it is important to realise that in the last resort we are dependent on the goodwill of the Ruler and his family, and that the human element is frail. Even the rudiments of the operation on which we are now embarking, are not, and never can be, understood by the Kuwaitis most concerned. To them the problem of safeguarding sterling is only an amiable expression of British nationalism against the United States, in fact little more than a whim to be indulged for the sake of 'auld lang syne', provided it becomes in no way a burden.[55]

The Ruler's signature of the investment proposals was finally secured in February 1953. The Kuwait Investment Board, which was initially provided with £27 million from Kuwait, consisted of four members: H. T. Kemp, Lord Piercy (a member of the Court of the Bank of England), Lord Kennet (a director of the British Bank of the Middle East), and C. P. L. Whishaw (a partner in the firm of Freshfield's, the Ruler's solicitors). Despite the establishment of the Kuwait Investment Board, the British were still far from sanguine. 'If we bring too much pressure to bear to slow down developments and increase investment,' cautioned Hay, 'we shall almost certainly be accused of appropriating Kuwait revenues for biased purposes.'[56] Reservations were also voiced by the Board of Trade about British policy with respect to the Ruler's surplus, one official opining: 'I must confess to some doubt about the underlying assumption . . . that our immediate aim should be to "sterilize" the Ruler's sterling because we cannot redeem it with goods. Is this really valid?'[57] The dilemma facing Britain was summed up by a Foreign Office official:

> The principle of suggesting ways in which Kuwait could use her riches, rather than finding arguments for and ways and means of keeping them locked up, may seem questionable, given the sterling area's present difficulties. But to use our influence in Kuwait towards a solution of this problem which is intended to help the U.K. rather than Kuwait, would be dubious ethics.[58]

Despite these concerns about the propriety of the investment proposals, the British remained convinced of the need to manage Kuwait surpluses in a way which would place as little strain as possible on the UK economy.[59] For example, when instructing the new Political Resident in the Persian Gulf, Bernard Burrows, of his principal duties in July 1953, the Foreign Office remarked:

> The expenditure of its [Kuwait's] large sterling revenue unless properly directed is capable of inflicting the most serious damage on the sterling area. Her Majesty's Government can no longer afford to confine themselves to the

---

[55] Letter from C. M. Pirie-Gordon to Hay, 11 Nov 1952, FO 371/98400.
[56] Telegram from Hay to the Foreign Office, No. 165, 3 March 1953, FO 371/104340.
[57] Letter from I. A. H. Moore to J. E. Coulson, 25 March 1953, FO 371/104341.
[58] 'Kuwait Revenues', Minute by C. T. Gandy, undated, FO 371/104341.
[59] Paul W. T. Kingston, *Britain and the Politics of Modernization in the Middle East, 1945–1958*, Cambridge: Cambridge University Press, 1996, pp. 42-4.

role authorised by the treaties and agreements in force and sanctioned by usage but must also interest themselves in all matters which affect the political and economic stability of Kuwait or which may affect the interests of the United Kingdom in the widest sense.[60]

Britain's determination to take a leading role in Kuwait's internal affairs was demonstrated by her renewed pressure on the Ruler to appoint a senior British adviser.

In April 1953, a meeting of officials of the Foreign Office, Treasury, Ministry of Fuel and Power, Commonwealth Relations Office, and Bank of England discussed the situation in Kuwait. While it was recognized that executive authority would have to remain in the hands of Kuwaitis, it was agreed that Britain should 'concentrate on building up the authority of British officials employed by the Kuwait authorities in an advisory capacity and on improving the means by which we are able to persuade the Ruler to accept Her Majesty's Government's advice'.[61] Doubt was expressed about whether Crichton and Hasted possessed either the technical knowledge to enable them to give the best advice or sufficient stature to ensure that the advice which they gave was accepted. Despite the Ruler's previous obduracy, the conclusion was reached that a senior adviser should be superimposed over the existing advisers. As a preliminary measure, the Foreign Office requested the head of the British Middle East Office, Sir Thomas Rapp, to embark on a study visit to Kuwait and report on the possible means of strengthening British influence there.[62] Rapp accepted the task, travelling to Kuwait in June.

Reporting on his findings, Rapp argued that 'The chief danger ... arises from the sudden acquisition of wealth and the adoption of a too ambitious development programme by a small state accustomed to personal rule and lacking the rudiments of a proper administrative system.'[63] 'Unless such a system is speedily introduced and development kept more in line with administrative capacity,' continued Rapp, 'a still more chaotic situation will ensue, which will be even more detrimental to us than to Kuwait itself. It is therefore essential that we should take a more direct interest in Kuwait's internal affairs than has hitherto been the case.' Nevertheless, Rapp was all too aware of the practical difficulties in achieving this aim, drawing attention to 'the tenuous nature of our rights in Kuwait, which are neither by length of association nor by the scope of our

---

[60] Letter from the Foreign Office to Burrows, No. 125 (EA 1053/8), 24 July 1953, FO 371/104270, cited in Jill Crystal, *Oil and Politics in the Gulf: Rulers and Merchants in Kuwait and Qatar*, Cambridge: Cambridge University Press, 1995, p. 67.
[61] Record of a meeting at the Foreign Office to discuss the situation in Kuwait, 16 April 1953, FO 371/104325.
[62] Telegram from the Foreign Office to Sir Thomas Rapp, No. 812, 12 May 1953, FO 371/104327.
[63] Letter from Rapp to Sir Winston Churchill, No. 20, 17 June 1953, FO 371/104328.

agreements by any means so firmly established as, for example, in Bahrain'.[64] Undaunted, Rapp concluded that 'The appointment of a Senior Adviser is imperative to exercise continuous influence on the Ruler, to supervise the introduction of the necessary administrative reforms and to coordinate the activities of the British Advisers.'[65] While in full sympathy with Rapp, the Foreign Office expressed reservations about the practicality of his recommendations in the light of the failure of high-level attempts to persuade the Ruler to accept a senior adviser during his visit to London for the coronation in June 1953.

The suggestion of using the opportunity provided by Abdullah's presence in London to impress upon him the rectitude of appointing a senior adviser was first made at an official meeting at the Foreign Office in April.[66] As the coronation approached, both the Minister of State at the Foreign Office, Selwyn Lloyd, and the Chancellor of the Exchequer, R. A. Butler, made representations to the Prime Minister, Winston Churchill, requesting him to receive the Ruler. 'Kuwait is of the greatest importance to us', stressed Butler, 'and I feel sure that a talk with you personally will do more than anything else to convince the Ruler of our interest in his territory and our ability to help him with the many problems created by his huge new wealth.'[67] More specifically, Lloyd urged Churchill to impress upon Shaikh Abdullah the necessity of a single British expert to deal with the continuing problems arising from Kuwait's rapid economic development.[68] During the meeting between Churchill and the Ruler on 10 June, the former lent his support to the idea of a senior British adviser to oversee economic and financial policy, pledging the British government to help in the selection of such an individual.[69] Abdullah, however, expressed satisfaction with existing arrangements, refusing to commit himself on further appointments. During discussions with Selwyn Lloyd two days later, the Ruler proved equally intractable, raising the question of his date gardens in southern Iraq as a 'counter-blast' to Britain's pressure for the appointment of a senior adviser.[70]

In 1871, the Turkish governor of Baghdad, Midhat Pasha, launched an expedition into the interior of the Arabian peninsula. In recognition of the assistance provided by Shaikh Abdullah (r. 1866–92), the Ottoman

[64] 'The situation in Kuwait', p. 2, 12 June 1953, enclosure to Rapp's despatch No. 20, 17 June 1953, FO 371/104328.
[65] Ibid., p. 3.
[66] Record of a meeting held at the Foreign Office to discuss the situation in Kuwait, 16 April 1953, FO 371/104325.
[67] Minute from R. A. Butler to the Prime Minister, 21 May 1953, FO 371/104328.
[68] Minute by Selwyn Lloyd to the Prime Minister, P.M./M.S./53/257, 10 June 1953, FO 371/104328.
[69] Minute by J. C. B. Richmond, 10 June 1953, FO 371/104272.
[70] 'Ruler of Kuwait's Date Gardens', Minute by Greenhill, 13 July 1953, FO 371/104388.

authorities rewarded him with extensive date gardens on the Shatt al-Arab in southern Iraq.[71] As part of the agreement reached with Shaikh Mubarak in November 1914, Britain promised to uphold his ownership of the gardens and guarantee their exemption from taxation in perpetuity.[72] This pledge, however, proved difficult to uphold, particularly after Iraq's acquisition of independent status in 1932. Not only did the Iraqis refuse to recognize the gardens' immunity from taxation, but they also tacitly supported moves to deprive the Shaikh of Kuwait of his title to the estates.[73] The tortuous legal proceedings caused acute embarrassment to the British. On the one hand, they were under a clear moral obligation to honour their 1914 undertaking, while on the other, they were constantly frustrated in achieving this by the independent state of Iraq. In 1933, for example, Shaikh Ahmad lost his title to most of one garden, necessitating the payment of compensation by the British.[74] Four-fifths of the remaining property became the subject of protracted litigation.

Although oil revenues soon eclipsed those from the date gardens, the Rulers of Kuwait clung tenaciously to their ownership claims. 'The Sheikh of Kuwait', recorded an official of the Foreign Office in 1953, 'is not unreasonably pressing for a settlement of this case in which we are clearly committed to give him satisfaction. He will unfortunately be inclined to measure the value of our protection by the outcome of this case.'[75] Two options faced the British: to attempt to buy themselves out of their obligation by providing the Ruler with compensation, or to persist with appeals to the Iraqi government and with legal representations in the Iraqi courts. Both remedies, however, presented problems. First, it was by no means certain that the Ruler would accept cash compensation from the British, an official of the Foreign Office conceding: 'He is immensely rich and the sum we are likely to offer him may be treated with contempt.'[76] Furthermore, it was feared that an offer of compensation could be represented as an open admission of failure to honour an obligation in full, thus undermining Britain's standing with the Ruler. In addition, the Foreign Office was worried about the reaction of the Treasury to the suggestion that Britain should compensate the Ruler. '[T]he Treasury will not

---

[71] Richard Schofield, *Kuwait and Iraq: Historical Claims and Territorial Disputes*, second edition, London: Royal Institute of International Affairs, 1993, p. 12; Maurice Mendelson and Susan Hulton, 'Iraq's Claim to Sovereignty over Kuwait', in Richard Schofield (ed.), *Territorial Foundations of the Gulf States*, London: UCL Press Limited, 1994, p. 119.
[72] H. V. F. Winstone and Zahra Freeth, *Kuwait: Prospect and Reality*, London: George Allen and Unwin, 1972, p. 76.
[73] Penelope Tuson, *The Records of the British Residency and Agencies in the Persian Gulf*, London: India Office Library and Records, 1979, p. 135.
[74] 'Ruler of Kuwait's Date Gardens', Minute by Greenhill, 13 July 1953, FO 371/104388.
[75] Minute by Greenhill, 7 July 1953, FO 371/104388.
[76] 'Ruler of Kuwait's Date Gardens', Minute by Greenhill, 13 July 1953, FO 371/104388.

easily be convinced that we ought to pay money to a man who already has far too much', warned an official.[77] To pursue the matter in the Iraqi courts, however, promised to be a lengthy and costly process with no guarantee of success. Britain's persistent failure to solve the problems presented by the date gardens did nothing to promote a more amenable attitude on the part of the Ruler to the engagement of a senior adviser.

On 13 July, the new Political Resident, B. A. B. Burrows, handed Abdullah a personal message from the Prime Minister, once more entreating him to engage a principal adviser.[78] Burrows, who admitted going to 'the limit of frankness' during his discussions with the Ruler, stressed the futility, and indeed danger, of applying further pressure.[79] Echoing the Political Agent's concerns, Burrows warned that to insist upon the appointment of a senior adviser would risk not merely the renewal of the Ruler's threat to abdicate, but also the withdrawal of his cooperation in financial matters. In future, concluded Burrows, British influence should be exercised principally through traditional channels, the most important being the Political Agent at Kuwait. This development had been pre-figured by discussions in London on the question of upgrading the position of the Political Agent.

Earlier in the year the managing director of the Kuwait Oil Company, C. A. P. Southwell, had expressed the view that Britain's representation at Kuwait was underpowered.[80] Southwell was particularly scathing of the Political Agent's subordination to the Political Resident, an anachronism which he felt did not take account of Kuwait's growing economic significance in relation to Bahrain. Sir John Maud of the Ministry of Fuel and Power was impressed by Southwell's reasoning and recommended that the Political Agent should be permitted to refer directly to the Foreign Office.[81] 'I suspect that this would make it very much easier for him to gain the confidence of the Ruler', opined Maud, 'and would help to compensate for the big show that the Americans appear to be putting up.'[82] Among the specific measures considered by the Foreign Office for altering Britain's representation in Kuwait were the removal of the Political Residency from Bahrain to Kuwait, the placing of the Political Agent under the direct control of the Foreign Office, and the upgrading of the Political Agent.[83] After some discussion a combination of the second two proposals was implemented. The Political Agent not only acquired additions to his staff,

---

[77] Minute by Ross, 14 July 1953, FO 371/104388.

[78] The text of the Prime Minister's message can be found in a telegram from the Foreign Office to the Bahrain Residency, No. 971, 31 July 1953, FO 371/104330.

[79] Letter from Burrows to the Marquess of Salisbury, No. 78 (11023/17/53), 20 Aug 1953, FO 371/104330.

[80] Minute by Rose, 8 April 1953, FO 371/104272.

[81] Sir John Maud to Pierson Dixon, 16 March 1953, POWE 33/1926.

[82] Ibid.

[83] Minute by Rose, 8 April 1953, FO 371/104272.

including an economic counsellor, but was also permitted to receive instructions from and report direct to the Foreign Office.[84]

Elucidating the new administrative arrangements, the Foreign Secretary informed the Political Resident that

> the Political Agent should maintain and indeed expand his function of being able to proffer advice to the Ruler, not only upon external affairs and other subjects within the traditional prerogative of the Agency, but also upon all matters concerning the good government of Kuwait. The ideal position would be that the Ruler should himself be inclined to turn naturally to the Political Agent for advice.[85]

Nevertheless, a note of caution was sounded by the Foreign Secretary who warned that 'Advice to the Ruler must . . . not be pressed beyond the point at which it defeats its own ends and arouses feelings which might weaken the position of the Agency'. 'In order to preserve the capacity to exercise influence and to sustain a favourable position *vis-à-vis* the Ruler and Kuwaiti opinion', concluded the Foreign Secretary, 'some sacrifice of interest to local susceptibilities and to inevitable if unwelcome movements of thought may become unavoidable.' Burrows had already reached a not dissimilar conclusion, remarking: 'A benevolent autocracy is likely to be the best government that Kuwait can have for a considerable time.'[86] Nevertheless, Burrows was forced to admit that 'while the Ruler is benevolent but not sufficiently autocratic the rest of his family are individually autocratic but rarely benevolent'.[87]

When the question of appointing a senior adviser was tentatively revived by the Foreign Office in 1954, Pelly was keen to inject a note of realism into the debate:

> I think the possibility of succeeding in this, never very good in recent years, now no longer exists. The Subah family are quite willing to co-operate with us within the traditional framework on which our relations have been built. . . . But when we try to bring about some major change in the traditional framework, the Subah will resist strongly any encroachment upon what has traditionally been regarded as their responsibility.[88]

---

[84] Letter from Foreign Office to Burrows, No. 125, 24 July 1953, FO 371/104270; Letter from the Foreign Office to Pelly, No. EA 1055/13, 25 July 1953, FO 371/104272. The enhanced status of the Political Resident did not mean that the Political Resident's role became redundant. Writing in 1956, G. W. Bell noted: 'We have found the practice whereby the Political Resident is held in reserve and occasionally used as a "big gun" to be most useful' (Letter from G. W. Bell to D. M. H. Riches, No. 10110/11/56, 29 April 1956, FO 371/120568).
[85] Letter from the Secretary of State to Burrows, No. EA 10111/24, 20 Nov 1953, FO 371/104264.
[86] Letter from Burrows to the Marquess of Salisbury, No. 79 (10122/6/53), 20 Aug 1953, FO 371/104330.
[87] Ibid.
[88] Letter from Pelly to Burrows, No. 1015/2, 9 Feb 1954, FO 371/109807.

Pelly was also sceptical about applying overt pressure on the Kuwaitis to accept a senior adviser. 'They are, of course, aware', he cautioned, 'of the value of Kuwait's oil to us and if we asked them to choose between accepting an adviser and losing our protection they would probably call our bluff.' Pelly's successor as Political Agent, G. W. Bell, was of a similar opinion. 'Before very long', he predicted, 'Kuwait nationalism will direct itself against all non-Kuwaitis in government service and if the number of British state servants is few and of the highest grade our position in Kuwait will be less vulnerable.'[89] Anticipating a gradual lessening of British influence in Kuwait, Bell concluded that 'So long as our fundamental interests in oil and sterling are unaffected, we may have to be less worried about some of our moral responsibilities.' The Foreign Office was persuaded by these arguments. 'Our position in Kuwait', concurred an official, 'must be flexible and we must take care not to jeopardise the position and influence we have got by seeking too brashly to extend them and to force advice down the Kuwaitis' throats.'[90] The maintenance of British influence, however, was menaced by the activities of British companies operating in the Shaikhdom.

III

With the encouragement of Hasted, the government of Kuwait committed itself to an ambitious development plan for the period 1952–7 involving capital expenditure of over £90 million. Commenting upon the scale of this programme, Rose noted: 'Kuwait is undoubtedly determined to become a modern welfare state in the quickest possible time.'[91] Nevertheless, the British identified a number of possible dangers in such rapid development. First, it was feared that if sufficient funds were not set aside for investment any future reduction in oil revenues would result in an inability to sustain development. Expanding on this point, Hay remarked that

> the attempt to create a super welfare state where everybody will get everything for nothing does give cause for alarm, not only because it means that none of the existing projects will pay for their maintenance, but also because the population will inevitably increase by leaps and bounds by the immigration of adventurers and vagrants from all over the Middle East.[92]

Furthermore, the Foreign Office feared that unless restraints were placed on the pace of development, the scale and rate of expenditure was likely to

---

[89] Letter from Bell to Fry, No. 10112/17/55, 15 Aug 1955, FO 371/114588.
[90] Letter from P. Broad to Bell, No. EA 1017/27, 3 Sept 1955, FO 371/114588.
[91] 'Progress on the recommendations in Sir Roger Makins' report on his visit to the Persian Gulf', Minute by Rose, 20 March 1953, FO 371/104270.
[92] Letter from Hay to Eden, No. 32, 19 March 1953, FO 371/104325.

Investment Problems, 1952–5 51

create an inflationary situation in Kuwait.[93] Moreover, Rose cautioned that the British firms might be tempted to exploit their favoured position in Kuwait to the detriment of British interests as a whole.[94]

Five principal British firms had acquired a foothold in Kuwait by the early 1950s. The 'big five', as they were known locally, were Taylor Woodrow, C. and D. William Press, Richard Costain, Holland, Hannen and Cubitt, and John Howard.[95] All development work was shared among these firms on a 'cost-plus 15 per cent' basis. Although this system had the effect of precluding competitive tendering, Hasted considered that it produced the greatest efficiency, as well as speed, in the development sphere.[96] Each of the big five was obliged to have a Kuwaiti partner who tended simply to provide local labour. The figure for profit gave its name to the so-called '15 per cent parties' which were staged to encourage smooth relations between visiting directors and their Kuwaiti partners.[97] Nevertheless, local antipathy towards the big five began to grow.

C. E. Loombe of the Bank of England, who visited Kuwait in early 1953, reported 'murmurs of discontent from the Kuwaitis' about the activities of the big five.[98] 'This is not surprising', continued Loombe, 'as most contractors are on a cost plus 15% basis and the tales one hears of what is included in "costs" can only reflect badly on British prestige.' Pelly was in full agreement. 'The British contractors' avidity and their tendency to meddle in politics for their own ends', he stressed,

> must be kept in bounds. As the Arabs crudely put it, many of them have come here like dogs around a camel's carcass. The harm they can do to our interests generally is not worth their profits. . . . The Kuwait merchant is the last person who you would think would need protecting against rapacity in business but in dealing with some Britons it is a pity for our sakes that he cannot be given it.[99]

John Howard and Company were described by Pelly as having the 'worst reputation for greed and sharp practice of any British firms here'.[100] With only slight exaggeration, the American consul in Kuwait described the

---

[93] 'Sir Roger Makins' report on the Persian Gulf', Minute by Greenhill, 20 March 1953, FO 371/104270.
[94] 'Progress on the recommendations in Sir Roger Makins' report on his visit to the Persian Gulf', Minute by Rose, 20 March 1953, FO 371/104270.
[95] The British firm of Ewbanks also operated in Kuwait, although the Political Agent described the distillation plant which they were constructing as 'a small development scheme on its own' (Letter from Pelly to Hay, No. 95/5/53, 31 March 1953, FO 371/104325).
[96] 'Kuwait': Draft Foreign Office Paper on Her Majesty's Government's position in and policy towards Kuwait, 15 April 1953, FO 371/104272.
[97] Letter from Pelly to Hay, No. 95/5/53, 31 March 1953, FO 371/104325.
[98] Copy of a note by C. E. Loombe given to Pelly, 10 Feb 1953, FO 371/104325.
[99] Letter from Pelly to Hay, No. 95/5/53, 31 March 1953, FO 371/104325.
[100] Letter from Pelly to Hay, No. 95/9/53, 8 April 1953, FO 371/104326.

British expatriates as 'turning Kuwait into an Anglo-Indian rest camp'.[101] Referring to the cost-plus system, the Foreign Office was forced to concede that 'there is reason to believe that British firms have regarded the present arrangement as an excellent opportunity to make a good thing out of Kuwait. This can only strengthen Fahad's position and redound to our disadvantage.'[102] Viewing the broader picture, Rose was concerned lest local criticism of the big five should undermine the prestige and influence of British officials in the Kuwait government.[103] His fears were soon realized in relation to Hasted.

Early in 1953, Shaikh Fahad engaged a Syrian engineer, Majadin Jabri, to head the public works department.[104] At the end of March, Hasted was obliged to place his executive staff under Jabri's control and confine himself to giving technical advice.[105] Although Hasted objected to these changes,[106] making dire prophecies of corruption and prejudice to sound development, Crichton welcomed them, believing that they would have the effect of curbing Hasted's more lavish schemes.[107] As suggested by Crichton's reaction to Hasted's demotion, relations between the two men had become increasingly strained. The Foreign Office described them as 'working on divergent lines',[108] while Victor Butler of the Ministry of Fuel and Power went so far as to characterize Crichton and Hasted as being at 'daggers drawn'.[109] During a lengthy meeting with Hay towards the end of April 1953, Crichton was purported to have 'detailed all his grouses about Hasted'.[110]

The growing enmity between the two men stemmed from differences in personality and policy objectives. Hasted was a dynamic figure who was described by Pelly as regarding development work with 'an almost fanatical enthusiasm'.[111] Indeed, he dismissed any suggestions that state revenues should be put aside for investment purposes as 'typical Treasury fussing'.[112]

---

[101] Rosemarie Said Zahlan, *The Making of the Modern Gulf States: Kuwait, Bahrain, Qatar, the United Arab Emirates, and Oman*, London: Unwin Hyman, 1989, p. 33.

[102] 'Kuwait': Draft Foreign Office Paper on Her Majesty's Government's position in and policy towards Kuwait, 15 April 1953, FO 371/104272.

[103] Minute by Rose, 18 Feb 1953, FO 371/104340.

[104] Crystal, *Oil and Politics in the Gulf*, p. 69.

[105] Telegram from Pelly to the Foreign Office, No. 85, 29 March 1953, FO 371/104272.

[106] Hasted claimed that he would never have come to Kuwait if he had known that he would be confined to an advisory role (Letter from W. F. Hasted to G. C. L. Crichton, 14 April 1953, HSTD 2/2).

[107] Telegram from Pelly to the Foreign Office, No. 85, 29 March 1953, FO 371/104272.

[108] Record of a meeting held at the Foreign Office to discuss the situation in Kuwait, 16 April 1953, FO 371/104325.

[109] 'Kuwait', Minute by Victor Butler, 16 April 1953, POWE 33/1926.

[110] Sir Rupert Hay's Diary, 28 April 1953, Private Papers of Sir Rupert Hay, Box 3.

[111] Letter from Pelly to Hay, No. 95/9/53, 8 April 1953, FO 371/104326.

[112] Ibid.

Crichton, on the other hand, was much more cautious, favouring a more equitable balance between investment and development, and bemoaning Hasted's financial irresponsibility and extravagance.[113] In April 1953, he went so far as to inform Hasted that 'there is little or no common ground or hope of understanding between us'.[114] Crichton's problems in dealing with Hasted were compounded by his inability to persuade the Ruler to introduce a proper budgetary system and the consequent lack of close liaison between the finance and development departments.[115] As a result, Crichton was unable to regulate the expenditure to which Hasted committed the Government of Kuwait. Commenting on the development expert's activities, Loombe recorded: 'I get the impression that Hasted has built up a small kingdom for himself and there is a danger that he will be carried away by his enthusiasm and the desire to see the results of his work in a short period.'[116]

Not surprisingly, the British companies operating in Kuwait had more sympathy for Hasted than for Crichton. Brigadier Guy Burton, a director of John Howard and Company, for example, forewarned that Britain's predominant influence in Kuwait would be eclipsed within eighteen months, blaming this state of affairs on Crichton's failure to support Hasted.[117] Moreover, the chairman of Holland, Hannen and Cubitt, Lord Ashcombe, predicted dire consequences for British interests as a result of Hasted's loss of executive control of development to Jabri.[118] Pelly, however, was impervious to the lamentations of the big five. For instance, he referred to Brigadier Burton's representations as 'intentionally misleading', describing the firm of John Howard and Company as 'one of those which has been pilloried (and in its case with some justification) for being here in order, with Hasted's help, to get everything possible out of Kuwait without caring much what they give in return'.[119] In addition, Pelly told Ashcombe that it would not be in Britain's interests 'if Kuwait were littered with white elephants ... in a couple of years as a result of the greed of British contractors'.[120] The preferential status enjoyed by the big five soon came under direct attack.

In February 1953, Rose had prophesied British firms would be displaced if they continued to exploit their position in Kuwait.[121] This fear

---

[113] Letter from Pelly to Hay, No. 2 (190/28/53), 24 Feb 1953, FO 371/104340.
[114] Letter from G. C. L. Crichton to W. F. Hasted, 18 April 1953, HSTD 2/2.
[115] Copy of a note by Loombe given to Pelly, 10 Feb 1953, FO 371/104325.
[116] Ibid.
[117] Letter from Brigadier Guy Burton to Sir Peter MacDonald, 26 March 1953, FO 371/104272.
[118] Telegram from Pelly to the Foreign Office, No. 8, 1 April 1953, FO 371/104325.
[119] Telegram from Pelly to the Foreign Office, No. 85, 29 March 1953, FO 371/104272.
[120] Telegram from Pelly to the Foreign Office, No. 8, 1 April 1953, FO 371/104325.
[121] Minute by Rose, 18 Feb 1953, FO 371/104340.

was soon realized. At the beginning of April, the Ruler issued instructions that the two-year contracts held by the big five were not to be renewed, and that subsequent contracts would be open to non-British firms.[122] Despite the more competitive environment in which the big five were forced to operate, Pelly asserted:

> I think that the time has come to impress on the contractors generally that their present policy of snarling with the disappointed rage of tigers in the jungle at the mere possibility of some of the good red joints of Kuwait oil revenues going to somebody else can only do damage to themselves and British interests in general.[123]

C. T. E. Ewart-Biggs of the Foreign Office was equally unsympathetic, remarking that the big five had already enjoyed 'a fair period of sheltered lactation'.[124]

One of the first development projects to be allocated under the new system was that for the construction of a four-berth quay which was badly needed to handle the heavy traffic passing through Kuwait Port.[125] Instead of allocating the work under contracts with the big five on a cost-plus 15 per cent basis, the government of Kuwait sought tenders from a number of different firms, both British and foreign. A list of fourteen was initially drawn up, including nine British firms, among them three from the big five. A subsequent list, nevertheless, excluded these three on the grounds that they already had sufficient work in Kuwait. A more plausible reason for their exclusion, however, centred on the desire of Kuwaitis not in partnership with the big five to see the introduction of other firms with whom they could enter into lucrative partnership arrangements. A further blow to the interests of the big five was dealt by the enforced resignation of Hasted, their greatest champion, in March 1954.[126] Local criticism of British business was not confined to the big five.

Under an exclusive concession granted by Shaikh Ahmad in 1947, the telecommunications company Cable and Wireless agreed to operate the telegraph service at Kuwait, in addition to providing 400 private telephone lines.[127] The former was efficient and remunerative, the latter, despite its gross inadequacy in relation to demand, was unprofitable. When the company was asked to expand the system to 2000 lines, it was only

---

[122] Minute by Rose, 8 April 1953, FO 371/104325.
[123] Letter from Pelly to D. A. Logan, No. 37/15/53, 9 May 1953, FO 371/104327.
[124] Minute by C. T. E. Ewart-Biggs, 30 Nov 1953, FO 371/104341.
[125] The following is based on a minute by Logan, 11 Aug 1953, FO 371/104329.
[126] Telegram from Pelly to the Foreign Office, No. 58, 18 March 1954, FO 371/109863. On the eve of his departure from Kuwait, Hasted opined: 'At the moment, chaos is supreme, with corruption a good second and engineering and ethical standards, except for the work of the British, of the lowest' (Letter from Hasted to Pelly, 3 April 1954, HSTD 2/2).
[127] The following is based on 'Kuwait: Cable and Wireless Limited: Telephone and Undertakings', Foreign Office minute (undated), FO 371/104383.

prepared to do so on condition that its charges could be increased. The resulting outcry in Kuwait led to negotiations for a modification in the concession under which the Ruler offered to purchase the existing system, the company merely acting as his agent. In November 1952, however, Shaikh Fahad informed the Political Agent that a similar 'nationalization' should be extended to the telegraph system. While the British were concerned that a nationalization of the telegraph service would represent an unwelcome precedent which might have repercussions in the oil industry,[128] the behaviour of Cable and Wireless was roundly condemned in official British circles. One Foreign Office official denounced the Company's conduct as 'disgraceful',[129] while another argued that if it failed to extend the telephone system 'a considerable blow will be dealt to British prestige in Kuwait'.[130] Cable and Wireless, however, remained intractable, refusing to undertake any such extension until negotiations over their concession had been completed.[131] By contrast, when the Ruler sought a revision of his oil concession in 1955, the negotiations, while complex, were pursued to a satisfactory conclusion.

The problems encountered by the big five led to a debate about the relationship which the KOC should foster with Kuwait. Traditionally, the company had attempted to maintain a separate existence, confining itself to the production of oil and eschewing involvement in local politics.[132] The result had been that the KOC was almost entirely self-sufficient, the only contribution to the economic activity of Kuwait, apart from payments of oil revenues, being the direct employment of some 2000 Kuwaitis and the use of a number of local building contractors.[133] The experience of the big five seemed to confirm the wisdom of this policy. Having taken Kuwaiti partners, the big five found that the envy of those who were not in partnership gave rise to a campaign of criticism of these arrangements. On these grounds the KOC's decision to keep integration with local Kuwaiti business interests to a minimum appeared to be vindicated. Nevertheless, the Company could not avoid dealing with the Ruler, who showed a determination to keep his concession arrangements in line with those of other Middle East oil producers.

Despite having achieved a 50/50 profit-sharing formula in December 1950, the Saudi Arabian government re-opened negotiations with the Arabian-American Oil Company in 1951 for a revision of the price on

---

[128] Letter from the Secretary of State to Hay, No. EA 1431/7, 21 March 1953; Minute by Greenhill, 28 April 1953, FO 371/104383.
[129] Minute by A. R. Sinclair, 1 May 1953, FO 371/104383.
[130] Minute by P. M. Maxey, 9 Dec 1953, FO 371/104383.
[131] Telegram from Pelly to the Foreign Office, No. 389, 8 Dec 1953, FO 371/104383.
[132] 'Kuwait', Minute by T. R. D. Belgrave, 15 Dec 1954, FO 371/109910.
[133] Ibid.

which oil profits were calculated.[134] These discussions ushered in a new agreement under which ARAMCO consented to make a retrospective payment to Saudi Arabia amounting to $70 million.[135] The Ruler of Kuwait, keen to secure an analogous agreement, called in the second half of 1954 for a revision of the Kuwait concession.[136] Initial objections were raised by the British half of the KOC, British Petroleum,[137] which argued that it could not consider an increase in payments until it received relief from United Kingdom income tax.[138] The Ruler was unimpressed with this argument, stressing that it was for the Company to settle its difficulties with the United Kingdom.[139] An impasse having apparently been reached, the Deputy Under-Secretary at the Foreign Office, Sir Harold Caccia, warned that 'the difficulties between the Kuwait Oil Company and the Ruler could blow up into something like another Abadan'.[140]

British Petroleum's inability to claim relief in the United Kingdom stemmed from the fact that the Kuwait income tax, introduced in 1951 as part of the revisions of the KOC concession, was not of general application and in consequence could not be accepted as a tax corresponding to those imposed on the Company in the United Kingdom.[141] In an attempt to overcome this problem, talks between representatives of the KOC and the government of Kuwait took place in Beirut at the end of April 1955. Despite the customary ill-feeling between the Ruler's representative, H. T. Kemp, and the managing director of the Kuwait Oil Company, C. A. P. Southwell,[142] an agreement was reached on 14 May. While the Ruler agreed to substitute the Kuwait income tax decree of 1951 for a new general income tax decree, the KOC consented to satisfy all his cash claims amounting to some £25 million.[143] As a result of the new agreement,

---

[134] Stephen Hemsley Longrigg, *Oil in the Middle East: Its Discovery and Development*, second edition, London: Oxford University Press, 1961, p. 210.

[135] Letter from Pelly to Harold Macmillan, No. 59, 11 May 1955, FO 371/114710.

[136] 'Kuwait Oil', Minute by Fry, 23 March 1955, FO 371/114709.

[137] In December 1954, at an extraordinary meeting of shareholders of the Anglo-Iranian Oil Company, it was agreed that in future the company would be known as British Petroleum. This change of name symbolized the diversification which had followed in the wake of the nationalization of Anglo-Iranian by Muhammad Musaddiq in 1951 (Bamberg, *History of the British Petroleum Company*, pp. 521–2).

[138] Memorandum of meeting in the KOC head office with the Ruler's representative, enclosed in Southwell's letter to Fry, 29 March 1955, FO 371/114709. In 1951, the Anglo-Iranian Oil Company had failed to secure relief in the United Kingdom for income tax paid in Kuwait under the concession revisions of that year. (See Chapter 1.)

[139] Telegram from Pelly to the Foreign Office, No. 41, 10 April 1955, FO 371/114709.

[140] 'Kuwait', Minute from Sir Harold Caccia to the Secretary of State, Foreign Affairs, 11 April 1955, FO 371/114709.

[141] Telegram from the Foreign Office to Kuwait, No. 91, 12 April 1955, FO 371/114709.

[142] See Letter from Pelly to Macmillan, No. 59, 11 May 1955, FO 371/114710.

[143] Memorandum of Agreement, 14 May 1955, enclosed in Southwell's letter to Fry, 17 May 1955, FO 371/114710.

British Petroleum reclaimed £10 million which had been paid in United Kingdom income tax.[144]

IV

Sir Rupert Hay, in his final despatch as Political Resident, reviewed developments in the Gulf, as well as giving an assessment of Britain's interests and commitments in the region.[145] 'Amid wars and revolutions', he wrote, 'the Gulf Shaikhdoms have shown a surprising political stability.' While conceding that little real affection was felt for the British, he emphasized that 'The Rulers realise that but for us they would long ago have lost their independence.' Commenting on internal threats to the position of the ruling families, Hay predicted that 'it will be some years before a large body of well-educated and politically-minded persons will be evolved to agitate successfully against the power of the Shaikhs'. Referring to the growth in Arab League interest in the Shaikhdoms, Hay opined: 'We have perhaps more to fear from external pressure than internal influences.' Nevertheless, he consoled himself with the thought that 'owing to lack of cohesion amongst the Arab States no serious attack on our position is likely to develop unless some superman emerges to unite them'. The elevation of Gamal Abdel Nasser to the status of Arab hero, following Britain's abortive attack on Egypt in 1956, provided such a figure.

[144] Telegram from the Foreign Office to Kuwait, No. 272, 10 Oct 1955, FO 371/114712.
[145] The following is drawn from a Letter from Hay to Churchill, No. 56 (10104/3/53), 25 June 1953, FO 371/104270.

3: Kuwait, Egypt, and the Suez Crisis 1956

[C]onflicts between Arabism and the material benefits of the 'British umbrella' are more than ever imminent.[1]

Her Majesty's Government has brought them [the al-Sabah] face to face with a struggle for power which must now develop far sooner than seemed likely before the present situation arose.[2]

Until the late 1940s, the British position in Kuwait had been unquestioned, both within and without the Persian Gulf. Locally, it had been tolerated because successive Rulers realized that Kuwait's independence rested upon the protection of the British government. Externally, Britain's presence was accepted because of its unobtrusive nature. Moreover, with the exception of Kuwait's strategic location, there was little in Kuwait for other powers to covet. By the mid-1950s, however, Britain's position in Kuwait was coming under growing pressure from external forces. Writing in 1955, the Political Agent, G. W. Bell, recorded: 'With the wealth which has fallen to Kuwait and the consequent envy with which the Arab world now looks to the Persian Gulf States, our position is no longer unassailed.'[3] Britain's position was further undermined by the worsening of her relations with Egypt in the mid-1950s, culminating in the Suez crisis of 1956.

---

[1] Letter from C. J. Pelly to B. A. B. Burrows, No. 1035/1, 22 March 1954, FO 371/109822.
[2] Telegram from G. W. Bell to the Foreign Office, No. 16, 6 Dec 1956, FO 371/120567.
[3] Letter from Bell to L. A. C. Fry, No. 10112/17/55, 15 Aug 1955, FO 371/114588.

I

In the immediate aftermath of the Second World War, Britain's position in the Arab world seemed stronger than ever.[4] She remained the mandatory power in Palestine and Transjordan, in addition to possessing treaties of alliance with the two leading independent states of the region, Egypt and Iraq. Moreover, the old French mandates of Syria and Lebanon were under effective British control. The only major challenge to British predominance was provided by the growing American influence in Saudi Arabia.[5] Britain's attempts to refashion her relationships with Arab countries in the post-war period, however, proved largely unsuccessful.

The exigencies of war had persuaded Britain to employ coercion to ensure the cooperation of Arab countries. The most notorious example of this is provided by British intervention in Egypt. In June 1940, the British Ambassador in Cairo, Sir Miles Lampson, had insisted that King Farouk dismiss the government of Ali Maher on account of its alleged sympathy for the Axis powers.[6] Although he acceded to this demand, Farouk refused to put the popular Wafdist party, which was prepared to cooperate with Britain, into power.[7] Britain's acceptance of Farouk's decision was only temporary. With news of General Rommel's advance on Egypt from Libya, Lampson surrounded the King's Abdin Palace with British tanks on 4 February 1942 and in effect presented Farouk with a stark choice between abdication and the formation of a Wafdist government under Nahas Pasha.[8] Such wartime incidents, however, left a legacy of bitterness which impeded Britain's attempts to establish new cooperative relations with the Arab world once peace had been restored. Egypt's growing resentment towards Britain, moreover, was fuelled by the latter's role in the creation of Israel.

Article 22 of the covenant of the League of Nations specified that certain former Ottoman territories had 'reached a stage of development where their existence as independent nations can be provisionally recognised subject to the rendering of administrative advice and assistance by a

---

[4] John Darwin, *Britain and Decolonisation: The Retreat from Empire in the Post-War World*, Basingstoke: Macmillan, 1988, p. 110.
[5] David Holden and Richard Johns, *The House of Saud*, London: Sidgwick and Jackson, 1981, pp. 135–40.
[6] Laila Amin Morsy, 'Britain's Wartime Policy in Egypt, 1940–42', *Middle Eastern Studies*, 25, 1 (1989): 66–9.
[7] Peter Mansfield, *The Arabs*, London: Penguin Books, 1985, p. 221.
[8] Janice J. Terry, *The Wafd, 1919–1952: Cornerstone of Egyptian Political Power*, London: Third World Centre for Research and Publishing, 1982, pp. 250–1; J. C. B. Richmond, *Egypt, 1798–1953: Her Advance towards a Modern Identity*, London: Methuen, 1977, p. 206. Gabriel Warburg argues that Lampson's primary objective on 4 February was to secure Farouk's abdication (Gabriel Warburg, 'Lampson's Ultimatum to Faruq, 4 February 1942', *Middle Eastern Studies*, 11, 1 (1975): 31).

Mandatory until such time as they are able to stand alone'.[9] During the San Remo Conference of allied powers in April 1920, Britain was granted a mandate for Palestine. This award, however, soon proved to be a poisoned chalice. In the inter-war years, Britain struggled to reconcile her conflicting commitments to both Jews and Arabs. By the late 1930s, faced with a deteriorating international situation and growing Arab unrest, Britain became convinced of the necessity of conciliating Arab opinion. The White Paper of May 1939 set a limit to Jewish immigration of 75 000 over a five-year period, in addition to offering the in-built Arab majority independence within ten years.[10] Britain's plans, however, were upset by the refusal of either side to accept the terms of the White Paper: while Zionists asserted the illegality of restrictions on immigration, the Arabs felt Britain's concessions did not go far enough.[11]

The radicalization of Jewish opinion as a result of the Holocaust, coupled with growing international sympathy for the Zionist cause,[12] made Britain's position in Palestine increasingly untenable. In February 1947, the Foreign Secretary, Ernest Bevin, announced that the whole question would be referred to the United Nations.[13] Six months later, Britain declared her intention to withdraw from Palestine by the middle of the following year.[14] The proclamation of the state of Israel on 14 May 1948 precipitated a general Arab–Israeli war. In the ensuing chaos, hundreds of thousands of Palestinians were forced to flee their homes,[15] while the armies of the Arab coalition ranged against Israel were defeated. Although Britain's judicious withdrawal had foreclosed a general Arab campaign against her interests in the Middle East, Britain's role in the creation of Israel left a legacy of resentment in the Arab world which was reinforced by the continuing Palestinian refugee problem.[16] 'Arabism, Islam and anti-

---

[9] Daniel Silverfarb, *Britain's Informal Empire in the Middle East: A Case Study of Iraq, 1929–1941*, New York: Oxford University Press, 1986, p. 6.

[10] Michael J. Cohen, *Palestine to Israel: From Mandate to Independence*, London: Frank Cass, 1988, p. 122.

[11] Ibid., pp. 123–5.

[12] See Zeev Tzahor, 'Holocaust Survivors as a Political Factor', *Middle Eastern Studies*, 24, 4 (1988): 432–44.

[13] A. N. Porter and A. J. Stockwell, *British Imperial Policy and Decolonization, 1938–1964*, 2 vols, Basingstoke: Macmillan, 1987, Vol. 1, p. 56; Ritchie Ovendale, *The Origins of the Arab–Israeli Wars*, London: Longman, 1984, p. 100.

[14] Michael J. Cohen, *Palestine and the Great Powers, 1945–1948*, Princeton, NJ: Princeton University Press, 1982, pp. 276–7.

[15] The precise number of Palestinian Arabs who became refugees as a result of the 1948 war is a disputed question. Arab leaders spoke of up to one million refugees, while Israelis suggested that the figure was closer to half a million. The most accurate estimate was probably made in September 1949 by the British Foreign Office when it concluded that the number of refugees was between 600 000 and 760 000 (Benny Morris, *The Birth of the Palestinian Refugee Problem, 1947–1949*, Cambridge: Cambridge University Press, 1987, pp. 297–8).

[16] By 1975, displaced Palestinian Arabs numbered 2.5 million (Mansfield, *Arabs*, p. 240).

imperialism', observed Sir John Troutbeck (British Ambassador, Baghdad, 1951–4), 'meet in concentrated fanaticism on the question of Israel.'[17]

Referring to the impact of Egypt's defeat at the hands of the Israelis in 1948–9, John Darwin has argued that 'Nothing could have been better calculated to . . . redouble Egyptian hostility to Britain on whose "betrayal" of the Palestine Arabs the catastrophe could conveniently be blamed.'[18] This feeling was given tangible expression in October 1951 when the Wafd government of Nahas Pasha unilaterally abrogated the 1936 treaty with Britain.[19] Not surprisingly, Britain's military installations in the Canal Zone soon became the target for Egyptian guerrillas. On 25 January 1952, the British Commander in Chief, General Erskine, ordered his forces to attack a unit of the Egyptian auxiliary police in Ismailia which he believed to be providing covert aid to the guerrillas.[20] When news of British actions reached Cairo, a frenzied mob burned the centre of the city, attacking British interests wherever it could. Nahas Pasha was dismissed and a succession of weak governments followed. It was against this background that a group of army officers, led by General Muhmammad Neguib and Colonel Gamal Abdel Nasser, staged a successful coup on 23 July 1952. Three days later King Farouk abdicated. In the power struggle between Neguib and Nasser which ensued, the latter emerged triumphant, becoming Prime Minister in April 1954 and President in June 1956.[21] It was the Suez crisis which elevated Nasser's status in the Arab world.

Initially, Britain had sought a rapprochement with Egypt, an aim which was facilitated by the new regime's willingness to surrender claims to the Sudan and support Sudanese self-determination.[22] The Foreign Secretary, Anthony Eden, persuaded the Cabinet of the futility of trying to keep British military forces in the Canal Zone in opposition to the wishes of the Egyptian government. By July Heads of Agreement were reached, later formalized in a new treaty signed in October, under which British forces were to leave Egypt by 18 June 1956.[23] This improvement in

---

[17] Cited in William Roger Louis, 'The British and the Origins of the Iraqi Revolution', in Robert A. Fernea and William Roger Louis (eds.), *The Iraqi Revolution of 1958: The Old Social Classes Revisited*, London: I. B. Tauris, 1991, p. 41.

[18] Darwin, *Britain and Decolonisation*, p. 207.

[19] William Roger Louis, *The British Empire in the Middle East, 1945–1951: Arab Nationalism, the United States and Postwar Imperialism*, Oxford: Clarendon, 1984, p. 732; Richmond, Egypt, p. 216.

[20] Jean and Simonne Lacouture, *Egypt in Transition*, London: Methuen, 1958, pp. 106–7.

[21] P. J. Vatikiotis, *The History of Modern Egypt: From Muhammad Ali to Mubarak*, fourth edition, London: Weidenfeld and Nicolson, 1991, pp. 384–8; P. J. Vatikiotis, *Nasser and His Generation*, New York: St Martin's, 1978, pp. 146–51.

[22] William Roger Louis, 'The Tragedy of the Anglo-Egyptian Settlement of 1954', in William Roger Louis and Roger Owen (eds), *Suez 1956: The Crisis and its Consequences*, Oxford: Clarendon, 1991, p. 51.

[23] David Carlton, *Britain and the Suez Crisis*, Oxford: Basil Blackwell, 1988, pp. 12–13.

Chapter 3

Anglo-Egyptian relations proved ephemeral, however. The formation in February 1955 of the Baghdad Pact, a defensive alliance between Iraq and Turkey which Britain subsequently joined, roused the ire of Nasser who perceived it as a threat to his regional leadership ambitions.[24] Not only did Nasser launch a sustained propaganda campaign against the Baghdad Pact,[25] but he also retaliated by forming a series of bi-lateral defence agreements with Saudi Arabia, Syria, and the Yemen.[26] In September 1955, moreover, Nasser announced a deal to purchase arms from the Soviet Union via Czechoslovakia, thus breaking the Western monopoly on the supply of weapons to Egypt. In an attempt to administer a sharp rebuke to Nasser, the United States withdrew their financial support for the construction of the Aswan dam, a project which Nasser claimed to be vital for the economic development of his country. With typical bravura, the Egyptian president responded on 26 July 1956 by declaring the nationalization of the Suez Canal.

Anthony Eden, who succeeded Winston Churchill as Prime Minister in April 1955, had viewed Nasser with increasing antipathy in the months leading up to the nationalization of the Canal. Indeed, Eden began to ascribe any dents to Britain's prestige in the region to Nasser's malign influence. This tendency reached a remarkable peak following King Hussein of Jordan's dismissal in March 1956 of the British commander of the Arab Legion, Sir John Glubb.[27]

In explaining his actions, King Hussein wrote: 'With Communism filtering into the Middle East and Cairo branding Jordan an "imperialist power" there was no alternative. Glubb had to go.'[28] Although delighted by news of Glubb's dismissal, Nasser was almost certainly not directly responsible for Hussein's decision and appears to have been as surprised as every-

---

[24] Elie Podeh, 'The Drift towards Neutrality: Egyptian Foreign Policy during the Early Nasserist Era, 1952–55', *Middle Eastern Studies*, 32, 1 (1996): 168; Elie Podeh, 'The Struggle over Arab Hegemony after the Suez Crisis', *Middle Eastern Studies*, 29, 1 (1993): 91; Richard L. Jasse, 'The Baghdad Pact: Cold War or Colonialism?', *Middle Eastern Studies*, 27, 1 (1991): 148. See also Elie Podeh, *The Quest for Hegemony in the Arab World: The Struggle over the Baghdad Pact*, Leiden: E. J. Brill, 1995.

[25] Phebe Marr, *The Modern History of Iraq*, Boulder, Colorado: Westview Press, 1985, pp. 118–19.

[26] R. Hrair Dekmejian, *Egypt under Nasser: A Study in Political Dynamics*, London: University of London Press, 1972, p. 42; W. Scott Lucas, 'The Path to Suez: Britain and the Struggle for the Middle East, 1953–56', in Anne Deighton (ed.), *Britain and the First Cold War*, Basingstoke: Macmillan, 1990, pp. 264–5.

[27] For an account of the events surrounding Glubb's dismissal, see Michael B. Oren, 'A Winter of Discontent: Britain's Crisis in Jordan, December 1955–March 1956', *International Journal of Middle East Studies*, 22 (1990): 171–84.

[28] Cited in Naseer H. Aruri, *Jordan: A Study in Political Development, 1921–1965*, The Hague: Martinus Nijhoff, 1972, p. 131.

one else.[29] In Eden's mind, however, Nasser was to blame, and during a telephone conversation with the Minister of State at the Foreign Office, Anthony Nutting, the Prime Minister is alleged to have exclaimed: 'I want Nasser murdered.'[30] Eden's determination not merely to redress the Suez Canal grievance but also to precipitate Nasser's removal is confirmed by the meeting of the Cabinet's Egypt Committee on 30 July which concluded that Britain's immediate objective should be 'to bring about the down fall [sic] of the present Egyptian Government'.[31] Eden also told the American President, Dwight D. Eisenhower, that 'The removal of Nasser and the installation in Egypt of a regime less hostile to the West must . . . rank high among our objectives.'[32] Despite American opposition to the use of force,[33] Britain together with France, which suspected Nasser of providing support to rebels resisting French rule in Algeria,[34] moved towards a military solution to the Canal dispute.

During a meeting at Chequers on 14 October 1956, the Deputy Chief of Staff of the French Air Force, Maurice Challe, presented a plan which would involve secretly encouraging Israel to attack Egypt, thus providing Britain and France with a justification for despatching their own forces to Egypt under the guise of separating the combatants and protecting the Canal.[35] This plan was given further definition during discussions between representatives of the British, French, and Israeli governments at Sèvres, Paris, on 22 October.[36] Two days later, the Israelis agreed to launch an attack on Egypt. 'I think we have to undertake this operation', wrote the Israeli Prime Minister, David Ben-Gurion, in his diary on the morning of 24 October. 'This is a unique opportunity that two "not so small" powers

---

[29] Uriel Dann, *King Hussein and the Challenge of Arab Radicalism: Jordan, 1955–1967*, New York: Oxford University Press, 1989, p. 32.
[30] Brian Lapping, *End of Empire*, London: Guild Publishing, 1985, p. 262.
[31] Carlton, *Suez Crisis*, pp. 36–7.
[32] Cited in Keith Kyle, *Suez*, London: Weidenfeld and Nicolson, 1991, p. 179.
[33] See W. Scott Lucas, *Divided We Stand: Britain, the United States and the Suez Crisis*, London: Hodder and Stoughton, 1991; Peter L. Hahn, *The United States, Great Britain, and Egypt, 1945–1956: Strategy and Diplomacy in the Early Cold War*, Chapel Hill, NC: The University of North Carolina Press, 1991, pp. 211–39; David Carlton, *Anthony Eden: A Biography*, London: Allen Lane, 1981, pp. 419–20; Geoffrey Warner, 'Review Article: The United States and the Suez Crisis', *International Affairs*, 67, 2 (1991): 310–12.
[34] Maurice Vaïsse, 'France and the Suez Crisis', in Louis and Owen, *Suez 1956*, pp. 137–8.
[35] Kyle, *Suez*, pp. 296–7; Carlton, *Suez Crisis*, p. 56; Roy Fullick and Geoffrey Powell, *Suez: The Double War*, London: Leo Cooper, 1990, pp. 77–8. W. Scott Lucas suggests that Eden's decision to collude with Israel represented not an irrational attempt to destroy Nasser, but a logical step designed to foreclose an Israeli attack on Jordan (Scott Lucas, 'The Path to Suez', p. 269. See also Zeid Raad, 'A Nightmare Avoided: Jordan and Suez 1956', *Israel Affairs*, 1, 2 (1994): 296–7).
[36] Britain was represented at these discussions by the Foreign Secretary, Selwyn Lloyd. For his own description of the Sèvres meeting, see Selwyn Lloyd, *Suez 1956: A Personal Account*, London: Jonathan Cape, 1978, pp. 181–5.

will try to topple Nasser, and we shall not remain alone against him while he becomes stronger and conquers all Arab countries.'[37]

Israeli forces launched their first assault on the Egyptian army in the Sinai on 29 October. A day later, Britain and France issued a joint ultimatum to the two combatants to withdraw their forces ten miles from the Canal. Even at this early juncture, Eden's duplicity began to be revealed, since the Israelis were nowhere near the Canal. The contradictions inherent in the British Government's position were highlighted by the Leader of the Opposition, Hugh Gaitskell. 'I do not think anybody will accuse me of lack of sympathy with Israel,' he commented,

> but I am bound to say that a proposal which is intended to stop the fighting and which involves the withdrawal of the Egyptians ten miles further within their own frontier and a withdrawal of the Israelis ten miles from the Canal Zone — which still leaves them at some points 160 miles inside Egypt — is hardly one which would commend itself on equitable grounds.[38]

The failure of the Opposition to give Eden's government unqualified support was compounded by the hostile international reaction to the first wave of Anglo-French attacks on Egypt on the night of 31 October/1 November.

Reflecting Commonwealth dismay over British actions, the Prime Minister of India, Jawaharlal Nehru, fulminated: 'After fairly considerable experience in foreign affairs, I cannot think of a grosser case of naked aggression than what England and France are attempting to do.'[39] Even more serious for Eden's government was the critical attitude adopted by the United States, exemplified by John Foster Dulles'[40] condemnation of his British and French allies at the United Nations General Assembly on 2 November.[41] On the same day, the Foreign Secretary, Selwyn Lloyd, urged that

> the Cabinet should take account of the strength of the feelings which the Anglo-French action had aroused in the United States. If no concession were made to those feelings, it was possible that oil sanctions might be imposed against us. We might then be compelled to occupy Kuwait and Qatar, the only suppliers of oil who were not members of the United Nations; and we should alienate, perhaps irretrievably, all the Arab States. The Government of Syria

---

[37] Cited in Mordechai Bar-On, 'David Ben-Gurion and the Sèvres Collusion', in Louis and Owen, *Suez 1956*, p. 153.
[38] Cited in Kyle, *Suez*, pp. 361–2.
[39] S. C. Gangal, 'India and the Commonwealth', in M. S. Rajan (ed.), *India's Foreign Relations during the Nehru Era*, Bombay: Asia Publishing House, 1976, p. 84.
[40] United States Secretary of State, 1953–9.
[41] Carlton, *Suez Crisis*, p. 72.

had already broken off relations with the United Kingdom. It was possible that Iraq, Jordan and Libya would follow her example.[42]

Selwyn Lloyd concluded his statement by warning: 'We could not hope to avoid serious difficulties with the Arab States for more than a very short time longer, certainly not for as long as it would take us to complete an opposed occupation of Egypt.' Despite the unfavourable climate of international opinion, Eden pressed ahead with the military operation, British and French paratroops landing at the northern end of the Canal on 5 November. A day later, however, with the Soviet Union threatening rocket attacks on Britain,[43] the British forces were ordered to cease fire. Although unrepentant about his handling of the Suez crisis,[44] Eden chose to resign as Prime Minister on grounds of ill-health on 9 January 1957.

The impact of the Suez crisis on Britain's standing in the world, and on the speed of subsequent British decolonization, has become a controversial question. In Brian Lapping's estimation, 'The Suez operation wrote *finis* not only to the British Empire but to all empires of western Europe.'[45] Others, however, have produced more cautious assessments. 'Suez did not trigger an imperial implosion nor instigate a sudden revulsion against colonial rule among the policymakers,' asserts John Darwin.[46] Support for this interpretation has come from A. N. Porter and A. J. Stockwell, who stress the continuities in British imperial policy which Suez did little to alter.[47] Looking at the international repercussions of the crisis, Nigel John Ashton stresses: 'accounts which see Suez as a decisive transition, with America taking over responsibility for the Middle East from Britain, are too revolutionary in their outlook'.[48] In a similar vein, David Carlton has observed that 'British influence in the region did *not* in fact collapse overnight following the Suez debacle.'[49] This evaluation is particularly appropriate when applied to Kuwait. Although British actions in 1956 threatened the stability of the al-Sabah regime and the viability of the imperial presence, British relations with Kuwait were not fundamentally altered by the Suez crisis. Indeed, the events of 1956 served to highlight the strength of the relationship which existed between Britain and the al-Sabah.

---

[42] Cabinet Conclusions, 2 Nov 1956, CM 77 (56), CAB 128/30 Part 2; Keith Kyle, 'Suez and the Waldegrave Initiative', *Contemporary Record*, 9, 1 (1995): 385.
[43] Kyle, *Suez*, p. 458.
[44] See 'The Economic Situation', Note by the Prime Minister, 5 Jan 1957, C.P. (57) 8, CAB 129/84.
[45] Lapping, *End of Empire*, p. 277.
[46] John Darwin, *The End of the British Empire: The Historical Debate*, Oxford: Blackwell, 1991, p. 70.
[47] Porter and Stockwell, *British Imperial Policy and Decolonization*, 1989, Vol. 2, pp. 29–32.
[48] Nigel John Ashton, *Eisenhower, Macmillan and the Problem of Nasser: Anglo-American Relations and Arab Nationalism, 1955–59*, Basingstoke: Macmillan, 1996, p. 99.
[49] Carlton, *Suez Crisis*, p. 101.

II

Traditionally the Gulf States had been relatively immune from outside influences. 'Compared to either the Mashreq or the Maghreb,' asserts Fred Halliday, 'the Gulf was politically isolated, anaesthetized from the effects of the Palestinian question and of the rise of Arab nationalism.'[50] As late as February 1952, C. M. Rose of the Foreign Office observed that 'The virus of Arab nationalism has so far had practically no impact on these Rulers or on their comparatively primitive populations.'[51] Furthermore, the Persian Gulf Rulers were naturally suspicious of pan-Arabism, fearing that it would be exploited by their powerful neighbours to advance territorial claims. '[T]he Rulers and people of the Gulf States', remarked Sir Rupert Hay, 'prefer our present mild tutelage to the possibility of absorption by a powerful Arab nation'.[52] Commenting on growing Arab League interest in Kuwait, moreover, an official of the Foreign Office consoled himself with the knowledge that 'the Kuwait ruling family knows the League are after their money and for this reason are reluctant to have dealings with it'.[53] This surmise was confirmed in discussions between the Ruler and the Political Agent, C. J. Pelly, during which the former asserted that in educational, social, and medical matters Kuwait would cooperate with the Arab League, but would have no dealings with it on political or defence questions.[54] Indeed, the 1950s witnessed the growth of 'oil nationalism', in which Gulf regimes resisted any form of Arab unity which might attenuate their new-found riches.[55] As John Marlowe puts it: 'In Kuwait the fewness of the inhabitants and the richness of the oil revenues . . . tended to minimize the attractions of an association which would involve the sharing of Kuwaiti wealth with other[s] less fortunately situated.'[56] Nevertheless, sandwiched between Iraq and Saudi Arabia at the head of the Gulf, Kuwait tended to be more open to new ideas than the other Gulf states.[57]

'The people of Kuwait (and this applies particularly to the ruling family)', suggested Rose, 'are more prone than those of the other protected

---

[50] Fred Halliday, 'The Gulf Between Two Revolutions: 1958–1979', in Tim Niblock (ed.), *Social and Economic Development in the Arab Gulf*, London: Croom Helm, 1980, pp. 214–15.

[51] 'The internal political situation in the Persian Gulf States', Minute by C. M. Rose, 8 Feb 1952, FO 371/98328.

[52] Letter from Sir Rupert Hay to Anthony Eden, 11 June 1952, FO 371/98333.

[53] Minute by D. A. Greenhill, 18 Dec 1953, FO 371/104266.

[54] Telegram from Pelly to the Foreign Office, No. 401, 23 Dec 1953, FO 371/104266.

[55] Riad N. El-Rayyes, 'Arab Nationalism and the Gulf', in B. R. Pridham (ed.), *The Arab Gulf and the Arab World*, London: Croom Helm, 1988, p. 84.

[56] John Marlowe, *The Persian Gulf in the Twentieth Century*, London: The Cresset Press, 1962, p. 198.

[57] See Saeed Khalil Hashim, 'The Influence of Iraq on the Nationalist Movements of Kuwait and Bahrain, 1920–1961', PhD. thesis, University of Exeter, 1984.

States in the Gulf to influences from the rest of the Arab world. This tends to make them less readily responsive to British advice and, on occasion, antipathetic to it in order to demonstrate their independence.'[58] Writing at the end of 1955, the Political Resident, Sir Bernard Burrows, observed:

> Even though most of the Gulf Arabs are parochially-minded and some of them inclined to be sceptical of the lack of positive achievements of the Arab League, and though most of them do not actively chafe against the relationship of their states with Her Majesty's Government, nevertheless, the themes of Arab unity and liberation from Western imperialism carry some mystical power among the younger and more idealistic members of society and command at least lip service from the rest.[59]

On the eve of the Suez crisis, moreover, the head of the Foreign Office's Eastern Department, D. H. M. Riches, conceded that 'The Egyptians, through their technicians and their visits to Kuwait, have certainly made some headway there. The Ruler is sensitive to possible criticism from Egypt.'[60]

The susceptibility of Shaikh Abdullah of Kuwait to the wishes of other Arab states was demonstrated as early as 1951 when he refused, despite British pressure, to condemn a Lebanese airline which had been running unauthorized services between Kuwait and Beirut.[61] Following visits to Kuwait in 1955 by Colonel Anwar Sadat, a close associate of Nasser and future President of Egypt, Abdullah allowed the education department to make a small contribution from Kuwait government funds to the Egyptian Arms Week. In justifying his actions to the Political Agent, the Ruler stressed the difficulty of his position and the inevitability of his 'going some way with Arab Nationalist feeling in order to avoid open criticism of his close ties with Her Majesty's Government'.[62]

Although not a development specifically in the Arab world, the nationalization by the Iranian premier, Musaddiq, of the Anglo-Iranian Oil Company with its great refinery at Abadan had a significant impact on Kuwait. The Political Agent, H. G. Jakins, reported that 'the *suq* [market-place] is full of talk of the decline of the British',[63] while the Kuwait administrative report for 1951 noted: 'The most important effect of the abandonment of Abadan was the emergence of a belief . . . that it was merely necessary to bark loudly and lengthily enough to make the British let go anywhere.'[64]

---

[58] 'Kuwait', Memorandum by Rose, 30 August 1952, FO 371/98352.
[59] Letter from Burrows to Selwyn Lloyd, No. 143, 24 Dec 1955, FO 371/120561.
[60] H. Rahman, *The Making of the Gulf War: Origins of Kuwait's Long-Standing Territorial Dispute with Iraq*, Reading: Ithaca Press, 1997, pp. 208–9.
[61] 'Relations with the rest of the Arab world', Minute by Rose, 8 Feb 1952, FO 371/98364.
[62] Letter from Burrows to Lloyd, No. 47, 7 May 1956, PREM 11/1472.
[63] Letter from H. G. Jakins to Hay, 16 Oct 1951, FO 371/91260.
[64] *Kuwait Administrative Report for 1951*, FO 371/98323.

Writing in 1952, moreover, Sir Rupert Hay opined that the 'catastrophe' at Abadan 'undermined our whole position in the Gulf'.[65]

Ruminating in March 1956 on the new influences on Kuwait, the Political Agent, G.W. Bell, observed: 'The Ruler is disturbed at the prospect of a situation developing in which traditional ties with Her Majesty's Government might be subject to increasing pressure from Egypt and Saudi Arabia.'[66] The Suez crisis provided just such a situation.

Reflecting on his political philosophy in 1957, Nasser asserted:

> It immediately became clear to us that Egypt, like the rest of the constituent parts of the Arab nation, would not be able to safeguard her security except when grouped with her sister countries in Arabism, in a strong union.... Arab nationalism for us acquired the characteristic of both a political doctrine and a strategic necessity.[67]

In an attempt both to assert Egypt's leadership role in the Arab world and to undermine the British presence in the Middle East, Nasser conducted a crude but effective propaganda campaign via Cairo's 'Voice of Arabs' radio station.[68] This tactic proved a particularly difficult one for Britain to counter. Referring specifically to the Gulf area, Selwyn Lloyd noted:

> The States are undoubtedly and inevitably subject to the influence of Arab nationalism of the particularly virulent kind manufactured in Egypt. They cannot be insulated against it. The main threat is not so much from the Egyptian teachers and experts employed by the Governments[69] ... as from the general psychological impact of Egyptian propaganda and prestige. It is difficult for us to compete in this field of 'Arab' thought where immoderation against the West is politically conventional and any attempt at counter-attack can be represented as unrespectable 'imperialism'.[70]

As Anglo-Egyptian relations worsened in the course of 1956, Burrows admonished:

> There is a body of opinion here among British officials and others with experience of local reactions, that even successful forcible action by us against Egypt would not have the effect of making it easier to maintain our positions here, but rather the reverse.

---

[65] William Roger Louis, 'Musaddiq and the Dilemmas of British Imperialism', in James A. Bill and William Roger Louis (eds), *Musaddiq, Iranian Nationalism and Oil*, London: I. B. Tauris, 1988, p. 230.

[66] Telegram from Bell to the Foreign Office, No. 45, 12 March 1956, FO 371/120568.

[67] Vatikiotis, *Nasser*, p. 229.

[68] Mansfield, *Arabs*, p. 250.

[69] By April 1956, the government of Kuwait employed 350 Egyptians (Letter from Bell to Riches, No. 1015/2/56, 9 April 1956, FO 371/120550).

[70] 'Persian Gulf', Note by the Secretary of State for Foreign Affairs, 14 May 1956, C.P. (56) 122, CAB 129/81.

... What is quite clear is that prolonged hostilities, i.e. for more than a few days, would have the worst possible effect on our position here. It is in this event that the loyalty of the security services in Kuwait would be particularly strained and that it might be necessary to bring in considerable British forces to maintain ourselves there at all.[71]

The first major test for the security services came in August on the eve of the Conference of Maritime Nations.

Meeting at Lancaster House in London between 16 and 23 August, the twenty-two-nation conference discussed their joint approach to the nationalization of the Canal, a majority supporting Dulles' proposal that it should be run by an international board on which Egypt would serve.[72] In protest at the calling of the conference, Nasser exhorted his fellow Arabs to hold a series of strikes.[73] In Kuwait, about 4000 people assembled outside the National Culture Club to decide what action should be taken. Pro-Nasser speeches and appeals for a strike were made mainly by Palestinian speakers. Although the crowd later dispersed quietly, a hard core of approximately 200 clashed with the security services who dispersed them with rifle butts. By 16 August, while government departments functioned normally, 90 per cent of the shops remained closed. In the evening, crowds gathered and a party of some twenty youths appeared carrying a picture of Nasser. Intervention by the security services once again succeeded in scattering the protesters. The tense atmosphere was heightened by reports of the stationing of French troops in Cyprus.[74] Strikes following France's arrest of Algerian leaders in October closed shops and offices.[75] During a mass meeting at the Kuwait secondary school on 28 October, two Algerians as well as a local doctor, Ahmad al-Khatib, made anti-French speeches.[76] The event was attended by Shaikh Abdullah Mubarak and the President of the department of education, Shaikh Abdullah Jabir, both of whom made handsome donations to Algerian rebel funds. As yet, there were few overt manifestations of anti-British feeling in Kuwait. News of the Anglo-French ultimatum and subsequent attack on Egypt transformed the situation, however.

The *Majlis* movement of the late 1930s had essentially been an elite phenomenon, the leadership consisting of merchant notables and disaffected

---

[71] Telegram from Burrows to the Foreign Office, No. 733, 13 Aug 1956, FO 371/120571.
[72] Kennett Love, *Suez: The Twice-Fought War*, London: Longman, 1970, pp. 405–6.
[73] The following is based on *Confidential Annex to Kuwait Diary No. 8*, covering the period 31 July–26 August 1956, FO 371/120551; Jill Crystal, *Oil and Politics in the Gulf: Rulers and Merchants in Kuwait and Qatar*, Cambridge: Cambridge University Press, 1995, p. 81.
[74] *Confidential Annex to Kuwait Diary No. 9*, covering the period 27 Aug–24 Sept 1956, FO 371/120551.
[75] Crystal, *Oil and Politics in the Gulf*, p. 81.
[76] Monthly diary: November 1956 in Burrows' letter to Riches, No. 10101/55/56, 10 Jan 1957, FO 371/126871.

members of the al-Sabah family. Later reform movements were more broadly based. They included not only young men who had been educated abroad, but also politically sophisticated Egyptians, Lebanese, Iraqis, and Palestinians who were working in Kuwait.[77] Since political parties were forbidden, reform-minded people had to pursue their activities through the medium of social clubs. In order to cloak their political activities still further, the clubs assigned honourary chairmanships to members of the ruling family.[78] By 1956, there were some seventeen clubs, the most important being the Teachers Club, the Graduate Club, and especially the National Culture Club (NCC) under the leadership of Ahmad al-Khatib,[79] who himself had studied at the American University of Beirut. While in Lebanon, he had became involved in George Habash's Arab Nationalist Movement. Profoundly influenced by this experience, al-Khatib developed into a leading opposition figure on his return home.

Founded in 1953, NCC membership was open not only to Kuwaitis but also to other Arabs. The NCC's publications, which by 1955 included a weekly newspaper called *Sada al-Iman*, reflected the ideas and trends of Arab nationalism.[80] Cooperation between the various clubs was facilitated by the formation of the Committee of Clubs. It was this organization which coordinated the protest at the attacks on Egypt. On 2 November, pamphlets were distributed by the Committee denouncing British actions and calling for strikes and a mass meeting for the following day.[81] In response, the police department produced public notices which forbade the proposed demonstrations. The scene was set, therefore, for a trial of strength between the authorities and the reformist movement.

At first almost all shops opened normally, only to put up their shutters when a crowd of several hundred attempted to hold a meeting in the main bazaar mosque. Meanwhile the police and security services engaged in a two-hour battle with demonstrators in the centre of Kuwait town. Bands of youths also roamed through the streets throwing stones indiscriminately and at one point even menacing the Political Agency. The al-Sabah's handling of the disorders, however, underlined the fundamental stability of the regime.

At the outset of the crisis, the Ruler confided in Bell that: 'In the com-

---

[77] Rosemarie Said Zahlan, *The Making of the Modern Gulf States: Kuwait, Bahrain, Qatar, the United Arab Emirates, and Oman*, London: Unwin Hyman, 1989, p. 32. See also Haya al-Mughni, *Women in Kuwait: The Politics of Gender*, London: Saqi Books, 1993, pp. 32–3.

[78] Falah al-Mdairis, 'The Arab Nationalist Movement in Kuwait from its Origins to 1970', PhD. thesis, University of Oxford, 1987, p. 151.

[79] Crystal, *Oil and Politics in the Gulf*, p. 82.

[80] Al-Mdairis, 'The Arab Nationalist Movement in Kuwait', p. 151.

[81] The following is based on *Confidential Annex to Kuwait Diary No. 11*, covering the period 28 Oct–28 Nov 1956, FO 371/120551, and monthly diary for November in Burrows' letter to Riches, No. 10101/55/56, 10 Jan 1957, FO 371/126871.

ing week I may be under pressure to do what I wish to avoid.'[82] Shaikh Abdullah, therefore, wisely removed himself to the remote island of Failaka, where he could not be contacted, leaving Abdullah Mubarak to deal with the security situation. Abdullah Mubarak, for all his faults, was nothing if not pro-British and assured Bell that Britain's interests would be protected.[83] Britain's heavy reliance on Abdullah Mubarak did have its disadvantages, however. 'We have unfortunately come closer to the reactionary elements of the Ruling family', acknowledged Bell, 'at precisely the time when we had hoped to work towards closer co-operation with the younger and more liberally minded members.'[84] During the Suez war, however, the al-Sabah demonstrated their ability to submerge individual animosities in the interests of preserving shaikhly rule. Despite the rivalry between Abdullah Mubarak and the head of the police department, Shaikh Sabah,[85] the latter placed his men under the former's general direction in the tense days which followed Anglo-French actions in Egypt.[86] Shaikh Fahad's absence from Kuwait in November also proved serendipitous since, as Bell put it: 'His antagonism to Shaikh Abdullah al-Mubarak and pressure from the Palestinians in his Department might well have caused him to agree to hasty decisions against our economic interests, decisions which in his absence could not be taken.'[87]

Abdullah Mubarak's robust handling of the disorders, which included personally administering a number of canings to those who hesitated to obey his orders, met with the approbation of the senior merchant class who threw their weight behind the regime.[88] In spite of their undoubted successes, therefore, the Committee of Clubs still faced a powerful force of opinion suspicious, if not hostile, to its reformist aims. In the short term, the al-Sabah's success in overcoming the immediate crisis served to protect British interests and foreclose the need for formal intervention,[89] a prospect which the Foreign Office viewed with horror. 'In present circumstances,' conceded one

---

[82] Sir Gawain Bell, *Shadows on the Sand*, London: C. Hurst and Company, 1983, p. 243.
[83] Ibid., p. 244.
[84] Letter from Bell to Burrows, 9 Nov 1956, FO 371/120557.
[85] In September 1956, Sabah had told the British Ambassador in Beirut, G. H. Middleton, that Britain should 'cut out the cackle and get on with the good work of eliminating Nasser' (Letter from Middleton to Burrows, No. 1632/43/56, 20 Sept 1956, FO 371/120684).
[86] Letter from Bell to Burrows, No. 1612A/100/56, 19 Nov 1956, FO 371/120684.
[87] Ibid.
[88] Ibid.
[89] In March 1956, an official of the Foreign Office expressed the view that 'in Kuwait it would be a fatal error to make use of British forces except in a moment of extreme emergency in order to restore order when the local forces had failed' (Letter from C. A. E. Shuckburgh to Sir Norman Brook, EA 1055/1G, 14 March 1956, FO 371/120571). In analysing the possibility of deploying British troops in the Gulf, another official opined: 'We might be driven to this as a last resort. But it would do great harm to our relations with the Shaikhdoms' (Minute by Riches, 25 April 1956, FO 371/120650).

official, 'for us to be known to be intervening militarily in Kuwait to safeguard our oil supplies would have a disastrous effect on our reputation elsewhere.'[90] Another official expressed fear that a military occupation of Kuwait would be represented as a 'second Port Said operation'.[91] Although intervention proved unnecessary, the impact of the Suez war on the long-term viability of the imperial presence in Kuwait remained a cause for concern.

Though not necessarily for the same reasons, British officials in the Gulf were as surprised and dismayed at the attack on Egypt as the local populations. In his memoirs, Bell recalled: 'In all our anxieties and in all our calculations we never envisaged the participation of Israel in a combined Anglo-French operation, and never were we given the slightest hint from London that such a course was even remotely contemplated . . . . We were told nothing of this confused and ill-advised intrigue.'[92] In stressing the absence of consultation, moreover, Burrows observed: 'The breakdown of the normal system of communications and of the normal trust between ministers and senior officials seems to demonstrate the degree of irrationality in the plans being hatched in the Government at this time.'[93] Once the Anglo-French operation had begun, both Bell and Burrows were quick to voice their concerns.

'[T]he Sheikhs and the more responsible of the older Kuwaitis have remained stoutly behind us', remarked Bell,

> but inevitably there is an increasing strain on their loyalty in the face of local and external pressure and uncertainty of the situation over the Canal. The conflict with the Egyptian Army and Egyptian casualties will intensify feeling against us and I foresee likelihood of deterioration in the situation here.[94]

Burrows expressed similar opinions. 'Apart from short term security danger of strain on loyalty of the responsible element', he asserted,

> I am particularly concerned at long term effect of this situation. Our continued attack on Egypt while doing nothing against Israel is the one thing that might make Kuwait and perhaps Qatar think of changing their relationship with us. Since the important object of our Middle East policy is to preserve our position here I submit that full weight should be given to this aspect.[95]

Burrows also warned that

> It is . . . clear that we draw very deeply on accumulated fund of goodwill of the Persian Gulf Rulers. Some of this goodwill is of course interested since in

---

[90] Minute by K. R. Oakeshott, 14 Dec 1956, FO 371/120619.
[91] Minute by Christopher Pirie-Gordon, 14 Dec 1956, FO 371/120619.
[92] Bell, *Shadows*, p. 242.
[93] Bernard Burrows, *Footnotes in the Sand: The Gulf in Transition, 1953–1958*, Salisbury: Michael Russell, 1990, p. 72.
[94] Telegram from Bell to the Foreign Office, No. 299, 3 Nov 1956, FO 371/120567.
[95] Telegram from Burrows to the Foreign Office, No. 989, 3 Nov 1956, FO 371/120567.

PLATE 1

Shaikh Abdullah and C. J. Pelly at the former's investiture with the KCMG in February 1953. (St Antony's College, Oxford)

Shaikh Fahad (1906–1959). (Kuwait Ministry of Information)

PLATE 3

Shaikh Abdullah, Sir William Fraser (Chairman, Anglo-Iranian Oil Company), Izzat Ja'far (Shaikh Abdullah's private secretary), June 1953. (From the BP Amoco Archive)

PLATE 4

Shaikh Abdullah in the boardroom of the Kuwait Oil Company, June 1953. The seated figure fourth from the right is the managing director of the Kuwait Oil Company, C. A. P. Southwell. The seated figures sixth and seventh from the left are Shaikh Abdullah's representative in London, H. T. Kemp, and the State Secretary of Kuwait, Abdullah Mulla Saleh. (From the BP Amoco Archive)

PLATE 5

C. A. P. Southwell and Shaikh Abdullah leaving Britannic House, June 1953. (From the BP Amoco Archive)

PLATE 6

Shaikh Sa'ad and Shaikh Abdullah Mubarak at a review of Kuwait's police and public security forces, April 1961. (Kuwait Ministry of Information)

PLATE 7

Discussions preceding Kuwait's achievement of full independence. From left to right: J. C. B. Richmond (Political Agent), Sir George Middleton (Political Resident), Edward Heath (Lord Privy Seal), Shaikh Abdullah. (Photograph Sir John Richmond)

PLATE 8

Shaikh Sabah (Heir Apparent and Prime Minister) and Shaikh Abdullah arrive for the opening of the first session of Kuwait's National Assembly, 29 January 1963. (Kuwait Ministry of Information)

some cases their own continued existence depends ultimately on our support but they must be weighing this factor with the disadvantages of acting against the emotions of the majority of their subjects.[96]

The role of Israel in the Suez war proved to be the most damaging revelation for Britain's standing in the Gulf. 'The most incomprehensible part of the matter to the Rulers, and the one most likely to provoke further reaction when it becomes generally understood,' remarked Burrows, 'is the way in which our attack on Egypt must facilitate further Israeli success against the Egyptian force in the Sinai.'[97] An official of the Foreign Office was forced to concede that 'I have no doubt that in all the Gulf States we are believed to have acted in collusion with Israel. So far we have done nothing which would help to dispel that impression.'[98] Referring specifically to Kuwait, Bell confessed that 'it is difficult to see how, in the face of an accepted and unquestioned view that we acted in collusion with Israel, we can hope to maintain our previous close relationship of confidence and trust'.[99] Indeed, local anger led to calls for the Ruler to boycott British commercial interests and to cancel existing contracts between state and British firms.[100] Although Britain's decision at the end of November to withdraw unconditionally from Egypt promoted an easing of tension, Bell recorded that

> there still exists a powerful body of opinion which sees Nasser . . . as a hero who has not hesitated to sacrifice Egypt's resources for the sake of Palestine, and among [the] Clubs and younger elements his appeal may well have increased rather than diminished.[101]

Britain's recognition of the strength of such sentiments fostered a debate about her future role in the Gulf.

The British Ambassador in Tehran, Sir Roger Stevens, was convinced of the necessity to undertake a fundamental reassessment of Britain's position.[102] First, Stevens questioned the strategic value of the Gulf. Taking account of not only the liquidation of the Indian empire, but also the loss of Britain's traditional footholds in Egypt, Jordan, and Iraq, Stevens argued that the Gulf had become 'a sort of double-ended cul-de-sac'. As regards the preservation of Britain's economic interests, Stevens was equally sceptical about the necessity of maintaining a formal British presence in the Gulf. '[I]t is not clear to me', he wrote,

---

[96] Telegram from Burrows to the Foreign Office, No. 971, 2 Nov 1956, FO 371/120567.
[97] Ibid.
[98] Minute by J. C. Moberly, 6 Nov 1956, FO 371/120567.
[99] Letter from Bell to Burrows, 9 Nov 1956, FO 371/120557.
[100] Telegram from Bell to the Foreign Office, No. 310, 7 Nov 1956, FO 371/120567.
[101] Telegram from Bell to the Foreign Office, No. 16, 6 Dec 1956, FO 371/120567.
[102] The following is based on a Letter from Sir Roger Stevens to Lloyd, No. 140, 8 Dec 1956, FO 371/120571.

that our political position in Kuwait and Qatar is essential to the maintenance of our commercial interests, nor am I sure how effective it is in the long run for ensuring that the Ruler of Kuwait does not try to spend his vast resources outside the sterling area. At any rate, recent events seem to have shown that our token military presence in the Gulf does not ensure the flow of oil any more than a military occupation foothold in the Plate would guarantee our supply of beef.

The British Ambassador in Baghdad, Sir Michael Wright,[103] was also convinced of the need for a fundamental revision of British thinking on the Gulf. Referring not merely to the strong tide of Arab nationalism but also to the growing perception that Britain's continued presence was anachronistic, Wright warned: 'If we take no new line we shall be accused of clinging to the past.'[104] His specific proposal related to the creation of a federation of Gulf states under British protection, coupled with their possible future association with the Baghdad Pact.

The man responsible for coordinating British policy in the Gulf, Sir Bernard Burrows, was unimpressed by the arguments presented by Wright and Stevens.[105] Indeed, he admitted that 'I disagree with so much of what is said in these despatches that it is hard to know where to begin.' In dismissing any thought of a British withdrawal from the Gulf, Burrows asserted:

> I do not know what is the justification for the assumption that the Gulf States and our relationship with them cannot continue more or less as they are. It is surely a principle borrowed from the Americans and alien to our system of political thought that anything which has existed for a hundred years, such as our relations with the Gulf States, must necessarily be wrong or must necessarily change.

Pressure for a British egress from the Gulf came not from the Rulers and their subjects, emphasized Burrows, but from foreign Arabs who had temporarily settled in the region. On the question of sponsoring constitutional change, Burrows regarded the idea of a federation as 'purely fanciful'. 'The Gulf States', he averred,

> are intensely parochial. Their interests and economic circumstances are different one from another and they have in many cases intense jealousies of their neighbours.[106] The commotion caused by our proposals to federate the

---

[103] Sir Michael Wright (1901–76); GCMG (1958), KCMG (1951), CMG (1945); Assistant Under-Secretary of State, Foreign Office, 1947–50; Ambassador to Norway, 1951–4; Ambassador to Iraq, 1954–8.
[104] Letter from Sir Michael Wright to Selwyn Lloyd, No. 5, 4 Jan 1957, FO 371/126923.
[105] The following is based on a Letter from Burrows to Lloyd, No. 12, 24 Jan 1957, FO 371/126915.
[106] As early as 1951, the Political Resident, Sir Rupert Hay, had opined: 'I am very doubtful whether it will be possible to achieve a real federation of all the Gulf Shaikhdoms owing to local jealousies and geographical factors' (Letter from Hay to the Secretary of State for Foreign Relations, No. 13, 29 Jan 1951, FO 371/91326).

states of the Aden Protectorate[107] should perhaps also be a warning against undue zeal in this direction at the present time.

Burrows concluded by urging that the preservation of existing relations with the Gulf should be regarded as a major British interest.

The Political Resident's views struck a chord in the Foreign Office. 'Any change in our relationship with the Persian Gulf States', declared an official, 'should only be made if it would improve our position or if our position could not be maintained without it.'[108] Selwyn Lloyd was in full agreement,[109] stressing the extent of Britain's interests in the Gulf, the most important being the supply of oil, 50 per cent of Britain's total needs being satisfied by Kuwait alone. Lloyd also perceived that the British presence acted as an obstacle to the spread of communist influence in the Middle East. As regards strategy, Lloyd saw the Gulf area as vital for assuring the communications of the Baghdad Pact countries in both peace and war.

The reservations voiced by Stevens and Wright about the viability of Britain's continued presence in the Gulf, therefore, did not prove influential. While Lloyd warned that 'We should seek generally to maintain our position by political rather than military means', no fundamental shift in British policy took place in the wake of the Suez crisis. Nor was Suez responsible for the problems associated with the widening of the Kuwait gap in the second half of 1956 and first half of 1957.

The Kuwait gap was a loophole through which residents of the sterling area were able to change their sterling into dollars or dollar securities. Typically, a Kuwaiti, having acquired dollars, would use them to purchase dollar securities from United States residents only to sell them at a premium to United Kingdom residents against sterling.[110] Kuwait could also be used by non-sterling area residents to purchase sterling below the official rate. These transactions were made possible because Kuwait had a free market in dollars and sterling,[111] the provisions of the Exchange Control Act of

---

[107] In 1955, the governor of Aden, Sir Tom Hickinbotham, pursued a policy of federating the states of the Aden Protectorate. By the end of 1956, however, the plan was shelved owing to both internal opposition and external pressure, especially from Egypt. (See Simon C. Smith, 'Rulers and Residents: British Relations with the Aden Protectorate, 1937–59', *Middle Eastern Studies*, 31, 3 (1995): 517–18.)

[108] Minute by John B. Denson, 9 March 1957, FO 371/126915.

[109] The following is based on 'Persian Gulf', Memorandum by the Secretary of State for Foreign Affairs, 7 June 1957, C (57) 138, CAB 129/87.

[110] *The Economist*, 13 July 1952. I am grateful to Catherine Schenk for this reference.

[111] For a discussion of the other principal free market territory in the sterling area, see Catherine R. Schenk, 'Closing the Hong Kong Gap: The Hong Kong Free Dollar Market in the 1950s', *The Economic History Review*, 47, 2 (1994): 335–53.

1947 never having been extended to the Shaikhdom.[112] 'The net effect', bemoaned a Treasury official, 'is that sterling has been transferred into dollars without any illegal act having been committed by anyone.'[113]

In June 1954, a working party consisting of representatives from the Treasury, Foreign Office, Colonial Office, and Bank of England, had reviewed the whole question of free market territories. A number of options for closing the Kuwait gap were considered, including expelling the Shaikhdom from the sterling area. 'Ejection', it was concluded, 'would increase the dollar cost of oil and might have serious political consequences which seem out of proportion with such damage as the sterling area may be suffering at the present moment through the existence of the free market.'[114] The Kuwait gap was also tolerated because the volume of transactions was not great. In the early 1950s, for example, the capital drain was around £36 million per annum.[115] In the second half of 1956, however, the sterling loss through the gap began to rise dramatically.

The precise cause of this sudden increase remained something of an enigma. At first it was thought that the loss might simply be a short-term reaction to the Suez crisis.[116] When the loss continued unabated in 1957, it was clear that a more fundamental shift was taking place reflecting a lack of confidence in the British government to control inflation.[117] At a meeting between Sir Leslie Rowan (Second Secretary, Treasury) and officials of the Bank of England, the former was described as being 'at his most impassioned' when discussing the Kuwait gap.[118] Unless something was done about it, argued Rowan, not only might sterling have to be devalued owing to the loss to the reserves, but also sterling area discipline would be undermined when it was discovered by member countries that dollars were being spent on dollar securities. The Treasury also described the Kuwait gap as driving 'a coach and four through a large part of our apparatus of dollar restrictions'.[119]

By mid-1957, the rate of loss, which had reached the alarming figure of

---

[112] In 1951, a Bank of England official noted: 'There is virtually no Exchange Control in the Persian Gulf Sheikdoms, and there is no possibility of inducing the local sheiks to introduce legislation for the purpose — let alone administering it adequately' ('Persian Gulf Sheikdoms', Note by H. H. Withrington, 29 Aug 1951, Bank of England, EC 5/434).

[113] 'The Kuwait Gap', Memorandum by J. G. Owens, 23 May 1957, T 231/832.

[114] 'Sterling Area Free Markets', Report of the Working Party, 15 June 1954, T 231/831. With respect to Hong Kong, Schenk argues that Britain perceived tangible economic and political advantages in preserving the colony's free market status (Schenk, 'Closing the Hong Kong Gap', pp. 338–46).

[115] Letter from D. R. Serpell to A. D. M. Ross, 27 April 1953, T 231/831.

[116] 'The Kuwait Gap', Paper by Owens, 23 May 1957, T 231/832.

[117] Schenk, 'Closing the Hong Kong Gap', p. 346.

[118] 'Kuwait Gap', Note by C. R. P. Hamilton, 16 May 1957, EC 5/434, cited in Schenk, 'Closing the Hong Kong Gap', p. 348.

[119] 'The Kuwait Gap', Draft memorandum by Owens enclosed in his letter to M. H. Parsons, 3 June 1957, EC 5/434.

around £15 million per month,[120] necessitated urgent action. Excluding Kuwait, and the other Persian Gulf states, from the sterling area was briefly reconsidered, only to be rejected in view of, as one Treasury official put it, 'the undesirability of doing anything which might make it more difficult to persuade their Rulers to invest their surplus oil revenues in sterling securities'.[121] At a meeting between the Chancellor of the Exchequer, Peter Thorneycroft, and the Governor of the Bank of England, C. F. Cobbold, on 28 June 1957, a number of possible solutions were discussed, including measures to prevent purchases of dollar securities by UK residents from non-UK residents of the sterling area.[122] Although favoured by the Chancellor, this proposal was questioned by the Governor on the grounds that it would be a retrograde step with respect to easing exchange controls, and would merely encourage the exploitation of other loopholes. Despite Bank of England reservations, the Treasury line prevailed. On 5 July, Thorneycroft issued an order under the Defence (Finance) Regulations prohibiting UK residents from acquiring foreign currency securities from anywhere in the Scheduled Territories of the sterling area outside the UK. That the closing of the Kuwait gap was not completely successful is demonstrated by the Treasury's continuing concern about the rate of loss through Kuwait, which stood at £8 million for August 1957.[123]

III

Recalling the strained atmosphere in Kuwait in the immediate aftermath of the Suez war, Bell wrote:

> I felt that nearly everything that my predecessors had achieved over the past fifty years in a place which had so long been traditionally pro-British, and the little I had done in the past fifteen months by way of maintaining and fostering confidence and friendship, had all evaporated.[124]

Referring to the situation in Kuwait and the other Shaikhdoms, an official of the Foreign Office was forced to concede that 'the Rulers must be under considerable pressure from popular opinion and torn between their loyalties to H.M.G. and to their fellow Arabs'.[125] It was probably no coincidence that the Ruler's British financial expert, Colonel Crichton, chose November 1956 to announce his resignation. Nevertheless, Bell consoled

---

[120] Note of a meeting in Sir Leslie Rowan's room, 15 May 1957, EC 5/434.
[121] 'The Sterling Area Free Markets in 1957', Draft paper by M. Rudd, 4 April 1957, T 231/832.
[122] 'Sterling Area Free Markets', Note of a meeting held in the Chancellor of Exchequer's room, 28 June 1957, EC 5/435.
[123] Note by J. M. Stevens, 27 Sept 1957, EC 5/435.
[124] Bell, *Shadows*, p. 245.
[125] Minute by Riches, 'Situation in the Persian Gulf', 13 Nov 1956, FO 371/120567.

himself with the thought that 'the removal of an Englishman from the prominent if largely ineffective position as Controller of Finance may in fact have done our general cause no harm'.[126] Moreover, despite the immediate turbulence which had followed in the wake of the Suez war, the al-Sabah demonstrated considerable skill in maintaining not merely their own position but also their relationship with Britain. For her part, Britain remained determined, despite some initial doubts, to preserve her position in Kuwait. The changing structures of power which resulted from the Suez war, however, militated against this objective. In succeeding years, moreover, pressure from the Arab world on Kuwait increased.

---

[126] Letter from Bell to Burrows, No. 3, 20 Feb 1957, FO 371/126869.

4: Kuwait and the Arab World, 1957-9

> [I]f the Sabah are confident... of their ability to combat criticism of the regime springing from internal forces, they are ... less confident in regard to the pressures which can be exerted against them by the rest of the Arab world.[1]
>
> With the formation of the united state of Syria and Egypt Kuwait will find it increasingly necessary to show that she is as good a supporter of Arabism as the rest.[2]

In his annual report for 1956, the Political Resident, Bernard Burrows, admitted that 'The year was probably the most difficult for us since the beginning of our connexion with Kuwait.'[3] Although Britain's relationship with the Shaikhdom remained outwardly intact, Burrows observed that 'Kuwait's characteristic as an independent Arab city state has become even more marked and our ability to influence its development has become less'.[4] This tendency was particularly pronounced in foreign affairs. Indeed, the Ruler increasingly sought to take the initiative in the conduct of relations with other Arab countries and demonstrated a concomitant unwillingness to be guided by British advice. Britain had little option but to acquiesce since, as Burrows conceded, 'Our position has become more exclusively dependent on the traditional goodwill and self-interest of the Shaikhs.'[5]

---

[1] Letter from G. W. Bell to Sir Bernard Burrows, No. 2, 23 Jan 1957, FO 371/126899.
[2] Minute by J. C. Moberly, 15 Feb 1958, FO 371/132810.
[3] Letter from Burrows to Selwyn Lloyd, No. 49, 15 April 1957, FO 371/126869.
[4] Ibid, cited in A. M. Gargash, 'Political Participation in Kuwait and the Arab Emirates: 1938-1979', PhD. thesis, University of Cambridge, 1989, p. 140.
[5] Letter from Burrows to Lloyd, No. 49, 15 April 1957, FO 371/126869.

I

'So far as the Persian Gulf States are concerned', wrote Burrows in October 1957, 'the primary purpose of our association with them is that we should look after their interests abroad'.[6] The growing sensitivity of the Arab world to the vestiges of Western imperialism, however, made the fulfilment of this objective increasingly problematic. As regards Kuwait, Britain remained powerless to resolve either the frontier demarcation with Iraq or Saudi Arabian claims to disputed islands in the Neutral Zone.[7] Entering a constructive dialogue with Saudi Arabia proved especially difficult following its severance of diplomatic relations with Britain in 1956. Ostensibly a mark of protest against the Suez war, this decision can be traced to Saudi resentment at Britain's handling of the Buraimi oasis dispute.[8]

In 1949, the Saudi Arabian King, Ibn Saud, demanded an adjustment of the border between his country and the Shaikdom of Abu Dhabi. In an attempt to consolidate Saudi claims, an armed party occupied one of the villages in the Buraimi oasis which formed part of the disputed area. Although Saudi Arabia agreed to submit the case to arbitration by an international tribunal, the discussions broke down in September 1955 amid allegations that the Saudis had resorted to bribery with a view to securing a favourable adjudication. A month later, Britain supported the expulsion of Saudi forces from Buraimi.

As has been noted with respect to Kuwait, the souring of relations with Saudi Arabia made the resolution of other disputes involving British protected states more difficult. With this in mind, an official of the Foreign Office warned that

> although the Ruler and many other Kuwaitis do still attach importance to our presence in the Gulf as a protective shield allowing them to enjoy their prosperity and to avoid the necessity of sharing their oil wealth with their neighbours, it is clear that they will watch increasingly closely our performance in relation to their disputes with their neighbours. They will want to be assured that they are getting value from a relationship which earns them so much criticism in other Arab countries.[9]

---

[6] Letter from Burrows to H. Beeley, No. 1034, 9 Oct 1957, FO 371/126905.
[7] Ibid.
[8] See Bernard Burrows, *Footnotes in the Sand: The Gulf in Transition, 1953–1958*, Salisbury: Michael Russell, 1990, pp. 87–111; J. B. Kelly, *Arabia, the Gulf and the West*, London: Weidenfeld and Nicolson, 1980, pp. 69–73; Glen Balfour-Paul, *The End of Empire in the Middle East: Britain's Relinquishment of Power in her Last Three Arab Dependencies*, Cambridge: Cambridge University Press, 1994, pp. 114–15; John Bulloch, *The Gulf: A Portrait of Kuwait, Qatar, Bahrain and the UAE*, London: Century Publishing, 1984, pp. 47–51; Tore Tingvold Petersen, 'Anglo-American Rivalry in the Middle East: The Struggle for the Buraimi Oasis, 1952–1957', *The International History Review*, 14, 1 (1992): 71–91.
[9] Minute by Moberly, 18 Dec 1957, FO 371/126905.

In some respects, however, the notion of British protection proved beneficial to the Ruler. As Burrows noted:

> It is convenient for him to be able to blame us if Kuwait cannot get all that it wants in its international relations and at the same time he can avoid the necessity of saying unpleasant things to his neighbours which he would find personally and politically distasteful.[10]

The new Political Agent in Kuwait, Aubrey Halford, agreed with Burrows' analysis. 'The Ruling Family', he observed,

> ... pay lip service to the fiction of Arab unity, but like all other Arabs, they have no intention that uncomfortable ideology should interfere with profitable practice. H.M.G. are invaluable in this context.... In short, anything which is easy and advantageous the Kuwaitis and their neighbours will settle by direct negotiation — anything which is difficult or un-Arab they are glad to hand to us.[11]

'The danger for us in Kuwait', concluded Halford, 'is that, while legally responsible for the defence of the State's interests, we may be allowing ourselves to slip into the role of mediator between her and her neighbours.' Moreover, Burrows expressed the concern that 'we shall only be able to ensure that Kuwait keeps its money in sterling if Kuwait is getting some fairly tangible benefit from us in return'.[12] Despite Burrows' warning, in the course of 1958 Kuwait's destiny became entangled in Britain's wider strategic and political goals in the Arab world.

In an effort to counter both mounting American pressure and internal political strife, the Syrian Baath Party, towards the end of 1957, began to look to Nasser to provide leadership.[13] In many ways the Egyptian President appeared to be the obvious figure to foster Syrian stability. His friend, Mohammed Heikal, recalled: 'Arabism took him for its hero and lifted him out of Egypt into an inter-Arab international role.'[14] Although some have doubted the depth of Nasser's ideological commitment to Arab nationalism,[15] from the mid-1950s he had increasingly espoused Arab unity. On the eve of the Suez war Nasser argued that 'Egypt must not live isolated from the rest of the Arabs, because once we are isolated, we shall be defeated separately.'[16] Two years later, he confessed that 'Arab

---

[10] Letter from Burrows to Beeley, No. 1034, 9 Oct 1957, FO 371/126905.
[11] Letter from Aubrey Halford to Burrows, No. 1034/6/57, 14 Nov 1957, FO 371/126905.
[12] Letter from Burrows to Beeley, No. 1034, 3 Dec 1957, FO 371/126905.
[13] A. L. Tibawi, *A History of Modern Syria including Lebanon and Palestine*, London: Macmillan, 1969, pp. 400–1.
[14] Derek Hopwood, *Egypt: Politics and Society, 1945–90*, third edition, London: HarperCollins, 1991, p. 58.
[15] See P. J. Vatikiotis, Nasser and His Generation, New York: St Martin's, 1978, pp. 225–48.
[16] Ibid., p. 228.

nationalism is not a word or a motto; it is a great and a high principle.'[17] Nevertheless, concerned that the ground had been insufficiently well-prepared, Nasser displayed initial diffidence in response to Baath requests for union between Egypt and Syria. He was won over, nevertheless, by assurances that the merger would be total, the Syrian political system following that of Egypt: all political parties were to be dissolved; the army had to withdraw from politics; state control and agricultural reform had to be extended to Syria. With these conditions accepted, the two countries announced on 1 February 1958 the formation of the United Arab Republic (UAR).[18]

Having harboured their own ambitions towards union with Syria since the end of the Second World War,[19] Iraqi leaders found Nasser's apparent triumph all the more galling. While conceding that the UAR appealed to 'extreme nationalists on every ground, to intellectuals and students partly for emotional reasons, and to the unthinking public', the British Ambassador in Baghdad, Sir Michael Wright, observed:

> the King and Crown Prince, most of the responsible politicians, the majority of the present Parliament, and powerful tribal leaders, while all favouring Arab unity in principle and on the right lines, see in this form of it a threat to the existence both of the regime and of Iraq itself.[20]

Equally concerned about the shift in the Middle Eastern balance of power symbolized by the UAR, King Hussein initiated discussions with Iraq for a union of the two Hashemite Kingdoms of Jordan and Iraq.[21]

This was not the first time that attempts had been made to promote unity between Jordan and Iraq.[22] Following his coronation in May 1946, King Abdullah of Jordan explored the possibility of establishing closer links with Iraq. The resulting 'Treaty of Brotherhood and Alliance', however, was an anodyne agreement with little practical significance. Shortly before his

---

[17] A. I. Dawisha, *Egypt in the Arab World: The Elements of Foreign Policy*, London: Macmillan, 1976, pp. 129–30.

[18] Despite initial euphoria, the union soon turned sour. Nasser's agricultural reforms were resented by Syrian landowners, while local politicians smarted at their loss of power. On 28 September 1961, the union experiment was brought to an abrupt end by the intervention of the Syrian army (Hopwood, *Egypt*, pp. 61–2).

[19] See Michael Eppel, 'Iraqi Politics and Regional Policies, 1945–9', *Middle Eastern Studies*, 28, 1 (1992): 108–113; Malcolm H. Kerr, *The Arab Cold War: Gamal 'Abd al-Nasir and his Rivals, 1958–1970*, third edition, London: Oxford University Press, 1971, p. 2.

[20] Matthew Elliot, *'Independent Iraq': The Monarchy and British Influence, 1941–58*, London: Tauris Academic Studies, 1996, p. 130.

[21] Phebe Marr, *The Modern History of Iraq*, Boulder, Colorado: Westview Press, 1985, pp. 121–2. In March 1956, Hussein had balked at the idea of a union which left no room for two kings (W. Scott Lucas, 'Redefining the Suez "Collusion"', *Middle Eastern Studies*, 26, 1 (1990): 95).

[22] The following is based on Bruce Maddy-Weitzman, 'Jordan and Iraq: Efforts at Intra-Hashimite Unity', *Middle Eastern Studies*, 26, 1 (1990): 65–75.

assassination in July 1951, Abdullah made another attempt, submitting proposals to his nephew, the Iraqi Regent, Abd al-Ilah, for a loose confederation between the two Hashemite Kingdoms. Although the Iraqis pursued Abdullah's ideas after his death, they met with opposition not merely from Jordanians jealous of their country's independence, but also from other Arab states fearful of a regional change in the balance of power. Ironically, it was just such concerns on the part of Iraq and Jordan, following the creation of the United Arab Republic at the beginning of 1958, which persuaded the two countries to cast aside past doubts and form their own union.

Towards the end of January, King Hussein voiced his fear that the formation of the UAR would give Egypt and Syria the initiative in the field of Arab unity.[23] With such concerns in mind, he despatched his Deputy Prime Minister, Samir Rifai, to Riyadh and the Chief of the Royal Court, Suleiman Touqan, to Baghdad in the hope of promoting a monarchical confederation. As a result of these contacts, the Arab Union of Jordan and Iraq was hastily declared on 14 February. In the war of words which ensued, Nasser denounced the 'collaborators of imperialism in Baghdad and Amman'.[24] While such statements represented little more than a crude attempt to discredit the Union, Britain did perceive the new structure, despite its inchoate nature, as a possible counterweight to Nasser and the UAR.

Even before the Suez affair, Britain had increasingly looked to Jordan and Iraq for the maintenance of her regional interests.[25] 'If we are to have any position in the Middle East,' noted Anthony Eden at the beginning of 1954, 'our authority must be based on relations with Jordan and Iraq.'[26] News of the Egyptian–Czech arms deal served to strengthen this policy. In December 1955, the Chief of the Imperial General Staff, Sir Gerald Templer, was despatched to Amman in an ultimately unsuccessful attempt to persuade Jordan to join the Baghdad Pact.[27] Despite initial shock at King Hussein's dismissal of Sir John Glubb in March 1956, the Cabinet concluded: 'Instead of seeking to conciliate or support Colonel Nasser, we should do our utmost to counter Egyptian policy and to uphold our friends

[23] Telegram from C. H. Johnston (British Ambassador, Amman) to the Foreign Office, No. 91, 25 Jan 1958, FO 371/134036.
[24] Lawrence Tal, 'Britain and the Jordan Crisis of 1958', *Middle Eastern Studies*, 31, 1 (1995): 42.
[25] Nigel John Ashton argues that Britain's support for an Iraqi–Jordanian axis should be seen as 'merely one aspect of promoting Iraqi leadership in the Arab world' (*Eisenhower, Macmillan and the Problem of Nasser: Anglo-American Relations and Arab Nationalism, 1955–59*, Basingstoke: Macmillan, 1996, p. 62).
[26] W. Scott Lucas, 'The Path to Suez: Britain and the Struggle for the Middle East, 1953–56', in Anne Deighton (ed.), *Britain and the First Cold War*, Basingstoke: Macmillan, 1990, p. 262.
[27] Uriel Dann, *King Hussein and the Challenge of Arab Radicalism: Jordan, 1955–1967*, New York: Oxford University Press, 1989, pp. 26–8.

in the Middle East. . . . We should seek to draw Iraq and Jordan more closer [sic] together.'[28] Indeed, the Foreign Office acted as a mediator between Baghdad and Amman, resulting on 14 March in a meeting in Iraq between Kings Hussein and Feisal.[29] Despite the unpromising results of this encounter, the British continued to support closer Iraqi–Jordanian links.

Referring in February 1957 to resistance in the Arab world to Egyptian leadership ambitions, the Official Cabinet Committee on the Middle East urged: 'It must be an aim of our diplomatic policy to encourage this centrifugal force and to seek to break up the Egyptian bloc.'[30] Writing soon after the establishment of the Arab Union, the British Ambassador to Jordan, C. H. Johnston, admitted: 'I have lost no opportunity over the last year of urging on King Hussein the advantages of a closer link with Iraq.'[31] In many ways, therefore, the creation of the Arab Union in February 1958 represented the realization of British hopes. 'In taking this step', emphasized the British Ambassador in Baghdad, Sir Michael Wright, 'the two countries know that it had our full support'.[32] Referring to the Arab Union, moreover, Johnston expressed satisfaction that 'the first real step towards Arab unity should have been taken on a pro-Western basis'.[33] The practical problems which faced Jordan and Iraq were, however, immense. Critics of the scheme, especially in Iraq, denounced it as a union between rulers, rather than between peoples.[34] Moreover, the Iraqi Prime Minister, Nuri al-Said, was concerned lest poverty-stricken Jordan should become a burden on his country.[35] 'Realizing that union with Jordan will mean economic sacrifices for Iraq,' elucidated Wright, 'Iraqi leaders have been much obsessed with [the] idea of Kuwait's joining [the] Union, and contributing to its support'.[36] Indeed, Iraq perceived that the financial resources of Kuwait were of vital importance in providing the Union with greater economic stability and viability. Viewing the situation from Amman, C. H. Johnston reported that the possibility of associating Kuwait with the Union was being 'widely discussed', the Shaikhdom being seen as 'a kind of Arab Eldorado'.[37]

---

[28] Scott Lucas, 'The Path to Suez', p. 268. See also David R. Devereux, *The Formation of British Defence Policy Towards the Middle East, 1948–56*, London: Macmillan, 1990, p. 181.
[29] Scott Lucas, 'Redefining the Suez "Collusion"', p. 94.
[30] 'Middle East Policy', Note by the Official Committee on the Middle East, 5 Feb 1957, ME (M) (57) 2, CAB 134/2230.
[31] Letter from Johnston to Lloyd, No. 13, 24 Feb 1958, FO 371/132854.
[32] Letter from Sir Michael Wright to Lloyd, No. 34, 25 Feb 1958, FO 371/134025.
[33] Telegram from Johnston to the Foreign Office, No. 156, 14 Feb 1958, FO 371/134023.
[34] Majid Khadduri, *Independent Iraq, 1932–1958: A Study in Iraqi Politics*, second edition, London: Oxford University Press, 1960, p. 345.
[35] Edith and E. F. Penrose, *Iraq: International Relations and National Development*, London: Ernest Benn, 1978, p. 131.
[36] Telegram from Wright to the Foreign Office, No. 590, 10 April 1958, FO 371/134054.
[37] Letter from Johnston to Lloyd, No. 13, 24 Feb 1958, FO 371/132854.

The prospects for associating Kuwait with the Arab Union were at first unfavourable. In the course of discussions with the Political Resident, Shaikh Abdullah made it clear that he did not intend to commit himself to either of the new political configurations.[38] However, during talks in the Lebanon with the Iraqi Foreign Minister, Taufiq al-Suwaidi, Abdullah was not unresponsive to the idea of cooperating more closely with his northern neighbour, provided that outstanding points of dispute, such as the demarcation of the boundary, could be resolved.[39] In the meantime, the Iraqis sought British support, even suggesting that Britain should recognize Kuwaiti independence as a prelude to the Shaikhdom's entry into the Arab Union.[40] Samir Rifai strongly endorsed the Iraqi position.[41]

The British clearly found themselves in a delicate position. On the one hand, there was a real danger that without external financial assistance the Union would collapse.[42] On the other, Shaikh Abdullah exhibited reluctance to commit himself to the Iraqi–Jordanian axis. In explaining this reticence, an official of the Foreign Office remarked: 'in view of the widespread enthusiasm in Kuwait for Nasser and the U.A.R., the Ruler considers that a real and immediate threat to his position would result if he were to attempt to take his country into the Union against the overwhelming wishes of popular opinion in Kuwait'.[43] Not unnaturally, Iraq's traditional claims to the Shaikhdom also made Abdullah intensely suspicious of Iraqi intentions.[44] In August 1957, the British Chargé d'Affaires in Baghdad, Richard Beaumont, noted: 'They [the Iraqis] feel that they must now take an active part to find an up-to-date substitute for the Pax Britannica which for fifty years or more has reigned in the Gulf. At the back of their minds there always lurks the idea of establishing a predominant position for themselves in Kuwait.'[45] The failure of the two countries in the mid-1950s to reach agreement on three inter-connected issues — the

---

[38] *Confidential Annex to Kuwait Diary No. 3*, covering the period 25 Feb–24 March 1957, FO 371/132750.

[39] *Confidential Annex to Kuwait Diary No. 4*, covering the period, 25 March–28 April 1958, FO 371/132750.

[40] Telegram from the Foreign Secretary to the Prime Minister, No. 89M, 8 March 1958, FO 371/132774.

[41] Telegram from Johnston to the Foreign Office, No. 314, 21 March 1958, FO 371/132774.

[42] 'Kuwait and the Arab Union', Minute by Sir W. Hayter, 14 March 1958, FO 371/132774.

[43] Ibid. See also Telegram from Burrows to the Foreign Office, No. 315, 15 March 1958, FO 371/132779. In his annual report for Kuwait, the new Political Resident, Sir George Middleton, noted that 'The establishment of the United Arab Republic met with universal acclaim, particularly among the younger generation, while the establishment of the Iraq–Jordan Union attracted corresponding hostility' (Letter from Sir George Middleton to Selwyn Lloyd, No. 9, 9 Feb 1959, enclosing annual review of events in the Persian Gulf for 1958, FO 371/140064).

[44] 'Kuwait', Brief by D. M. H. Riches, 3 March 1958, FO 371/132774.

[45] H. Rahman, *The Making of the Gulf War: Origins of Kuwait's Long-Standing Territorial Dispute with Iraq*, Reading: Ithaca Press, 1997, p. 222.

supply of water to Kuwait from the Shatt al-Arab, the leasing of Kuwaiti territory to Iraq for the development of a port at Umm Qasr, and the demarcation of the frontier — merely heightened mutual antipathy.[46] Against this background, Burrows stressed: 'it is essential that we should speak mainly in terms of seizing [the] opportunity to improve Kuwait–Iraq relations rather than press him to associate with the Union'.[47] In a similar vein, Halford argued: 'If Kuwait is ever to grow into a closer association with Iraq and Jordan this process must . . . be allowed to develop slowly and as far as possible spontaneously.'[48] Matters came to a head during the Ruler's visit to Iraq between 10 and 15 May 1958.

On the evening of his arrival, Abdullah was called upon by the British Ambassador, Sir Michael Wright. In the course of discussions, the former prophetically warned that to build up the Union in opposition to the UAR, far from providing security, would increase tension and the danger of revolution.[49] During talks with King Feisal II, the Crown Prince, and Iraqi leaders, Shaikh Abdullah proved impervious to any reasoning on the common danger presented by Nasser to the independence of the pro-Western Arab monarchies, and was entirely unresponsive to any suggestion of associating Kuwait with the Union.[50] In further conversations with Wright, moreover, he expressed annoyance that Britain had discussed with the Iraqis matters affecting Kuwait without first consulting him.[51] Summing up the results of the Ruler's visit to Iraq, Wright came to the unwelcome conclusion that in the absence of financial contributions from Kuwait, the Union would increasingly look to Britain and the United States for support.[52]

Examining the reasons for Abdullah's reluctance to join the Union, Burrows noted:

> there can be little doubt that any such step . . . would intensify internal opposition in Kuwait, and would attract propaganda attacks from outside from which Kuwait is at present more or less free. Iraq could only help to deal with this kind of situation by sending troops to Kuwait which is the last thing that the Ruler or any other Kuwaiti would wish.[53]

---

[46] Ibid., pp. 193-231.
[47] Telegram from Burrows to the Foreign Office, No. 373, 29 March 1958, FO 371/132774.
[48] Telegram from Halford to the Foreign Office, No. 69, 24 Feb 1958, FO 371/132779.
[49] Telegram from Wright to the Foreign Office, No. 764, 11 May 1958, FO 371/132775.
[50] Telegram from Wright to the Foreign Office, No. 793, 14 May 1958, FO 371/132775.
[51] Telegram from Wright to the Foreign Office, No. 798, 14 May 1958, FO 371/132775. See also Ritchie Ovendale, *Britain, the United States, and the Transfer of Power in the Middle East, 1945–1962*, London: Leicester University Press, 1996, p. 191.
[52] Telegram from Wright to the Foreign Office, No. 818, 16 May 1958, FO 371/132775. In June, following resignation threats by Nuri, Britain and the United States agreed to make a contribution of $29 million towards the Union budget ('Arab Union Finances', Minute by E. M. Rose, 16 June 1958, FO 371/134055).
[53] Telegram from Burrows to the Foreign Office, No. 563, 19 May 1958, FO 371/132775.

The Iraqis, however, were not prepared to accept the Ruler's decision. On 31 May, Nuri informed Wright that if Kuwait did not accede to the Arab Union Iraq would revive its territorial claims to the Shaikhdom.[54] Referring to the Iraqi premier's demeanour during the meeting, Wright recorded: 'I have had some experience of storms with Nuri but few as severe as this one.' Nuri's mood had scarcely improved when he met the Foreign Secretary, Selwyn Lloyd, the following month. During the encounter, the irritated Iraqi premier was reported to have thumped the table, demanding acceptance of his policy towards Kuwait.[55]

Iraq's position was clarified in a note delivered to the British Embassy on 5 June. It claimed not only the islands of Warba and Bubiyan, but also all the territory down to Kuwait Bay.[56] In analysing this development, Wright stressed:

> the Iraqi and the Jordanian Governments and regimes are fighting, not only for their own survival within the new Union based on friendly partnership, but also for the principles of both Arab unity . . . and of the maintenance of active friendship with the West.[57]

In just over a month, however, the Hashemite monarchy in Iraq was swept away, precipitating the collapse of the Arab Union.

Iraq's growing political instability is reflected by the fact that the last ten years of monarchical rule witnessed some twenty different cabinets.[58] In August 1954, Nuri became Iraqi Prime Minister for the twelfth time. Reflecting eighteen months later upon the challenges which had faced the aging premier, Wright commented: 'The old champion had rolled up his sleeves and walked down the pavilion steps to bat on a rapidly crumbling wicket.'[59] Indeed, the absence of civil liberties, coupled with the slow rate of social progress despite rapidly increasing oil revenues,[60] aroused growing disaffection with the monarchical regime. In December 1954, the British Ambassador in Baghdad, Sir John Troutbeck, admitted: 'we have a country

---

[54] Telegram from Wright to the Foreign Office, No. 941, 2 June 1958, FO 371/132776.
[55] Saeed Khalil Hashim, 'The Influence of Iraq on the Nationalist Movements of Kuwait and Bahrain, 1920-1961', PhD. thesis, University of Exeter, 1984, p. 279.
[56] Telegram from Wright to the Foreign Office, No. 977, 6 June 1958, FO 371/132776. See also Richard Schofield, *Kuwait and Iraq: Historical Claims and Territorial Disputes*, second edition, London: Royal Institute of International Affairs, 1993, pp. 99–100; Ovendale, *Transfer of Power in the Middle East*, p. 192.
[57] Telegram from Wright to the Foreign Office, No. 989, 8 June 1958, FO 371/132776.
[58] Marion Farouk-Sluglett and Peter Sluglett, 'The Social Classes and the Origins of the Revolution', in Robert A. Fernea and William Roger Louis (eds), *The Iraqi Revolution of 1958: The Old Social Classes Revisited*, London: I. B. Tauris, 1991, p. 128.
[59] Cited in William Roger Louis, 'The British and the Origins of the Iraqi Revolution', in Fernea and Louis, *The Iraqi Revolution*, p. 33.
[60] Oil revenues for 1958 stood at more than £84 million (Penrose and Penrose, *Iraq: International Relations*, p. 167; Daniel Silverfarb, 'The Revision of Iraq's Oil Concession, 1949–52', *Middle Eastern Studies*, 32, 1 (1996): 87).

with all the material means for progress at its disposal but with an administration so rotten and chaotic that it is more than doubtful whether it can take advantage of them'.[61] It was the repercussions of the Suez affair, however, which inflicted terminal damage on the standing of Nuri and the Hashemite dynasty in Iraq.

On 2 November 1956, at the height of the Suez crisis, Selwyn Lloyd warned of the possibility of the fall of Nuri and the overthrow of King Feisal.[62] This view was confirmed by Sir Michael Wright at the beginning of 1957:

> The action of Her Majesty's Government, because it was linked with action by Israel, placed him [Nuri] personally, as well as the King and Crown Prince and all those in Iraq who had so actively pursued a policy of friendship with Her Majesty's Government, not only in the gravest political difficulty but in danger of their lives, and imperilled the continued existence of the regime and the monarchy.[63]

Although the Iraqi government's face-saving protest at British actions, in addition to the imposition of martial law, allowed the Iraqi regime to weather the immediate storm, its prospects for long-term survival were dealt a severe blow. Referring to the Iraqi monarchy, Rashid Khalidi has noted: 'one of its few remaining assets, its prestige in the Arab world, was irrevocably shattered by the attack on Egypt of its protector Britain'.[64] Further damage was inflicted on the embattled Iraqi regime by Syria's announcement on 23 November 1956 of the discovery of an Iraqi plot to topple the Syrian government.[65] Such was the decline in Iraq's standing that by the end of the year she was 'almost completely isolated in the Arab world'.[66] From early 1957, Iraq tried to counteract Egypt's bid for Arab hegemony by drawing closer to the other monarchical regimes.

The bitter memory of Ibn Saud's ejection of the Hashemites from the Hijaz in 1926 had proved a lasting impediment to the establishment of close relations between Hashemite Iraq and Saudi Arabia. The formation in

---

[61] Cited in Louis, 'The British and the Origins of the Iraqi Revolution', in Fernea and Louis, *The Iraqi Revolution*, p. 36.

[62] Cabinet Conclusions, 2 Nov 1956, CM 77 (56), CAB 128/30 Part 2.

[63] Cited in Louis, 'The British and the Origins of the Iraqi Revolution', in Fernea and Louis, *The Iraqi Revolution*, p. 43.

[64] Rashid Khalidi, 'Consequences of the Suez Crisis in the Arab World', in William Roger Louis and Roger Owen (eds), *Suez 1956: The Crisis and its Consequences*, Oxford: Clarendon, 1991, p. 383.

[65] Patrick Seale, *The Struggle for Syria: A Study of Post-War Arab Politics, 1945–1958*, new edition, London: I. B. Tauris, 1986, pp. 278–9. See also Andrew Rathmell, *Secret War in the Middle East: The Covert Struggle for Syria, 1949–1961*, London: Tauris Academic Studies, 1995, pp. 111–24.

[66] Elie Podeh, 'The Struggle over Arab Hegemony after the Suez Crisis', *Middle Eastern Studies*, 29, 1 (1993): 100–1.

1955 of the Baghdad Pact, which Saudi Arabia perceived as a tool for the promotion of Iraqi interests, merely fuelled Saudi–Hashemite enmity. Egypt's opposition to the pact was strongly supported by Saudi Arabia, and in October 1955 the two countries formed a military alliance of their own. They also joined forces in a successful campaign to prevent Jordan from acceding to the Baghdad Pact.[67] The Egyptian–Saudi combination was short-lived, however. Concerned that Nasser's growing popularity would undermine the foundations of royal power, and alienated by Egypt's flirtation with communist Russia, King Saud (r. 1953–64) began to doubt the wisdom of alignment with Egypt.[68] As early as August 1956, the British Ambassador in Jedda, R.W. Parkes, felt able to report that 'the attraction of a ride on the Egyptian bandwagon has largely passed'.[69] Saud's alienation from the Egyptian leader was completed by the uncovering of an assassination plot. 'I gave him [Nasser] 40 million dollars and other help besides', complained Saud, 'and in return he tried to assassinate me.'[70]

Tensions between Saudi Arabia and Iraq were eased following a meeting between Saud and Crown Prince Abd al-Ilah in Washington in February 1957. King Hussein's displacement of his nationalist Prime Minister, Suleiman al-Nabulsi,[71] in April, moreover, allowed Jordan to join what the British Chargé in Baghdad described as the 'Monarchistic Trade Union'.[72] At the time of al-Nabulsi's dismissal, both Saudi Arabia and Iraq had sent troops to Jordan in order to forestall Syrian intervention.[73] King Saud's re-positioning of his country within the Arab world was further underlined by visits to Baghdad in May and to Amman in June.[74] The royalist coalition, however, was never cohesive. Despite perceiving the UAR as a threat to the Arab monarchies, Saud would only contemplate closer association with the Hashemite Kingdoms if Iraq first consented to withdraw

---

[67] Nadav Safran, *Saudi Arabia: The Ceaseless Quest for Security*, Ithaca, NY: Cornell University Press, 1988, p. 79.

[68] Mordechai Abir, *Saudi Arabia in the Oil Era: Regime and Elites; Conflict and Collaboration*, London: Croom Helm, 1988, pp. 78–81; A. R. Kelidar, 'The Arabian Peninsula in Arab and Power Politics', in Derek Hopwood (ed.), *The Arabian Peninsula: Society and Politics*, London: George Allen and Unwin, 1972, p. 154.

[69] Letter from R.W. Parkes to Lloyd, No. 57, 11 Aug 1956, PREM 11/5068.

[70] Elie Podeh, 'Ending an Age-Old Rivalry: The *Rapprochement* between the Hashemites and the Saudis, 1956–1958', in Asher Susser and Aryeh Shmuelevitz (eds), *The Hashemites in the Modern Arab World: Essays in Honour of the Late Professor Uriel Dann*, London: Frank Cass, 1995, p. 100.

[71] For an account of the circumstances surrounding the dismissal of al-Nabulsi, see Robert B. Satloff, *From Abdullah to Hussein: Jordan in Transition*, New York: Oxford University Press, 1994, pp. 164–5.

[72] Elie Podeh, *The Quest for Hegemony in the Arab World: The Struggle over the Baghdad Pact*, Leiden: E. J. Brill, 1995, p. 231.

[73] John Marlowe, *Arab Nationalism and British Imperialism: A Study in Power Politics*, London: The Cresset Press, 1961, p. 151.

[74] Ibid., p. 148.

from the Baghdad Pact.[75] Weakened by the absence of Saudi Arabia, the Iraqi–Jordanian union proved no match for the UAR.

US policy-makers judged that 'most Jordanians [were] convinced they were in the wrong union'.[76] On the day of the Arab Union's inception, furthermore, Wright observed lugubriously: 'there will be the problem of selling the confederation to the Iraqi man in the street, who is likely to be somewhat unimpressed by its advantages as compared with those of joining the United Arab Republic'.[77] Wright went so far as to suggest that if a plebiscite were held, a large majority of Iraqis would vote in favour of joining not the Arab Union but the United Arab Republic.[78] Nevertheless, the lack of political freedoms in Iraq prevented the popular voice from being heard.

The inability of opposition politicians in Iraq to effect change through the ballot box, coupled with the government's monopoly on the instruments of repression, dictated that radical change could only be achieved through the intervention of the military.[79] Drawing on the Egyptian example, moreover, the Iraqi army came to realize that the overthrow of a 'corrupt regime' could be achieved with both relative ease and popular approbation.[80] A few days before the military coup of 14 July 1958, King Hussein had warned his cousin of a plot against the Iraqi government.[81] By requesting the movement of Iraqi troops to Jordan, however, Hussein unwittingly precipitated the downfall of his Hashemite brethren. Taking advantage of the troop movements, the chairman of the 'Free Officers', Brigadier Abdul Karim Qassem, seized power in a bloody military coup.[82] On the morning of 14 July, King Feisal, Crown Prince Abd al-Ilah, and the rest of the royal family were killed as they were leaving the palace through the kitchen door. Nuri Said's demise was equally ignominious. Spotted leaving a friend's house dressed in a woman's cloak, he was shot and, after a swift burial, his body was disinterred and dragged through the streets of Baghdad. Within a few hours, therefore, the Hashemite dynasty which had ruled Iraq since 1921 was expunged from the political scene.

---

[75] Telegram from Johnston to the Foreign Office, No. 115, 4 Feb 1958, FO 371/134036.

[76] Douglas Little, 'A Puppet in Search of a Puppeteer? The United States, King Hussein, and Jordan, 1953–1970', *The International History Review*, 17, 3 (1995): 526.

[77] Cited in Louis, 'The British and the Origins of the Iraqi Revolution', in Fernea and Louis, *The Iraqi Revolution*, p. 47.

[78] Letter from Wright to Selwyn Lloyd, No. 34, 25 Feb 1958, FO 371/134025.

[79] Farouk-Sluglett and Sluglett, 'Social Classes', in Fernea and Louis, *The Iraqi Revolution*, p. 131.

[80] Uriel Dann, *Iraq Under Qassem: A Political History, 1958–1963*, New York: Praeger, 1969, p. 19.

[81] Tal, 'Britain and the Jordan Crisis', p. 43.

[82] For accounts of the coup, see Majid Khadduri, *Republican Iraq: A Study in Iraqi Politics since the Revolution of 1958*, London: Oxford University Press, 1969, pp. 38–61; Penrose and Penrose, *Iraq: International Relations*, pp. 199–209.

II

Commenting on the Iraqi Revolution, Peter Mansfield has noted: 'At one blow the strongest and most effective pro-Western bastion in the Arab world had fallen.'[83] In his memoirs, moreover, Harold Macmillan recalled that the events of 14 July had had the effect of 'destroying at a blow a whole system of security which successive British Governments had built up'.[84] One of the first acts of Qassem's revolutionary government was to withdraw from the Arab Union.[85] Britain and the United States, however, acted swiftly to shore up those states which remained friendly towards the West. On 14 July, the Lebanese President, Camille Chamoun, sent a desperate message to Washington warning that if he did not receive immediate support his regime would be overthrown.[86] A month earlier, the United States Secretary of State, John Foster Dulles, had prophesied: 'If Chamoun calls on us and we do not respond that will be the end of every pro-Western government in the area.'[87] With such concerns in mind, America despatched marines from the Sixth Fleet to Beirut. Fearing a fate similar to that of his Iraqi cousin, King Hussein requested British military support on 16 July, the first contingent of troops arriving in Amman within twenty-four hours.[88] In Kuwait, by contrast, there was a marked reluctance to accept military aid despite British and American concerns about the stability of the Shaikhdom.

On the day of the Iraqi Revolution the Director of Central Intelligence in America, Allen Dulles, suggested that 'The fate of Kuwait is presently in the balance.'[89] In a similar vein, Selwyn Lloyd observed, during a meeting with John Foster Dulles on 17 July, that 'If a coup could be carried out in Baghdad, there was an equal danger of one in Kuwait.'[90] 'It would not be impossible,' warned Lloyd, ' . . . for the Ruler to abdicate, for Abdullah Mubarak to be killed and for Shaikh Fahad to become the Ruler after which he might seek to join the UAR.'[91] Persuaded by Lloyd's dire predictions, the US Secretary of State declared that 'it would be foolish for the U.S. and the U.K. to move into Lebanon and Jordan and not plan at the

---

[83] Peter Mansfield, *The Arabs*, Penguin Books, 1985, p. 263.
[84] Harold Macmillan, *Riding the Storm, 1956–1959*, London: Macmillan, 1971, p. 511.
[85] Dann, *Iraq Under Qassem*, p. 52.
[86] Kamal S. Salibi, *The Modern History of Lebanon*, London: Weidenfeld and Nicolson, 1965, p. 202.
[87] Douglas Little, 'His Finest Hour? Eisenhower, Lebanon, and the 1958 Middle East Crisis', *Diplomatic History*, 20, 1 (1996): 41.
[88] See Tal, 'Britain and the Jordan Crisis', pp. 39–57.
[89] *Foreign Relations of the United States, 1958–1960, Volume 11: Lebanon and Jordan*, Washington DC: United States Government Printing Office, 1992, p. 212.
[90] Little, 'Eisenhower, Lebanon, and the 1958 Middle East Crisis', p. 48.
[91] *Foreign Relations of the United States, 1958–1960. Volume 12: Near East Region; Iraq, Iran, Arabian Peninsula*, Washington DC: United States Government Printing Office, 1993, p. 776.

same time to hold other areas of greater intrinsic importance'.[92] A day after the Dulles–Lloyd encounter, the American President, Dwight D. Eisenhower, sent a message to the British Prime Minister, Harold Macmillan, in which he opined: 'we must, I think, not only try to bolster up both . . . Lebanon and Jordan, we must also, and this seems to me even more important, see that the Persian Gulf area stays within the Western orbit'.[93]

The prospect of intervention in Kuwait was weighed up by Macmillan. In his diary, the Prime Minister confided: 'The Gulf is very uncertain — but we have plans for Bahrein and Kuwait, in case of need. But there is the usual dilemma. Should we go in now? If so it is 'aggression'. Shall we wait? If so, we may be too late.'[94] Despite the finely balanced arguments presented by the Prime Minister, concerns about the possible repercussions of uninvited intervention proved decisive. 'I think it would be an act of great folly', opined C. A. E. Shuckburgh of the Foreign Office, 'to send forces into Kuwait without the Ruler's authority'.[95] Moreover, Her Majesty's Minister in Washington, Lord Hood, stressed that, in contemplating a military occupation of Kuwait, Britain risked forfeiting the goodwill and support of the al-Sabah.[96] As a result of such considerations, senior members of the ruling family were consulted. In response, Shaikh Abdullah Mubarak expressed confidence at being able to maintain order,[97] while the Ruler argued that a British military presence would merely exacerbate tensions, thus heightening the threat to shaikhly rule.[98] In conversations with Halford on 27 July, nevertheless, he expressed pessimism about the prospects for the survival of hereditary monarchs in the Middle East.[99] A few days later, he informed Halford of his intention to explore the possibility of Kuwaiti membership of the Arab League.[100]

In March 1945, a loose confederation of Arab states, the Arab League, was inaugurated in Cairo. Although Anthony Eden had made a public dec-

---

[92] Ibid., p. 777. Towards the end of 1958, the Foreign Office recalled that 'At the height of the Middle East crisis in the summer, Mr. Dulles took a strong line about the justice of intervention in Kuwait' ('Points for a Middle East Policy — Part II', Foreign Office paper for the Cabinet Official Committee on the Middle East, 19 Nov 1958, OME (58) 46, CAB 134/2342).

[93] Little, 'Eisenhower, Lebanon and the 1958 Middle East Crisis', p. 49. See also Ritchie Ovendale, 'Great Britain and the Anglo-American Invasion of Jordan and Lebanon in 1958', *The International History Review*, 16, 2 (1994): 298.

[94] Macmillan diaries, volume 5 second series, 18 July 1958, MSS Macmillan dep. d. 32. See also Macmillan, *Riding the Storm*, p. 523.

[95] Minute by C. A. E. Shuckburgh, 19 July 1958, FO 371/132757.

[96] Telegram from Lord Hood to the Foreign Office, No. 1979, 19 July 1958, FO 371/132779.

[97] Telegram from Kuwait to the Foreign Office, No. 320, 15 July 1958; Telegram from Kuwait to the Foreign Office, No. 334, 17 July 1958, PREM 11/2752.

[98] Telegram from Halford to the Foreign Office, No. 416, 30 July 1958, PREM 11/2752.

[99] Telegram from Halford to the Foreign Office, No. 390, 27 July 1958, FO 371/132776.

[100] Telegram from Halford to the Foreign Office, No. 420, 31 July 1958, PREM 11/2752.

laration of support for Arab unity at the Mansion House on 29 May 1941,[101] in the aftermath of war Britain increasingly looked askance at the League, perceiving its activities as detrimental to British interests. In February 1954, the then Minister of State at the Foreign Office, Selwyn Lloyd, went so far as to state: 'it would be intolerable if Kuwait should ever be allowed to join the League'.[102] Shaikh Abdullah's advocacy of Kuwaiti membership of the League, therefore, was viewed unfavourably by the British. While admitting that 'Pan-Arab sentiments can already find expression in Kuwait', the Foreign Office predicted that 'the entry of Kuwait into the Arab League would much increase the possibilities and provide a far greater number of points around which radical Nationalist sentiment could crystallize'.[103] Moreover, Halford feared that Kuwait's adherence to the League could be represented as a further personal triumph for Nasser and yet another grievous blow to Britain, while Burrows warned of the impression being given that Kuwait was escaping from Britain's grasp.[104] The Foreign Office shared Burrows' concerns, arguing that 'if the Ruler weakens the ties between Great Britain and Kuwait it will be a step along a road which will mean that Kuwait will be swallowed up in the U.A.R. Kuwait would become an outlying province of Egypt whose revenues would be sucked out for distribution in Egypt.'[105] Such fears were heightened following Shaikh Abdullah's well-publicized meeting with Nasser in Damascus on 20 July 1958, during which the Egyptian leader may have urged Kuwaiti membership of the Arab League.[106]

In order to prevent Kuwait from falling under Nasser's spell, the Foreign Office considered occupying Kuwait and running it as a crown colony.[107] C. A. E. Shuckburgh, furthermore, suggested reviving the idea of a union between Iraq and Kuwait in order to create a counterweight to Egypt.[108] The Head of the Eastern Department, D. M. H. Riches, however, was cautious about this proposal, stressing: 'our interest lies in keeping Kuwait independent and separate if we possibly can in line with the idea of maintaining the four principal oil producing areas under separate political control'.[109] The problems presented by Kuwaiti membership of the Arab League remained, however.

[101] See Michael Cohen, 'A Note on the Mansion House Speech, May 1941', *Asian and African Studies*, 11, 3 (1977): 375–86.
[102] A meeting held on 23 Feb 1954 to discuss Mr E. B. Wakefield's impressions of the situation in Kuwait, FO 371/109807.
[103] Telegram from the Foreign Office to Bahrain, No. 1494, 11 Aug 1958, FO 371/132786.
[104] Letter from Halford to Burrows, No. 1075/58, 15 Oct 1958; Letter from Burrows to Riches, No. 1034, 22 Oct 1958, FO 371/132555.
[105] Telegram from the Foreign Office to Bahrain, No. 1461, 8 Aug 1958, FO 371/132786.
[106] 'Kuwait', Minute by D. M. H. Riches, 14 Aug 1958, FO 371/132786.
[107] 'Policy in the Middle East', Paper by the Foreign Office, 21 July 1958, FO 371/132545.
[108] Minute by Shuckburgh, 24 July 1958, FO 371/132545.
[109] Minute by Riches, 8 Aug 1958, FO 371/132545.

In justifying his insistence on joining the League, Abdullah not only argued that it would provide Kuwait with security in the Arab world, but also stressed the impracticality of relying on Britain to conduct his affairs with fellow Arab states.[110] These sentiments struck a chord with Burrows who noted: 'In addition to doubting our ability to help him against dangers threatening from the Arab world he has found many reasons in the last two years to doubt our political wisdom in Middle East affairs.'[111] Abdullah's particular grievance related to what he regarded as Britain's failure adequately to protect him from Iraqi pressure for Kuwait's inclusion in the Arab Union.[112]

Soon after the formation of the Arab Union, the Foreign Office had stressed that

> support for Iraq and Jordan is of such importance to the maintenance of our position in the Middle East as a whole, not least in the Persian Gulf, that we must help the Iraqis to produce the most favourable possible conditions for an approach to the Ruler of Kuwait.[113]

The Foreign Office also urged that 'We must . . . be ready to take some risk in our relations with Kuwait if by so doing there is a real chance of bringing her into the Arab Union.'[114] In a candid moment Sir William Hayter (Deputy Under-Secretary of State, Foreign Office) admitted that 'we are going much further than Bernard Burrows deems wise in pressing the Iraqi case on the Ruler of Kuwait'.[115] Halford described the Ruler's feelings towards Britain as amounting to 'something near betrayal'.[116] Abdullah even charged Britain with having 'deserted' him.[117] In these circumstances, it seems likely that the threat to join the League represented a reaction to his feeling of isolation during negotiations with Nuri in May.[118] Support for this interpretation is given by his willingness to drop the idea of joining the League in return for a written undertaking that Britain would continue to protect Kuwait.[119] Nevertheless, he insisted on being given some latitude in the conduct of relations with neighbouring Arab states.[120] This develop-

---

[110] Telegram from Halford to the Foreign Office, No. 420, 31 July 1958, PREM 11/2752.
[111] Telegram from Burrows to the Foreign Office, No. 985, 2 Aug 1958, PREM 11/2752.
[112] Telegram from the Foreign Office to Baghdad, No. 35, 19 Aug 1958, FO 371/132776.
[113] Telegram from the Foreign Office to Baghdad, No. 492, 22 Feb 1958, PREM 11/2403.
[114] 'Kuwait and the Arab Union', Foreign Office Paper, 14 March 1958, PREM 11/2403.
[115] Letter from Hayter to Wright, 3 April 1958, FO 371/134054.
[116] Letter from Halford to Middleton, No. 1, 6 Jan 1959, FO 371/140064.
[117] *Confidential Annex to Kuwait Diary No. 8,* covering the period 29 July–25 Aug 1958, FO 371/132523.
[118] Later, the Ruler claimed that the idea of joining the Arab League first came to him during his unhappy visit to Iraq (Telegram from Halford to the Foreign Office, No. 420, 31 July 1958, FO 371/132786).
[119] Telegram from Halford to the Foreign Office, No. 499, 18 Aug 1958, PREM 11/2752.
[120] 'Kuwait: International Relations', Memorandum by the Secretary of State for Foreign Affairs, 3 Nov 1958, Annex B: Memorandum by the Kuwait Government, 30 Sept 1958, C. (58) 228, CAB 129/95.

ment had been supported by Burrows as early as December 1957. In response to the growing impression in Kuwait that Britain's performance in the conduct of foreign relations had been 'far from brilliant', Burrows suggested that the Shaikhdom should be permitted to 'do more of its own dirty work in dealing with its neighbours'.[121] The letter of assurance of 23 October 1958, therefore, not only committed the British government to 'continue to be ready, as in the past, to provide any support which may be necessary in connection with Kuwait's relations with other countries', but also acknowledged the Ruler's 'intention to deal with certain matters affecting Kuwait's relations with other Arab States' by his own efforts.[122] Despite Halford's depiction of the letter as a 'remarkably good bargain from our point of view',[123] Kuwait's growing freedom in the conduct of foreign relations inescapably opened up the whole question of its international status.

At the same time as the Ruler requested recognition of his right to conduct relations with other Arab states, he also noted: 'To create a friendly atmosphere in the Arab world for Kuwait it would help if the neighbours see that Kuwait is taking an active part expected of her in some of the international bodies which have been formed for the purpose of looking after the various normal walks of life.'[124] In particular, the Ruler sought membership of the International Telecommunications Union (ITU), as well as certain maritime conventions, the latter being especially important in view of the imminent delivery of the first Kuwaiti-owned ocean-going ship. In weighing up the advantages and disadvantages of the Ruler's proposals, the Foreign Secretary, Selwyn Lloyd, remarked: 'In the last resort Her Majesty's Government are unable to resist a determined demand from the Ruler for concessions of this nature; and indeed it would be impolitic to try to do so.'[125] Furthermore, Lloyd noted that 'Her Majesty's Government's position resembles that of agent much more than that of a controller of Kuwait's foreign relations.' The matter reached the Cabinet on 11 November 1958.[126]

During discussions, Lloyd admitted that if Britain acceded to the

---

[121] Letter from Burrows to Beeley, No. 1034, 3 Dec 1957, FO 371/126905, cited in Abdul-Reda Assiri, *Kuwait's Foreign Policy: City-State in World Politics*, Boulder, Colorado: Westview Press, 1990, p. 7.
[122] 'Kuwait: International Relations', Memorandum by the Secretary of State for Foreign Affairs, 3 Nov 1958, Annex A: Substantive letter of assurance to the Ruler of Kuwait, 23 Oct 1958, C. (58) 228, CAB 129/95.
[123] Telegram from Halford to the Foreign Office, No. 499, 18 Aug 1958, PREM 11/2752.
[124] 'Kuwait: International Relations', Memorandum by the Secretary of State for Foreign Affairs, 3 Nov 1958, Annex B: Memorandum by the Kuwait Government, 30 Sept 1958, C. (58) 228, CAB 129/95.
[125] 'Kuwait: International Relations', Memorandum by the Secretary of State for Foreign Affairs, 3 Nov 1958, C. (58) 228, CAB 129/95.
[126] The following is based on Cabinet Conclusions, 11 Nov 1958, CC 80 (58), CAB 128/32 Part 2.

Ruler's request, it would be tantamount to conceding that Kuwait was fully responsible for the conduct of its international relations, a concession which might weaken the British position in the Persian Gulf. On the other hand, Lloyd reiterated the inadvisability of impeding Kuwait's growing independent status, warning that Britain risked forfeiting the goodwill of the Ruler. By allowing the Ruler to develop Kuwait's international personality, Lloyd suggested, his confidence would be retained without the substance of his relationship with Britain being modified. The Cabinet was persuaded by the Foreign Secretary's arguments, but recommended that the decision should not be given undue publicity.[127] Kuwait's advance towards independent status also raised the question of the appointment of Arab consular representatives to the Shaikhdom.

'The irreducible interest of the United Kingdom in Kuwait', opined Selwyn Lloyd in January 1959, 'is that Kuwait shall remain an independent state having an oil policy conducted by a Government independent of other Middle Eastern producers ... and also having a policy independent of Communist or satellite influence.'[128] Although Lloyd perceived that it was in Britain's national interest to support the Shaikhdom's assumption of independent status, he warned that this development would unavoidably lead to direct contacts between Kuwait and other Arab states.[129] Indeed, the Ruler had informed the British government that he was coming under mounting pressure for the establishment in Kuwait of Arab consuls.[130] In the course of Cabinet discussions on this question, Lloyd warned that such consuls could become focal points for intrigue against not only the Ruling family, but also British interests.[131] The Cabinet agreed with Lloyd's analysis, recommending that if the Ruler felt it necessary to make some concession to Arab opinion it would be more preferable for him to join the Arab League than to accept consular representatives. When Halford raised the matter with the Ruler at the beginning of February, however, he expressed a willingness neither to accept consuls, nor join the League.[132] Although this was in many ways the most satisfactory solution from Britain's perspective, Halford voiced concern that, if Shaikh Abdullah hastily reversed his decision, it could be represented as a political defeat for the British gov-

---

[127] Over the next two years, Kuwait became a full member of the International Telecommunications Union, the Universal Postal Union, the International Civil Aviation Organization, the Intergovernmental Maritime Consultative Organization, the World Health Organization, and the United Nations Educational, Scientific, and Cultural Organization ('Kuwait's Foreign Affairs', Arabian Department Memorandum, 27 Oct 1960, FO 371/148948).

[128] 'International Status of Kuwait', Memorandum by the Secretary of State for Foreign Affairs, 26 Jan 1959, ME (M) (59) 3, CAB 134/2230.

[129] Ibid.

[130] Minutes of a meeting of the Middle East Committee, 28 Jan 1959, ME (M) (59) 2, CAB 134/2230.

[131] Cabinet Conclusions, 29 Jan 1959, CC 3 (59), CAB 128/33.

[132] Telegram from Halford to the Foreign Office, No. 93, 5 Feb 1959, FO 371/140118.

ernment. 'The Ruler, of course, wants it both ways', observed Halford, ' — our support and also freedom to appear independent of it.'[133] While Britain's support for Kuwaiti membership of the League was predicated on the assumption that the principal pressures facing the Shaikhdom would be external ones, at the beginning of 1959 the stability of the ruling family was rocked by internal strife. The first anniversary of the creation of the United Arab Republic provided the spark which ignited a full-scale challenge to the al-Sabah.[134]

Some nationalist exuberance had been anticipated. The director of Cairo's 'Voice of the Arabs' radio station, Ahmad Said, had been invited by the reformist weekly *ash-Sha'ab* to give two speeches, while the Committee of the Clubs was known to be planning a celebration in a local secondary school. What did cause surprise, however, were the forceful terms in which the reformists expressed their twin desires: immediate reforms, including popular participation in the government, and the chance to make an effective expression of their pan-Arabism. The speeches began in earnest on the afternoon of 1 February before a crowd of some 20 000. The leader of the reformists, Ahmad al-Khatib, began proceedings followed by Jasim al-Qatami, a former member of the police department who had resigned his post at the time of Suez in protest at the banning of demonstrations. Carried away by the occasion, al-Qatami departed from his prepared text, declaring:

> The Sabah became the Rulers of Kuwait 300 years ago. They ruled autocratically and arbitrarily then. They cannot expect to do the same in the latter part of the twentieth century. Either they grant the people the necessary reforms at once, or the people will take power for themselves.

The al-Sabah's response to this challenge amounted to a mixture of repression and concession. On 3 February, al-Qatami was summoned to the public security department where he was abused by Shaikh Abdullah Mubarak and dismissed from his post as director of the Kuwait Cinema Company. He was also forbidden employment in the Shaikhdom for an unspecified period. In addition, four clubs — the Graduate, Teachers, Cultural, and Arab Union — were closed, while publication of the reform-minded newspapers *al-Fajr* and *ash-Sha'ab* was indefinitely suspended. Finally, Ahmad Said's second speech, which was to have been given at the Graduate Club, was cancelled.

In explaining the psychology which underpinned the al-Sabah's repressive measures, Halford noted: 'if enlightened rulers such as the late King Faisal of Iraq can share the same atrocious fates as the most

---

[133] Letter from Halford to Middleton, No. 1039/59, 25 Feb 1959, FO 371/140119.
[134] The following is based on Letter from Halford to Middleton, No. 5, 11 Feb 1959, FO 371/140081.

obscurantist of feudal tyrants, there seems little point in encouraging the "people" to expect greater political freedoms'.[135] While the Ruling family rejected the promotion of popular participation in the business of government, it did seek to quell internal opposition by reforming the administration with a view to eliminating the most flagrant abuses. This new approach was discussed during the meetings of the Supreme Council which were held in the aftermath of the UAR anniversary celebrations.

Created in 1956 as an advisory body, the Supreme Council consisted of ten members, all of whom were drawn from the al-Sabah family.[136] The chief targets of criticism in the Council's deliberations were Shaikh Abdullah Mubarak and Shaikh Sabah al-Ahmad, son of the late Ruler and half-brother of Shaikh Jabir al-Ahmad, the future Amir of Kuwait. Both Abdullah Mubarak and Sabah al-Ahmad had sought to win popular acclaim by protecting reformists and expressing solidarity with the cause of Arab unity.[137] Indeed, Abdullah Mubarak had given his blessing to the celebrations in honour of the foundation of the UAR. The events of 1 February, however, underscored the dangers to the whole family which individual indiscretions could create. Criticism of the wayward Shaikhs in the Supreme Council was led by Abdullah Mubarak's old adversary, Shaikh Fahad. The Council also resolved to enact internal reforms in order to eliminate the more flagrant abuses of power. Ironically, having initiated the attack, it was Fahad who was the principal victim of the family's attempts to put its own house in order.

In the drive against incompetence, extravagance, and corruption, Fahad, whose departments were popularly believed to be the most culpable on these counts, was an obvious target. His vulnerability was increased by the erosion of his position within the ruling family consequent upon his prolonged absences from Kuwait.[138] As the Political Agent recorded: 'Being on the spot is more than half the battle in Arabia.'[139] In an effort to counteract his waning influence within the family, Fahad had attempted to draw closer to Britain, even to the point of publicly praising British policy in the Gulf.[140] Fahad's blatant attempt at ingratiation not only stood in marked

---

[135] Letter from Halford to Lloyd, No. 31, 11 June 1959, FO 371/140083.

[136] Jill Crystal, *Oil and Politics in the Gulf: Rulers and Merchants in Kuwait and Qatar*, Cambridge: Cambridge University Press, 1995, p. 71.

[137] Letter from Halford to R. A. Beaumont, No. 10112/59, 25 June 1959, FO 371/140286. Towards the end of 1958, the Foreign Office had predicted that 'even our most loyal Arab friends will feel the need to come to terms to some extent with the new move towards Arab unity' ('Points for a Middle East Policy — Part I (Final Version)', Foreign Office paper for the Cabinet Official Committee on the Middle East, 15 Dec 1958, OME (58) 56, CAB 134/2342).

[138] Telegram from Halford to the Foreign Office, No. 316, 17 May 1959, FO 371/140083.

[139] Letter from Halford to Beaumont, No. 10112/59, 25 June 1959, FO 371/140286.

[140] Minute by W. J. Adams, 19 May 1959, FO 371/140083.

contrast with his anti-British reputation but also provided him with little protection from the mounting pressure on his position. Matters came to a head when the new President of the finance department, Shaikh Jabir, refused to honour public works department cheques amounting to £12 million until such time as Fahad produced proper accounts.[141] In mid-May 1959, Shaikh Fahad resigned his official posts and retired into private life.[142]

Fahad's relinquishment of the administrative empire which he had established since the early 1950s was described by an official of the Foreign Office as 'a striking indication of the Ruling Family's determination to make their regime more efficient and less vulnerable to criticism'.[143] In a similar vein, Halford observed:

> The Sabah are like gannets or guillemots or any social creature that lives in colonies. They have a highly developed instinct for preservation of the species as a whole. They can make sacrifices, accept restrictions, even to their personal detriment, if the common good of the whole requires it.[144]

The risk remained, however, that Fahad would seek to resurrect his fortunes. In 1952, following the threatened resignation of the advisory health department committee, he had been dismissed by the Ruler, only to be reinstated after a short period in the wilderness.[145] His sudden death on 16 June 1959, nevertheless, foreclosed this possibility and allowed the al-Sabah to deflect public criticism of shaikhly rule as Kuwait moved rapidly towards independence.

---

[141] *Confidential Annex to Kuwait Diary No. 5*, covering the period 28 April–25 May 1959, FO 371/140067.
[142] Telegram from Halford to the Foreign Office, No. 315, 17 May 1959, FO 371/140083.
[143] Minute by Adams, 19 May 1959, FO 371/140083.
[144] Letter from Halford to Beaumont, No. 10112/59, 25 June 1959, FO 371/140286.
[145] Crystal, *Oil and Politics in the Gulf*, p. 69.

5: Kuwait's Progress towards Independence, 1959-61

> The essential consideration must be ... that in the course of nature Kuwait, because of her cohesive political identity, backed by great wealth, must some day achieve complete independence .... I submit that we must accept this necessity and be prepared to meet it before it becomes too urgent and a cause of dissension between us.[1]

Kuwait's growing stature as an independent state was symbolized not merely by its membership of international bodies but also by the Ruler's insistence on conducting direct relations with neighbouring Arab countries. In an effort to retain the goodwill of the ruling family, Britain was prepared to acquiesce in this process. Indeed, despite the fall of the Hashemite regime in Iraq, the importance which Britain placed on monarchical rule in Kuwait remained undiminished. Writing in June 1959, the Political Agent, Aubrey Halford, remarked: 'In the last analysis, British interests in Kuwait will only prosper if internal stability can be maintained. For that basic condition we have no choice but to rely on the Sabah Family, at least for the foreseeable future.'[2] Applying the lessons of Suez to Kuwait, moreover, Halford cautioned: 'we should never allow ourselves to be forced into the position where British and Arab nationalist interests can come into conflict with each other'.[3] In a similar vein, the Foreign Office had urged with respect to the Gulf that 'the United Kingdom should appear to be taking something of a back seat, and that any necessary guidance to the Rulers must be unobtrusive'.[4] With such considerations firmly in mind, Britain

---

[1] Letter from A. S. Halford to Selwyn Lloyd, No. 42, 13 Aug 1959, FO 371/140084.
[2] Letter from Halford to Lloyd, No. 31, 11 June 1959, FO 371/140083.
[3] Letter from Halford to Lloyd, No. 42, 13 Aug 1959, FO 371/140084.
[4] 'Points for a Middle East Policy — Part I (Final Version)', Foreign Office paper for the Cabinet Official Committee on the Middle East, 15 Dec 1958, OME (58) 56, CAB 134/2342.

proved willing to facilitate Kuwait's progress to full independent status, starting with the revision of extra-territorial rights and culminating in the abrogation of the 1899 Exclusive Agreement.

I

Britain's extra-territorial rights placed her subjects and all foreigners, other than subjects of the Ruler or, with the exception of Pakistan, nationals of Muslim states, beyond the jurisdiction of Kuwaiti courts. Cases involving those outside Kuwaiti jurisdiction were tried by a specially convened British court. Although this arrangement had been a common feature of British relations with non-European states from the mid-nineteenth century, it was becoming increasingly unusual by the mid-twentieth.[5] As early as July 1958, A. K. Rothnie (Assistant Political Agent, Kuwait) had described extra-territoriality as an 'anachronism'.[6] A year later, Halford characterized Britain's residual jurisdiction as a 'wasting asset', in addition to emphasizing 'the anomaly of pushing Kuwait into independence, while clinging to an outmoded expedient for exercising covert control'.[7] Echoing Rothnie's views, Halford reinforced his position by referring to British jurisdiction as 'an anachronism offensive to nationalism'.[8] In a similar vein, D. J. McCarthy (Assistant Political Agent, Kuwait) commented: 'Our interests here are after all bigger than jurisdiction, and to suffer avoidable political trouble over it would not in any cold-blooded sense be rational or productive.'[9] McCarthy also stressed the sagacity of making an early gesture and 'not waiting till the concessions are dragged out of us piecemeal and as apparent victories over the "colonialists"'. By the mid-1950s, moreover, the growing number of expatriates was turning the system into an administrative burden. In the two years from 1953 to 1955, for example, the number of cases heard by the British court rose from 4 to over 200.[10] The Ruler was also finding dual jurisdiction increasingly onerous.

Referring to extra-territoriality at the end of June 1959, the Ruler

---

[5] In 1909, Britain agreed to transfer jurisdiction over all British subjects in Siam to Siamese law (David K. Wyatt, *Thailand: A Short History*, New Haven, Connecticut: Yale University Press, 1984, p. 206). Britain's extra-territorial rights in China were resigned in 1942 following the Japanese invasion of China (C. P. Fitzgerald, *The Birth of Communist China*, Harmondsworth: Penguin Books, 1964, p. 97).
[6] Minute by C. H. Haines, 1 July 1958, FO 371/132611.
[7] Letter from Halford to Lloyd, No. 31, 11 June 1959, FO 371/140083.
[8] Telegram from Halford to the Foreign Office, No. 40, 17 June 1959, FO 371/140244.
[9] Letter from D. J. McCarthy to M. C. G. Man (Bahrain Residency), No. 16427/59, 13 Aug 1959, FO 371/140245.
[10] Jill Crystal, *Oil and Politics in the Gulf: Rulers and Merchants in Kuwait and Qatar*, Cambridge: Cambridge University Press, 1995, p. 72.

informed Halford that 'The time might be coming — and sooner rather than later — when this convenient arrangement might turn into a most inconvenient irritant to relations between us.'[11] Shaikh Abdullah clarified his views a few months later, describing British jurisdiction as 'embarrassing to him and derogatory to Kuwait'.[12] It is also clear that he was under mounting pressure from Shaikhs Abdullah Mubarak and Jabir who were finding British jurisdiction burdensome in conducting their departmental activities.[13] The momentum for change was maintained by the Assistant State Secretary, Ashraf Lutfi, who, during a meeting with the new Political Agent, J. C. B. Richmond, stressed the importance which the Ruler attached to the question.[14]

Reviewing the whole issue, R. A. Beaumont (Head of the Arabian Department, Foreign Office) remarked:

> It is likely to become politically impossible for us to resist indefinitely the Ruler's demand for a reduction of our jurisdiction. To so do would sour our relations with the Ruling Family to a point where our oil interests and, possibly, the Ruler's continued investment in sterling might be affected.[15]

Moreover, Beaumont saw positive advantages in promoting Kuwait's independent status in the context of potential threats to its separate existence from powerful neighbours. Deterrence could be achieved, he argued, either through a British military presence, which would be politically dangerous, or through 'achieving such a degree of international recognition of Kuwait as a political entity that a would-be aggressor would pause before the international complications which an invasion might provide'.[16]

When the matter was brought before Cabinet at the beginning of December 1959, the Foreign Secretary, Selwyn Lloyd, urged his colleagues to support a reduction of British jurisdiction in the interests of preserving the Ruler's confidence.[17] Nevertheless, he expressed the hope that the cession of jurisdiction would be accompanied by legal reform in Kuwait, including the introduction of appropriate civil and criminal codes. The Cabinet was persuaded by Lloyd's arguments. Explaining the considerations which underpinned Britain's decision to comply with the Ruler's request, Richmond recorded:

---

[11] Telegram from Halford to the Foreign Office, No. 43, 30 June 1959, FO 371/140244.
[12] Letter from McCarthy to Sir George Middleton, No. 16427/59, 6 Oct 1959, FO 371/140246.
[13] Letter from Middleton to Lloyd, No. 87, 29 Oct 1959, FO 371/140246.
[14] Letter from J. C. B. Richmond to Middleton, No. 16427/59, 15 Oct 1959, FO 371/140247.
[15] 'Jurisdiction in Kuwait', Minute by R. A. Beaumont, 23 Oct 1959, FO 371/140247.
[16] Ibid.
[17] Cabinet Conclusions, 3 Dec 1959, CC 61 (59), CAB 128/33.

it would not make sense to have a row with the Ruler over a jurisdictional anachronism when our prime if not only concern in Kuwait is the preservation of our share in, and access to, the largest reservoir of soft currency oil in the world.[18]

The first transfer of jurisdiction took place on 25 February to coincide with the tenth anniversary of the Ruler's accession.[19] When the Foreign Office's legal adviser, C.H. Haines, questioned the wisdom of Britain's acquiescence in the Ruler's request, A. R. Walmsley of the Foreign Office's Arabian Department stressed the 'political necessity' of driving forward as fast as possible with the transfer of jurisdiction.[20] Developments in the judicial sphere were mirrored by Kuwait's growing independence in financial matters.

Throughout the Persian Gulf, the Indian rupee circulated as the customary currency. By the 1950s, however, a number of problems associated with this practice were being experienced. The common currency, for instance, facilitated smuggling between the Gulf and India, especially in gold.[21] Furthermore, as the Foreign Secretary understated in 1954: 'It is, at the least, inconvenient that the monetary authority controlling the Gulf currency should be fifteen hundred miles away and only incidentally concerned with Gulf interests'.[22] Indeed, it proved difficult to replenish existing notes, the condition of which was becoming progressively worse, with new ones from India. The illogicality of persisting with the rupee was also highlighted by the diminishing proportion of trade between India and the Gulf. With an eye to the future, moreover, C. E. Loombe of the Bank of England observed: 'Nationalism in Kuwait is showing signs of developing and on this ground alone some plans for the introduction of a currency . . . may be expected in spite of the opposition to a change by the gold dealers.'[23] In 1953, and again three years later, the question of a new currency for Kuwait was considered in the finance department,[24] only to be deferred. It was not until 1959 that a decisive change took place, the initiative coming from India.

At the end of 1958, the Reserve Bank of India estimated that gold

---

[18] Letter from Richmond to Middleton, No. 16427/59, 10 Dec 1959, FO 371/140248.

[19] 'Transfer of Jurisdiction in Kuwait', Minute by Beaumont, 26 Sept 1960, FO 371/149112. The final transfer of jurisdiction was made on 1 April 1961 (*Parliamentary Debates, Commons*, vol. 642, 19 June 1961, col. 934).

[20] Minute by A. R. Walmsley, 25 April 1960, FO 371/149115.

[21] 'Persian Gulf Currency', Draft brief enclosed in W. Armstrong's (Treasury) letter to D. W. S. Hurst (Commonwealth Relations Office), No. OF 89/204/01 C, 24 Sept 1953, OV 72/6.

[22] Letter from the Secretary of State for Foreign Affairs to Bernard Burrows, No. 48, 2 April 1954, OV 72/7.

[23] Letter from C. E. Loombe to D. R. Serpell, 27 Jan 1954, OV 72/7.

[24] 'Indian Currency in Kuwait', Memorandum by G. C. L. Crichton, 18 March 1956, FO 371/120613.

smuggling from the Gulf was costing the Indian reserves £30–35 million annually.[25] In an effort to counteract this drain, India resolved to replace the rupee notes circulating in the Gulf with new notes of a different colour which became known as the external rupee.[26] The Indians made this decision in the full knowledge that it might stimulate the Persian Gulf states to introduce their own currency. Indeed, even before the changeover was completed on 21 June 1959, members of the Kuwait finance department were talking openly of the imminent introduction of a separate currency.[27] By October, Shaikh Jabir was requesting Bank of England advice on the establishment of a new currency.[28] In response, the Bank sent Loombe, along with another official, R. H. Turner, to Kuwait in November.

The two officials had four meetings, the department of finance being represented by its deputy director, Sayed Ahmad. The President of the finance department, Shaikh Jabir, chaired two of the meetings. In the course of discussions, the Kuwaitis indicated that they wanted the new currency to be linked to sterling and that they intended Kuwait to remain within the sterling area.[29] In many ways, this represented the fulfilment of earlier British hopes. Writing in May 1958, for example, D. Watkinson of the Bank of England's Overseas Division stressed: 'whether the initiative for a new currency comes from India or Kuwait, our basic aim could be the same, namely, to steer the proposals in the direction of a single Persian Gulf currency backed by sterling'.[30] However, the Kuwaitis' proposals were tempered by their desire for the new currency authority to assume responsibility for exchange control.

In reviewing the exchange control question, Richmond stressed that Kuwait was already treated with 'exceptional liberality': Britain viewed requests from the ruling family for foreign exchange with considerable latitude, while Kuwait as a whole enjoyed the advantage of a free market in sterling.[31] Analysing the situation from the Kuwaiti perspective, on the other hand, Richmond noted:

> Kuwait is emerging from a semi-colonial status and Arab Nationalist sentiments reinforce their natural desire for complete freedom to deal with their

---

[25] Telegram from the Foreign Office to Kuwait, No. 2164, 6 Dec 1958, OV 72/8.

[26] 'Persian Gulf Currency', Minute from Sir Roger Makins to the Prime Minister, 30 Jan 1959, FO 371/140154; 'Persian Gulf Currency', Paper enclosed in J. E. Lucas' (Treasury) letter to J. A. Snellgrove (Bank of England), 29 Oct 1963, OV 72/9.

[27] Telegram from Halford to the Foreign Office, No. 363, 7 June 1959, FO 371/140156.

[28] Telegram from Richmond to the Foreign Office, No. 632, 19 Oct 1959, FO 371/140157.

[29] 'Kuwait Currency', Note by Loombe, 4 Dec 1959 enclosed in J. M. Stevens' (Bank of England) letter to Sir Roger Stevens, 15 Dec 1959, FO 371/140157.

[30] 'Persian Gulf Currency', Note by D. Watkinson, 22 May 1958, OV 72/7.

[31] Letter from Richmond to Beaumont, No. 1119/60, 24 May 1960, FO 371/148997.

own money. They are sensitive to jibes from other Arabs that it is used to support a tottering British Empire.[32]

With such considerations in mind, Richmond saw the new currency board's assumption of exchange control as a 'logical move'.[33] On 8 February 1961, an informal request for the transfer of exchange operation was made by the Finance Department.[34] In April, the month that saw the introduction of the new dinar into Kuwait, Richmond conveyed to Shaikh Jabir Her Majesty's Government's willingness to relinquish exchange control. For his part, Jabir expressed gratification with Britain's decision and assured Richmond that Kuwait would be willing to administer the system on the same broad principles as the Bank of England.[35] Kuwait's growing freedom of action in financial matters raised the question of future investment policy.

II

In their two-volume study *British Imperialism*, P. J. Cain and A. G. Hopkins seek to explain the expansion and contraction of the British empire with reference to changes in the metropolitan economy. The central figures in their analysis are the so-called 'gentlemanly capitalists', land-owners and financiers from the south of England who possessed the same social background and perceptions of national interest as the governing class. According to Cain and Hopkins, 'gentlemanly interests which sustained the empire down to World War II also managed and to some extent planned its demise thereafter'.[36] During the Second World War, and more importantly thereafter, contend Cain and Hopkins, British policy-makers sought to preserve 'sterling's role in financing international trade and investment, and with it the maintenance of the earning power of the City of London'.[37] This was achieved through the operation of the sterling area where 'the pound was nursed within a framework of controls in which the empire ... had a starring if also involuntary role'.[38] Cain and Hopkins suggest that Britain's changing attitude towards the value of the sterling area by the late 1950s is central to accounting for rapid decolonization in succeeding years. On the one hand, they suggest that British investors were seeking opportunities outside the sterling area, and on the other, that the build-up of large sterling

---
[32] Ibid.
[33] Letter from Richmond to Beaumont, No. 1119/60, 6 Nov 1960, FO 371/149001.
[34] Letter from Richmond to Beaumont, No. 1119/61, 12 Feb 1961, FO 371/156859.
[35] Letter from Richmond to Beaumont, No. 1119/61, 12 April 1961, FO 371/156860.
[36] P. J. Cain and A. G. Hopkins, *British Imperialism: Crisis and Deconstruction, 1914–1990*, London: Longman, 1993, p. 265.
[37] Ibid., pp. 265–6.
[38] Ibid., p. 266.

balances by members of the area came to be seen as a 'problem instead of an asset'.[39] This second consideration was particularly influential, argue Cain and Hopkins, once sterling became convertible in 1958 since 'balances could be drawn on more freely', thus raising the spectre of a run on the pound.[40] The essence of the Cain and Hopkins thesis has been restated by Gerold Krozewski, who suggests that the closing of the dollar gap and the return to convertibility in the late 1950s, 'undermined much of the rationale of the sterling area', thus easing the path to decolonization.[41] In keeping with Cain and Hopkins, Krozewski argues that large sterling balances became a 'potential burden'.[42]

The arguments presented by Cain and Hopkins, and Krozewski, are unsatisfactory with respect to Kuwait. First, they ascribe an exaggerated importance to 1958. Sterling balances represented the foreign reserves of the overseas sterling area. Even before 1958, the monetary authorities of Kuwait, and most other sterling area territories, had been free to draw on central reserves in London to meet foreign exchange needs.[43] Moreover, Kuwait's special position as a free market territory in the sterling area had meant that sterling could readily be converted into dollars. The Shaikhdom's sterling balances, therefore, were no more liquid after 1958 than they had been before. As regards the build-up of sterling balances by Kuwait, while they undoubtedly caused concern, it would be an exaggeration to suggest that Britain perceived them as a liability instead of an asset. Indeed, Catherine Schenk's contention that sterling balances were not a dangerous and volatile factor in the British external economy[44] is supported by the example of Kuwait.

Standing at £260 million at the end of 1958, the Persian Gulf's sterling balances, the bulk of which were Kuwaiti, were surpassed only by those of West Africa, Malaya, and Australia.[45] In 1959, it was estimated that the Gulf's balances were equivalent to over a quarter of Britain's gold and foreign exchange holdings.[46] The concern was that if either the existing Rulers, or new hostile regimes, decided to diversify the accumulated wealth, severe strain would be placed on sterling. Apart from the drain on the central

[39] Ibid., p. 288.
[40] Ibid.
[41] Gerold Krozewski, 'Sterling, the "Minor" Territories, and the End of Formal Empire, 1939–1958', *The Economic History Review*, 46, 2 (1993): 241. See also Gerold Krozewski, 'Finance and Empire: The Dilemma Facing Great Britain in the 1950s', *The International History Review*, 18, 1 (1996): 49.
[42] Krozewski, 'Sterling and the End of Formal Empire', p. 251.
[43] Catherine R. Schenk, *Britain and the Sterling Area: From Devaluation to Convertibility in the 1950s*, London: Routledge, 1994, p. 27.
[44] Ibid., pp. 17–49.
[45] Ibid., pp. 50–3.
[46] 'Persian Gulf States and the Sterling Area', Draft paper by J. A. Ford, 2 April, 1959, T 236/5181.

reserves of the sterling area, it was feared that any move by Kuwait to weaken the link with sterling would be likely to affect confidence in sterling as an international currency. Despite these worries, the Treasury felt the balance of advantage rested with maintaining the Persian Gulf's sterling balances. 'It seems to me', wrote one official, 'that it would be a faint-hearted banker who would discourage a customer from depositing large sums in his account because of doubt about his own ability to repay them. It would not be much of a tribute to the standing of London as a financial centre, if we were to take the line that only New York can handle business on such a scale.'[47] Indeed, the Treasury declared:

> The disadvantages of the continued accumulation of large sterling balances by Kuwait are not, so far as the United Kingdom overseas monetary position is concerned, such as to call for any measures to alter or terminate the existing arrangements whereby the surplus revenues of Kuwait are invested in the United Kingdom.[48]

From the Kuwait perpective, Catherine Schenk's characterization of the sterling balances as a 'niggling potential discomfort' which 'did not present a real obstacle to British foreign and domestic economic policy'[49] seems apt. The only change which Britain was prepared to countenance was Kuwaiti investment in sound Arab projects and this for essentially political, rather than economic, reasons.

In April 1960, Shaikh Jabir gave Richmond an assurance that there was no question of changing the basic policy of investing Kuwait's surpluses in London.[50] At the beginning of the following month, nevertheless, the Treasury argued:

> In principle ... H.M.G. should support any move to invest part of Kuwaits [sic] surplus in Arab projects, because this would remove any stigma of imperialism and would also remove the existing criticism that the Ruler had no interest in Arab development.[51]

Reflecting such pressures, Sayed Ahmad informed W. P. Cranston (Economic Counsellor to the Political Resident) that some diversification of Kuwait's investments was under consideration. He was quick to stress, however, that such investments would be 'kept to the minimum necessary to satisfy the critics'.[52]

---

[47] 'Kuwait's Sterling Balances', Minute by A. W. Taylor, 22 April 1959, T 236/5181.
[48] 'The Persian Gulf States and the Sterling Area', Note by the Treasury, 10 Nov 1959, T 236/5181.
[49] Catherine Schenk, 'Finance and Empire: Confusions and Complexities: A Note', *The International History Review*, 18, 4 (1996): 872.
[50] Letter from Richmond to Walmsley, No. 1117/60, 26 April, 1960, T 236/6314.
[51] 'Kuwait Investment Policy', Minutes of a meeting held in the Treasury, 5 May 1950, T 236/6314.
[52] Letter from W. P. Cranston to Beaumont, No. 1117/60, 17 May 1960, FO 371/148997.

In July 1960, Kuwait concluded an agreement to extend a loan of £1 million to Jordan.[53] The process of investing in Arab countries was accelerated by the renewal of the Iraqi threat to Kuwait in mid-1961 (see Chapter 6). '[I]t may well be', observed Cranston,

> that the promise of substantial Kuwaiti financial contributions to future Arab economic development may be part of the price which Kuwait will have to pay in order to secure her future independence and to remove the current feeling of resentment, not wholly justified, that Kuwait is retaining all her wealth for herself and not sharing it with her neighbours.[54]

In July 1961, King Hussein of Jordan specifically told Kuwait that it could not expect help from other Arab countries unless it showed willingness to provide financial assistance.[55] The strength of this sentiment was reinforced by the frosty reception which greeted Shaikh Jabir as he toured Arab capitals in the aftermath of Iraq's revival of her claims to the Shaikhdom.[56]

At a meeting between officials of the Foreign Office, Treasury, and Bank of England, the political desirability of Kuwaiti investment in other Arab states was accepted.[57] At the beginning of 1962, Kuwait established the Kuwait Fund for Arab Economic Development (see Chapter 6). The principle that the Kuwait Investment Board (KIB) had sole responsibility for the management of Kuwait's surplus capital had been broken a year earlier with the establishment of a separate investment committee within the department of finance.[58] Britain was prepared to acquiesce in this development provided that Kuwait's balances held in London were maintained.[59] Furthermore, in order to make the KIB more accountable, the Foreign Office supported the appointment of a Kuwaiti member.[60] The Board's chairman, H. T. Kemp, nevertheless, resisted this proposal, stressing that both the Ruler and the finance department already had full control over general policy if they chose to exercise it.[61] As an indication of this, the 40 per cent sterling backing for the Kuwaiti dinar was withdrawn from the

---

[53] Letter from Richmond to J. G. S. Beith, No. 1032/60, 30 July 1960, T 236/6314.
[54] Letter from Cranston to A. Mackay (Treasury), No. 11116/61, 16 July 1961, FO 371/156860.
[55] Telegram from John Henniker-Major (British Ambassador, Amman) to the Foreign Office, No. 591, 25 July 1961, FO 371/156852.
[56] *Kuwait: Annual Review for 1961*, enclosed in Richmond's letter to Lord Home, No. 3, 4 Jan 1962, DEFE 7/1950.
[57] Letter from Walmsley to A. K. Rothnie, No. BK 1114/32, 8 Nov 1961, FO 371/156865.
[58] 'Kuwait', Minute by J. E. Lucas, 14 March 1961, T 236/6315.
[59] 'Kuwait Investment Policy', Note by Lucas, 7 March 1961; 'Kuwait Investment Board', Note by Lucas, 6 April 1961, T 236/6315; 'Kuwait Investment Policy', Foreign Office Note, 28 March 1961, FO 371/156864.
[60] Letter from Beaumont to Richmond, No. BA 1114/83, 27 July, FO 371/148998.
[61] 'Kuwait Director on the Kuwait Investment Board', Minute by Beaumont, 12 Aug 1960, FO 371/148999.

assets of the KIB.[62] Britain's relaxation of her control of investment policy is mirrored in her relations with oil companies operating in Kuwait.

The signature of political agreements between the British government and oil companies operating in Kuwait had been designed to ensure that the former's protecting role was recognized by all parties. On 5 March 1934, the Kuwait Oil Company signed an agreement by which it consented to conduct its local relations, except as regards routine commercial business, through the Political Agent. Although the KOC was accused of not always complying with this undertaking,[63] the political agreement did provide the basis for regulating the tripartite relationship between Ruler, protecting power, and oil company. The progressive erosion of Kuwait's subordinate status, however, made the practice of signing political agreements obsolete.

In 1960, with the Ruler on the verge of awarding a concession for the Kuwait off-shore area, the Foreign Office argued against insisting upon the signature of a political agreement.[64] This proposal received support from the Ministry of Power, Treasury, Ministry of Defence, and Admiralty.[65] When the allocation of the off-shore concession to Shell Oil was announced, therefore, Britain did not seek to accompany it with a political agreement. The award of the concession to the part British-owned company, however, was the source of gratification for Britain. 'This is very satisfying,' enthused an official of the Foreign Office, 'both intrinsically for British interests involved and as an indication of the Ruler's preference for things British (including sterling).'[66] The concession was also welcomed since it preserved the 50/50 profit-sharing formula which had been undermined in 1958 by the Ruler's granting of a concession for the Neutral Zone off-shore area to the Japanese-owned Arabian Oil Company on the basis of a 57/43 division of profit in favour of Kuwait.[67] The Japanese bid also provided for all payment in dollars.[68] Britain was prepared to tolerate this arrangement provided that payments from the KOC continued to be made in sterling.[69] 'To permit payment in dollars', remarked Halford, ' . . .

---

[62] 'Kuwait Investment Policy', Bank of England note enclosed in J. M. Stevens' letter to Sir Denis Rickett, 28 March 1961, T 236/6315.

[63] Letter from W. R. Hay to Burrows, No. 122/26/49, 2 May 1949, R/15/5/268.

[64] Letter from Beaumont to A. B. Powell (Ministry of Power), No. BA 1536/53, 28 Oct 1960, FO 371/149092.

[65] Letter from Beaumont to Richmond, No. BA 1536/66, 28 Nov 1960, FO 371/149093.

[66] Minute by W. N. Hillier-Fry, 30 Nov 1960, FO 371/149093.

[67] Letter from Halford to D. M. H. Riches, No. 10814/58, 13 May 1958, T 236/5201; Stephen Hemsley Longrigg, *Oil in the Middle East: Its Discovery and Development*, second edition, London: Oxford University Press, 1961, p. 310; George Lenczowski, *Oil and State in the Middle East*, New York: Cornell University Press, 1960, p. 85; Benjamin Shwadran, *The Middle East, Oil and the Great Powers*, third edition, Jerusalem: Israel Universities Press, 1973, p. 424.

[68] 'Kuwait/Saudi Arabian Neutral Zone Seabed Concession', Minute by Mary Hedley-Miller, 9 May 1958, T 236/5201.

[69] Letter from N. M. P. Reilly to Hedley-Miller, No. 10814/13/57, 12 June 1957, T 236/5199.

is an insurance premium against demand for part payment in dollars by the Kuwait Oil Company's off-takers or conversion of part of Kuwait's sterling investments.'[70] Accounting for the Ruler's decision to grant the concession to a Japanese concern, an official of the Foreign Office suggested that the Ruler 'wished to show that he was a good Arab and a good Asian'.[71] Halford, moreover, recorded that 'Arab nationalists view the award as a major setback for the Western oil companies and hail the Japanese as heralds of a new golden age.'[72] The undermining of Britain's formal protection over Kuwait, symbolized by the lapsing of her role in the conduct of relations with the oil companies, led inevitably to pressure for a revision of the 1899 agreement.

III

In September 1960, an official of the Foreign Office remarked: 'we may take it that Kuwait will soon be taking a further step forward (and effectively the last) towards the attainment of full independence'.[73] This prophecy was shortly to be realized. At the beginning of 1961, the Ruler indicated to Richmond not only his belief that the provisions of the 1899 agreement were obsolete, but also his desire to study the possibility of replacing it with a new agreement more consonant with the evolving status of Kuwait.[74]

As early as April 1960, Richmond had opined: 'I would see no real loss in our dropping the concept of "protection". It would in many ways improve our relations if the change came about. We have at present, in Kuwait, as formerly in Jordan, responsibility without power.'[75] In sponsoring Kuwait's application for membership of UNESCO (the United Nations Educational, Scientific, and Cultural Organization) in May, the British government advised the organization's Director General that it 'regarded Kuwait as responsible for the conduct of her international relations'.[76] Commenting on Kuwait's growing international personality, the Foreign Secretary, Selywn Lloyd, stressed: 'The 1899 Agreement is ... clearly

---

[70] Telegram from Halford to the Foreign Office, No. 3, 5 Jan 1958, FO 371/132841.
[71] Minute by P. H. Gore-Booth, 12 May 1958, T 236/5201. The Ruler may also have been influenced by the fact that King Saud had already awarded the concession for his half of the Neutral Zone to the Japanese concern with a 56/44 split in profits in favour of Saudi Arabia ('Kuwait Neutral Zone Sea-Bed Oil Concessions', Draft Paper for Official Committee on Middle East (undated), FO 371/132841).
[72] Letter from Halford to Riches, No. 10814/58, 13 May 1958, T 236/5201.
[73] Minute by Hillier-Fry, 20 Sept 1960, FO 371/148948.
[74] Telegram from Richmond to the Foreign Office, No. 6, 4 Jan 1961, FO 371/156834.
[75] Letter from Richmond to Beaumont, No. 1041/60, 18 April 1960, FO 371/148948.
[76] Glen Balfour-Paul, *The End of Empire in the Middle East: Britain's Relinquishment of Power in her Last Three Arab Dependencies*, Cambridge: Cambridge University Press, 1994, p. 119.

inconsistent with the international status which Kuwait was now assuming in practice'.[77] Nevertheless, in subsequent Cabinet discussions it was decided that the initiative for altering the agreement should rest with the Ruler.[78] His approach to Richmond in January 1961 set in train a debate about the form which future relations with Kuwait should take.

Previous British attempts to revise defensive alliances with Middle Eastern countries had proved difficult. Under the 1936 Anglo-Egyptian treaty, Britain had been permitted to station forces in the Suez Canal Zone for a further twenty years. In the aftermath of the Second World War, Egypt requested a revision of this agreement. During 1946, the two sides were edging towards consensus on the basis of a withdrawal of British troops from Egypt by the end of 1949.[79] Britain's refusal to countenance Egypt's request for unification with Sudan, however, led to the collapse of the negotiations in December 1946. Britain also experienced acute complications in reforming her post-war relationship with Iraq.

At the San Remo Conference of allied powers in April 1920, Britain acquired the mandate for Iraq. Relations between the two countries were regulated by a treaty signed in October 1922 under which the Iraqi king, Feisal, bound himself to accept British advice on all matters affecting Britain's international interests. In an attempt to reduce her financial commitments, Britain informed the Iraqi government in September 1929 of her willingness to liquidate the British mandate. Although entering the League of Nations in 1932, Iraq's independence, like that of Egypt, was circumscribed by the suffocatingly close relationship which she still possessed with Britain. Under the 1930 Anglo-Iraqi treaty of alliance, Britain's sovereign rights over the military bases at Habbaniyya and Shaiba, near Baghdad and Basra respectively, were recognized. In addition, Britain reserved the right to use all of Iraq's military facilities in time of war. As Daniel Silverfarb has noted: 'while Iraq became an independent state in 1932, it was still involuntarily bound to Britain in a subordinate relationship'.[79a]

In an attempt to deflect both internal and external criticism of Iraq's relationship with Britain, the Iraqi leadership sought to revise the terms of the 1930 treaty after the end of the Second World War. The Foreign Secretary, Ernest Bevin, proved keen to facilitate their request, and initial discussions opened in Baghdad in May 1947, concluding with the signing

---

[77] 'Kuwait: The Exclusive Agreement of 1899', Memorandum by the Secretary of State for Foreign Affairs, 9 May 1960, C (60) 81, CAB 129/101.

[78] Cabinet Conclusions, 17 May 1960, CC 31 (60), CAB 128/34.

[79] For an account of the negotiations see William Roger Louis, *The British Empire in the Middle East, 1945–1951: Arab Nationalism, the United States and Postwar Imperialism*, Oxford: Clarendon, 1984, pp. 232–53.

[79a] Daniel Silverfarb, *Britain's Informal Empire in the Middle East: A Case Study of Iraq, 1929–1941*, New York: Oxford University Press, 1986, p. 22.

of the treaty of Portsmouth on 15 January 1948. In return for agreeing to share the military bases provided under the 1930 treaty, Britain was conceded unrestricted rights to use them in either peace or war. The treaty of Portsmouth also contained the ambiguous formula that 'His Majesty the King of Iraq agrees to afford, in case of need and on request, all necessary facilities for the movement of units of His Britannic Majesty's forces in transit across Iraq.'[80] In addition, Britain retained the right to send warships into the Shatt al-Arab, Iraq's principal waterway, without prior permission, and extracted a promise from Iraq that it would purchase military equipment from Britain. In consequence, the treaty of Portsmouth did little to alter fundamentally Britain's dominant position in Iraq.

The publication of the terms of the treaty in Iraq, however, incited a spontaneous storm of protest. In response to the popular outcry, the Regent, Abd al-Ilah, announced that 'no treaty whatever not ensuring the rights of the country and its national aspirations will be ratified'.[81] On 27 January, the Iraqi premier, Salih Jabr, was forced to resign. A week later the Iraqi government informed Britain that the new treaty was 'not a fit instrument for strengthening the ties of friendship between Iraq and the United Kingdom'.[82] In keeping with Britain's reversion to the 1936 Anglo-Egyptian treaty following the collapse of discussions with Egypt, Iraq's abandonment of the treaty of Portsmouth obliged Britain to fall back on the hated 1930 Anglo-Iraqi treaty.

With the unwelcome precedent of Iraq in mind, Richmond remarked:

> Having been in Baghdad when the Portsmouth Treaty blew up in our face and having observed at longer range the limited success which attended the Baghdad Pact I am perhaps unduly pessimistic about treaties between a great power and a little one in an area where the nationalism of the inhabitants of the little one is growing rapidly stronger. But making every allowance for my own bias I think we ought to see if we can avoid the difficult task of defining Anglo-Kuwait mutual obligations in a written document.[83]

R. S. Crawford of the Foreign Office articulated similar concerns. 'Any reformulation of our obligations to Kuwait', he stressed, 'is bound to expose us to attack elsewhere.'[84] Moreover, the Head of the Arabian Department, R. A. Beaumont, emphasized the need to avoid giving the appearance of signing an 'unequal' treaty with Kuwait.[85] The Lord Privy Seal, Edward Heath, also added his voice to the debate, warning:

---

[80] Daniel Silverfarb, *The Twilight of British Ascendancy in the Middle East: A Case Study of Iraq, 1941–1950*, Basingstoke: Macmillan, 1994, pp. 134–5.
[81] Ibid., p. 150.
[82] Ibid., p. 154.
[83] Letter from Richmond to Middleton, No. 1041/61, 18 Jan 1961, FO 371/156834.
[84] Minute by R. S. Crawford, 6 March 1961, FO 371/156834.
[85] Letter from Beaumont to Middleton, 30 March 1961, DEFE 7/1949.

A new agreement between the United Kingdom and Kuwait which stated the obligation of Her Majesty's Government to assist Kuwait in maintaining her independence would be liable to invite attack both on Her Majesty's Government for imposing, and on the ruler of Kuwait for accepting, what would be represented as an imperialist relationship out of line with developments elsewhere in the modern world.[86]

During Cabinet deliberations in April 1961, Heath presented three possible alternatives to his colleagues for the reformulation of relations with Kuwait.[87] The first would have involved an exchange of notes abrogating the 1899 Agreement, accompanied by an oral and unpublished assurance that the United Kingdom recognized their continuing obligation to assist in maintaining Kuwait's independence. The second would entail an exchange of notes which, while abrogating the 1899 Agreement, would state that this did not affect Britain's responsibility to defend Kuwait. The final option would record the same obligations, but in a formal treaty. In the course of discussions, the point was made that 'A formal treaty would serve the interests neither of Kuwait nor of Her Majesty's Government. Experience in Jordan[88] and Iraq indicated that the existence of such a treaty could be a standing invitation to its abrogation.' In consequence, the Cabinet decided to offer the Ruler a choice of the first two courses outlined by Heath. Underpinning British calculations, however, was the traditional determination to ensure that Kuwait's independent existence was preserved. Reflecting this perennial concern, Heath emphasized:

> Access to Kuwait's oil resources on the best financial terms possible remain vital interests for the United Kingdom and these would be endangered should Kuwait lose her independence. It therefore remains in the interest of Her Majesty's Government to continue to afford assistance to Kuwait in maintaining its independence.[89]

In a similar vein, the Foreign Secretary, Lord Home, remarked:

> Access to the oil of Kuwait on present terms strengthens the position of British oil companies and of the British economy in their relations with other oil-producing countries and prevents the latter holding Britain and indeed Western Europe to ransom.[90]

---

[86] 'Kuwait: Future Relations with the United Kingdom', Memorandum by the Lord Privy Seal, 5 April 1961, C (61) 49, CAB 129/104.

[87] Cabinet Conclusions, 13 April 1961, CC 20 (61), CAB 128/35 Part 1.

[88] In March 1957, Jordan abrogated the 1946 Anglo-Jordanian treaty of alliance (Kamal Salibi, *The Modern History of Jordan*, London: I. B. Tauris, 1993, p. 191; Naseer H. Aruri, *Jordan: A Study in Political Development, 1921–1965*, The Hague: Martinus Nijhoff, 1972, p. 135; John Marlowe, *Arab Nationalism and British Imperialism: A Study in Power Politics*, London: The Cresset Press, 1961, p. 144).

[89] 'Kuwait: Future Relations with the United Kingdom', Memorandum by the Lord Privy Seal, 5 April 1961, C (61) 49, CAB 129/104.

[90] Letter from the Secretary of State to Sir William Luce, No. 77, 25 May 1961, FO 371/156673.

While the precise form of the new Anglo-Kuwaiti relationship caused intense discussion in British governmental and official circles, it was also keenly debated among Kuwaitis. In the Supreme Council there was a division of opinion on the question of whether any specific reference to future military assistance being provided by Britain should be made.[91] During Cabinet discussions on 13 April 1961, the Prime Minister, Harold Macmillan, had urged that 'Any new agreement must recognise our right to intervene if Kuwait's independence were threatened and this would ... equally involve recognising our obligation to do so'.[92] The Foreign Office was sceptical about this assertion, one official minuting: 'I very much doubt whether the Ruler would be prepared to sign any agreement which gave us the right to intervene in Kuwait otherwise than with the agreement of the Government of Kuwait.'[93] This prediction proved accurate since the Ruler, although agreeing to adopt the second of Heath's proposals, made it clear that Kuwait would not recognize the right of uninvited intervention.[94] In the end, a form of words was devised which met Kuwaiti concerns.

On 19 June 1961, the exchange of notes between Britain and Kuwait took place. After consenting to terminate the 1899 Agreement and expressing hope that relations between the two countries would continue to be governed by a spirit of close friendship, the British note stated: 'Nothing in these conditions shall affect the readiness of Her Majesty's Government to assist the Government of Kuwait if the latter request such assistance.'[95] Within a few days, the Kuwaitis invoked this clause in order to deter renewed Iraqi claims to the Shaikhdom.

---

[91] Letter from Richmond to Crawford, No. 10221/61, 9 March 1961, FO 371/156834.
[92] Cabinet Conclusions, 13 April 1961, CC 20 (61), CAB 128/35 Part 1.
[93] 'Anglo-Kuwaiti Relations', Minute by Beaumont, 17 April 1961, FO 371/156835.
[94] Telegram from the Foreign Office to Bahrain, No. 501, 28 April 1961, FO 371/156835.
[95] *Exchange of Notes regarding Relations between the United Kingdom of Great Britain and Northern Ireland and the State of Kuwait, 19 June 1961*, London: HMSO, 1961, Cmd. 1409.

6: Dependence and Independence 1961–5

> The Department's view . . . has always been that Kuwait is unlikely to remain independent, in the foreseeable future, unless she is militarily protected, and known to be militarily protected, by H.M.G.[1]

> A stretch of sand with an income of £170 million per annum is too big a prize to remain in isolation.[2]

Some have argued that the process of withdrawal from empire in the postwar world merely represented a re-formulation of the imperial relationship, an attempt by Britain to return to 'informal empire'.[3] In some senses such an interpretation is appropriate to Kuwait. Although Kuwait's use of the term Amirate, following the exchange of letters of June 1961, was intended to emphasize Kuwait's new status, its independence was circumscribed by continuing dependence on British military support. Nevertheless, the cover provided by the British military umbrella was not sufficient to ensure Kuwait's survival. The Amirate also needed Arab political support. Indeed, it was the apparently incompatible combination of British military and Arab political support which represented the twin pillars of Kuwait's separate existence. This was graphically illustrated within days of Kuwait's nominal independence.

I

On 14 July 1958, the Head of the Eastern Department at the Foreign Office, D. M. H. Riches, predicted that the new regime in Baghdad would

---

[1] Minute by A. R. Walmsley, 8 Sept 1959, FO 371/140084.
[2] 'Kuwait: Political Situation', Note by C. E. Loombe, 14 Dec 1961, OV 72/13.
[3] William Roger Louis and Ronald Robinson, 'The Imperialism of Decolonization', *Journal of Imperial and Commonwealth History*, 22, 3 (1994): 462–511.

'prosecute the Iraqi claim to Kuwait with greater vigour than the previous Iraqi Government'.[4] Although in the longer term this prophecy proved accurate, in the short term relations between Iraq and Kuwait experienced a marked improvement.

On the eve of the July revolution, relations between the two countries had reached their nadir as Iraq revived her territorial claims to Kuwait in an effort to frighten the Ruler into bringing the Shaikhdom into the Arab Union (see Chapter 4). When Shaikh Abdullah visited Baghdad at the end of October 1958, the new Iraqi premier, Abdul Karim Qassem, greeted him warmly and expressed admiration for his achievements in Kuwait.[5] Moreover, Qassem made no mention of Iraqi claims to Kuwait. For his part, the Ruler was reported to have been 'much impressed' by the personality of the new Iraqi leader.[6] Such was the initial improvement in relations with Iraq that Riches even suggested Kuwait might be tempted to dispense with British protection altogether.[7] Iraq's apparent acceptance of Kuwait's independent existence was highlighted by her support for the Shaikhdom's application to join international organizations.[8] In late October 1960, furthermore, the al-Sabah felt sufficiently confident to invite Qassem to Kuwait to discuss the border question.[9] Just days before the Anglo-Kuwaiti exchange of letters, the British Ambassador in Baghdad, Sir Humphrey Trevelyan,[10] informed the Foreign Office that the Iraqi leader was 'playing up Iraq's close connections and friendship with Kuwait and might well not wish to prejudice his relations with the Sheikh by attacking an agreement made by him'.[11] In keeping with other Arab states, he expressed satisfaction at news of the abrogation of British protection, although ominously

[4] 'Events in Iraq in relation to the Eastern Department countries of Kuwait, Saudi Arabia, and Iran', Minute by D. M. H. Riches, 14 July 1958, FO 371/132502.
[5] Telegram from Aubrey Halford to the Foreign Office, No. 645, 4 Nov 1958, FO 371/132623. See also Sir Rupert Hay, *The Persian Gulf States*, Washington, DC: The Middle East Institute, 1959, pp. 146-7.
[6] Letter from Halford to Sir George Middleton, No. 1035/58, 18 Dec 1958, FO 371/132623.
[7] 'Kuwait/Iraq', Minute by Riches, 12 Nov 1958, FO 371/132623.
[8] Richard Gott, 'The Kuwait Incident', in D. C. Watt (ed.), *Survey of International Affairs 1961*, London: Oxford University Press, 1965, p. 525, n. 1; Ritchie Ovendale, *Britain, the United States, and the Transfer of Power in the Middle East, 1945–1962*, London: Leicester University Press, 1996. p, 228; H. Rahman, *The Making of the Gulf War: Origins of Kuwait's Long-Standing Territorial Dispute with Iraq*, Reading: Ithaca Press, 1997, pp. 238, 240.
[9] Richard Schofield, *Kuwait and Iraq: Historical Claims and Territorial Disputes*, second edition, London: Royal Institute of International Affairs, 1993, p. 103.
[10] Humphrey Trevelyan (1905-1985); Baron (1968), KG (1974), GCMG (1965), KCMG (1955), CMG (1951); entered the Indian Civil Service, 1929; entered Foreign Service, 1947; Counsellor in Baghdad, 1948; UK High Commission for Germany, 1951–3; Chargé d'Affaires, Peking, 1953–5; Ambassador to Egypt, 1955–6; Under-Secretary at the United Nations, 1958; Ambassador to Iraq, 1958–61; Deputy Under-Secretary of State, Foreign Office, 1962; Ambassador to the USSR, 1962–5; High Commissioner in South Arabia, 1967.
[11] Morice Snell-Mendoza, 'In Defence of Oil: Britain's Response to the Iraqi Threat towards Kuwait, 1961', *Contemporary British History*, 10, 3 (1996): 45.

made no reference to Kuwaiti independence.[12] The improvement in Kuwaiti–Iraqi relations proved illusory.

Qassem chose a Baghdad press conference held on 25 June not only to declare that Kuwait was an 'integral part' of Iraq, but also to announce his intention to reduce Shaikh Abdullah's position to that of *qaimmaqam*, or district governor, of Kuwait.[13] Furthermore, the Iraqi premier denounced those Kuwaitis who had exchanged notes with Britain on 19 June as 'irresponsible people who are under the sway of imperialism'.[14] 'No individual, whether in Kuwait or outside,' he fulminated, 'has the right to dominate the people of Kuwait, for they are people of Iraq.'[15] In justifying Iraq's renewed claim, Qassem relied upon arguments first advanced by Taufiq al-Suwaidi nearly a quarter of a century earlier, namely that Kuwait was historically part of the Basra province and that the 1899 Agreement with Britain had been invalid since Shaikh Mubarak, an Ottoman *qaimmaqam*, had no authority to conclude it.[16]

The legality of Qassem's insistence on Iraqi ownership of Kuwait is open to doubt. As regards the question of succession to the Ottoman title to Kuwait, Maurice Mendelson and Susan Hulton argue that the link between the Ottoman empire and Kuwait was broken in 1914 when the al-Sabah rebelled against their former overlords.[17] Even if the relationship between Kuwait and the Ottomans survived the war, continue Mendelson and Hulton, the title to Kuwait would have been inherited by the modern state of Turkey, rather than Iraq. Under the 1923 treaty of Lausanne, however, Turkey renounced 'all rights and title whatsoever over or respecting the territories situated outside' its present borders.[18] Furthermore, the Ottoman empire's relationship with Kuwait was historically that of suzerain, rather than sovereign, making Iraq's claims to sovereignty invalid. Husain M. al-Baharna, moreover, emphasizes that the exchange of letters between Nuri Said and Shaikh Ahmad in July–August 1932, under which Iraq recognized Kuwait's existing boundaries, was binding on both parties.[19] Despite the legal dubiousness of Qassem's reasoning, he continued to pursue his country's irredentist claims to Kuwait.

[12] Schofield, *Kuwait and Iraq*, p. 105.
[13] Majid Khadduri, *Republican Iraq: A Study in Iraqi Politics since the Revolution of 1958*, London: Oxford University Press, 1969, p. 166.
[14] Abdul-Reda Assiri, *Kuwait's Foreign Policy: City-State in World Politics*, Boulder, Colorado: Westview Press, 1990, p. 19.
[15] John Bulloch, *The Gulf: A Portrait of Kuwait, Qatar, Bahrain, and the UAE*, London: Century Publishing, 1984, p. 62.
[16] Schofield, *Kuwait and Iraq*, p. 105.
[17] Maurice Mendelson and Susan Hulton, 'Iraq's Claim to Sovereignty over Kuwait', in Richard Schofield (ed.), *Territorial Foundations of the Gulf States*, London: UCL Press, 1994, p. 127.
[18] Ibid., p. 123.
[19] Husain M. al-Baharna, *The Arabian Gulf States: Their Legal and Political Status and Their International Problems*, second edition, Beirut: Librairie Du Liban, 1975, pp. 256–7.

Chapter 6

The Iraqi Prime Minister's approach to Kuwait stood in marked contrast with the apparent improvement in relations between the two countries following the Iraqi Revolution. Qassem's growing belligerence was prefigured on 30 April when he warned Kuwait against joining the British Commonwealth.[20] Majid Khadduri suggests that the idea to annex Kuwait began at this time.[21] The spur for Qassem's actions, however, would appear to have been the abrogation of the 1899 Agreement and the exchange of notes on 19 June 1961. 'The signature of the new Anglo-Kuwait agreement', minuted an official of the Foreign Office, 'seems to have made him [Qassem] very angry and also perhaps to have convinced him that with the possibility of Kuwait joining the Arab League and perhaps the United Nations, he would have to reassert Iraq's claim to Kuwait before it was too late.'[22] Benjamin Shwadran, furthermore, suggests that Qassem's pronouncement was designed both to forestall other possible claimants and to test the reaction of the British.[23] Whether Qassem ever intended to prosecute his claim with military force is a controversial question.

John Bulloch argues that the Iraqi premier did not intend to attack or annex Kuwait, but was merely 'seizing the moment to restate his country's historic claims to Kuwait'.[24] Indeed, from the outset Qassem asserted his intention to achieve his objective through peaceful means.[25] The day after Qassem's Baghdad press conference, an official of the Foreign Office admitted that

> Although the possibility of his having a rush of blood to the head cannot be excluded, it seems on the whole unlikely that he will resort to military action in view of the current strength of the opposition in Iraq and the need to keep a large amount of the army available for internal security.[26]

---

[20] Letter from M. C. G. Man to Air Marshal Sir Charles Elworthy, No. 1054, 12 May 1961, FO 371/156835.
[21] Khadduri, *Republican Iraq*, p. 169.
[22] 'Qasim's Policy towards Kuwait', Minute by G. F. Hiller, 26 June 1961, FO 371/156845.
[23] Benjamin Shwadran, 'The Kuwait Incident', *Middle Eastern Affairs*, 13, 1 (1962): 6.
[24] Bulloch, *The Gulf*, p. 62.
[25] Khadduri, *Republican Iraq*, p. 166.
[26] 'Qasim's Policy towards Kuwait', Minute by Hiller, 26 June 1961, FO 371/156845, cited in Snell-Mendoza, 'In Defence of Oil', p. 50. Tension between the Kurdish leader, Mulla Mustafa al-Barzani, and Qassem heightened following the former's visit to Moscow in October 1960 to plead the cause of the Iraqi Kurds with the Soviet Union. Growing disorder culminated in the launching of a major military campaign against the Kurds in September 1961. By the time of Qassem's fall in February 1963, two-thirds of the Iraqi army was engaged in the struggle with Kurdistan. (See Phebe Marr, *The Modern History of Iraq*, Boulder, Colorado: Westview Press, 1985, pp. 176–9; Uriel Dann, *Iraq Under Qassem: A Political History, 1958–1963*, New York: Praeger, 1969, pp. 332–47.) In September 1961, Qassem accused the British Embassy in Baghdad of being behind the Kurdish rising and having spent between £400 000 and £500 000 for the purpose (Telegram from Sir Humphrey Trevelyan to the Foreign Office, No. 1285, 23 Sept 1961, FO 371/157680).

On 27 June, the British Consul General in Basra was forced to concede that 'no reliable informant has seen or heard any unusual troop movements'.[27] The Consul General also reported that Qassem's threats in respect of Kuwait were not taken seriously by Iraqi public opinion.[28] The Ruler of Kuwait, however, was less phlegmatic and on the last day of June requested formal British assistance under the terms of the notes which had been exchanged only eleven days earlier.[29] In response, the Iraqi representative at the United Nations insisted that his country would not resort to the use of force in pursuing its claim to Kuwait.[30]

Despite mounting evidence to the contrary, the Foreign Secretary, Lord Home, warned his Cabinet colleagues on 29 June that there were indications that the Prime Minister of Iraq might move armoured forces to Basra in preparation for an attack on Kuwait.[31] With the Suez precedent firmly in mind, the Cabinet was in agreement on the importance of receiving 'clear and public support' from the United States government in the event of the deployment of British forces.

The prospects for Anglo-American cooperation were not good. A month before Qassem revived Iraqi claims to Kuwait, the Permanent Under-Secretary at the Foreign Office, F. R. Hoyer Millar, bemoaned the lack of Anglo-American planning for the Persian Gulf, warning of 'serious consequences in the event of a sudden emergency arising in the area'.[32] 'It is also really rather ludicrous', he elucidated, 'that there should be an American Admiral stationed in Bahrain alongside a British Admiral ... both of them apparently working in water-tight compartments and not having much idea of what the other is doing.' Discussing the possibility of American assistance in defending Kuwait two days after Qassem's Baghdad press conference, the Foreign Office observed:

> The United States authorities have shown increasing reluctance even to discuss military plans for the area. The State Department have been most careful to avoid any commitment that the United States Government would support the United Kingdom Government if the latter took action in Kuwait.[33]

---

[27] Telegram from Her Majesty's Consul General (Basra) to the Foreign Office, No. 45, 27 June 1961, DEFE 11/411.
[28] British Consulate-General, Basra, monthly summary, July 1961, FO 371/157661.
[29] Telegram from Kuwait to the Foreign Office, No. 314, 30 June 1961, FO 371/156874.
[30] Telegram from Sir Patrick Dean (United Kingdom Mission to the United Nations) to the Foreign Office, No. 1106, 6 July 1961, FO 371/156850.
[31] Cabinet Conclusions, 29 June 1961, CC 36 (61), CAB 128/35 Part 1.
[32] Minute by F. R. Hoyer Millar, 25 May 1961, FO 371/156694.
[33] 'The Possibility of Assistance from the United States in Defending Kuwait', Minute by Walmsley, 27 June 1961, FO 371/156874.

Moreover, the US State Department described Qassem's claim to Kuwait as 'basically [an] inter-Arab controversy'.[34] Furthermore, the State Department expressed fear that 'gratuitous USG entry' into the dispute would merely 'goad Qasim to new intemperance'.[35] Despite the unpromising signals emanating from Washington, US support for possible British intervention in Kuwait was sought.

Anticipating the Ruler's request for help, a message was sent to the United States Secretary of State, Dean Rusk, expressing the hope that the British and American governments would 'act with the closest co-operation'.[36] In asking the State Department for 'full political support', the Foreign Office emphasized: 'The importance of Kuwait to the Western World is such . . . that we cannot take the risk of allowing Qasim to seize it unopposed'.[37] In reply, Rusk assured Home that 'We understand the depth of your obligation, we agree that the independence of Kuwait must not be destroyed by force, and we are prepared to render the full political support you request.'[38] Rusk also offered to prevail upon Saudi Arabia, with which Britain had no diplomatic relations, to mediate in the dispute. In the meantime, the British military build-up proceeded apace. The first contingent of 600 British troops arrived in Kuwait on 1 July. Within five days, this number had risen to 7000.[39]

The lack of hard evidence of a tangible military threat from Iraq has led some to doubt the sincerity of Britain's motives. Marwan Iskandar asserts that Britain's willingness to come to Kuwait's aid resulted from a determination to 'revenge their fiasco in Suez in 1956'.[40] In a similar vein, John Bulloch argues that the Iraqi threat to Kuwait was perceived as an opportunity to 'show that Britain was still a force East of Suez, and that it did still have a special role in the Arab world'.[41] Mustafa Alani has expanded this interpretation, suggesting that the threat to Kuwait from Iraq was contrived in order to 'assert Britain's role in Kuwaiti affairs and to preserve Britain's interests and position there'.[42] In order to pre-empt an Arab solution to the problem, argues Alani, Britain had to give the Iraq–Kuwait dispute the appearance of a military confrontation. This was

---

[34] *Foreign Relations of the United States, 1961–1963. Volume 17: Near East, 1961–1962*, Washington, DC: United States Government Printing Office, 1994, p. 163.

[35] Ibid.

[36] Miriam Joyce, 'Preserving the Sheikhdom: London, Washington, Iraq and Kuwait, 1958–1961', *Middle Eastern Studies*, 31, 2 (1995): 286.

[37] Ibid., p. 287.

[38] Letter from Alfred W. Wells (United States Embassy, London) to A. C. I. Samuel (Private Secretary to the Secretary of State for Foreign Affairs), 30 June 1961, FO 371/156876.

[39] Schofield, *Kuwait and Iraq*, p. 108.

[40] Marwan Iskandar, *The Cloud Over Kuwait*, New York: Vantage Press, 1991, p. 54.

[41] Bulloch, *The Gulf*, p. 63.

[42] Mustafa M. Alani, *Operation Vantage: British Military Intervention in Kuwait 1961*, Surbiton: LAAM, 1990, p. 133.

achieved through the use of inaccurate intelligence reports which exaggerated the scale and imminence of the Iraqi menace.[43] Alani concludes:

> It is difficult to resist the belief that the so-called 'Kuwait crisis' was pure fiction, from which fictitious heroes and villains have emerged. While Iraq has been branded as an aggressor, Britain has cultivated the image of a saviour, and Kuwait, rather unjustifiably, the potential victim. Britain not only created the Iraqi threat, she has also been credited for deterring that threat.[44]

While it is true that Britain did view the immediate military threat from Iraq as remote, Alani's interpretation is open to question. On the one hand, Morice Snell-Mendoza, having full regard to the extent of Britain's economic interests in Kuwait, has convincingly argued that if Qassem's claims were an opening gambit with no military menace, he was 'foolish to think that Britain could afford to operate on that assumption'.[45] Similarly, Nigel John Ashton has shown that although the evidence of an Iraqi move on Kuwait was sketchy, Britain felt compelled to take pre-emptive action owing to doubts about her military capacity to reverse an invasion once it had taken place.[46]

On the other hand, Britain was acutely aware of the possible damage that a prolonged occupation of Kuwait could inflict not only on the legitimacy of the al-Sabah regime,[47] but also on her own standing in the Arab world. As the US Embassy in London recalled: 'the Foreign Office and undoubtedly other members of the Government were reluctant actually to put troops on the ground because of the adverse political results which might flow from such an action'.[48] Throughout the crisis, moreover, Sir Humphrey Trevelyan in Baghdad brought a moderating influence to bear on British policy. On 27 June, for example, he stressed:

> It is clearly preferable from a political point of view, that the Arab States should take the lead in defending Kuwait. They could not be expected to approve the presence of British troops in Kuwait and the despatch of British troops would enable Qasim to conduct effective anti-imperialist propaganda and allege that Kuwait's independence is a sham.[49]

---

[43] Ibid., pp. 108, 250.
[44] Ibid., p. 254.
[45] Snell-Mendoza, 'In Defence of Oil', p. 40.
[46] Nigel John Ashton, 'A Microcosm of Decline: British Loss of Nerve and Military Intervention in Jordan and Kuwait, 1958 and 1961', *The Historical Journal*, 40, 4 (1997): 1073–4; Nigel Ashton, 'Britain and the Kuwaiti Crisis, 1961', *Diplomacy and Statecraft*, 9, 1 (1998): 166.
[47] Ashton, 'Microcosm', p. 1080.
[48] Nigel John Ashton, *Eisenhower, Macmillan and the Problem of Nasser: Anglo-American Relations and Arab Nationalism, 1955–59*, Basingstoke: Macmillan, 1996, p. 227.
[49] Telegram from Trevelyan to the Foreign Office, No. 644, 27 June 1961, PREM 11/3427.

Referring to the impact of Britain's military action on the Arab world, moreover, Trevelyan warned: 'We shall have plenty of sympathy if we defeat Qasim's crude tactics, but little if we have to use British forces for more than a brief period.'[50] The Political Resident, Sir William Luce, was in full agreement, remarking: 'it seems inevitable that the longer we keep any troops in Kuwait the greater will become the pressure to force us out of the Gulf area altogether'.[51] As early as the end of the first week in July, Luce was reporting that 'The rift in Arab views is closing and the whole weight of Arab Nationalist publicity is now swinging back to its traditional target of British imperialism.'[52] 'Since the Iraqi attack has not in fact developed,' echoed Macmillan, 'all the pressure will be turned on us.'[53] In these circumstances, and in contrast with the interpretation of Alani, Britain was keen to promote an Arab solution to the problem.

In an attempt to cultivate Arab support, the Ruler despatched Shaikh Jabir to various regional capitals with instructions to inform his hosts that Kuwait was prepared to ask Britain to withdraw on condition of Kuwait's admittance to the Arab League and the provision of an Arab or United Nations force to replace the British one.[54] On the whole, Britain was prepared to support such moves. '[W]hile the continuance of Kuwaiti independence remains a basic principal of our policy,' insisted Luce, 'we should seek to achieve this by emerging from the immediate situation in a way which does not alienate Kuwait from the Arab world nor draw us into increasing military commitments'.[55] 'I fully agree with Luce's emphasis on the danger of isolating Kuwait from the Arab world', wrote Trevelyan.[56] 'It is equally important', he added, 'that we should retire from the foreground of the picture and that we should not destroy our strong position by getting into conflict with those Arab States which support Kuwait's independence.' Lord Home, furthermore, predicted that a prolonged stay by British troops 'would be likely to create strains inside Kuwait and with other Arab countries'.[57] Macmillan was in full agreement, commenting: 'The sooner we can reduce to a mission (the airfield) or retire altogether, the better.'[58] The Cabinet Official Committee on the Middle East, moreover,

---

[50] Telegram from Trevelyan to the Foreign Office, No. 939, 17 July 1961, DEFE 11/413.
[51] Letter from W. H. Luce to Sir Roger Stevens, No. 1035/61, 16 July 1961, FO 371/156884.
[52] Telegram from Luce to the Foreign Office, No. 422, 7 July 1961, FO 371/156880.
[53] Macmillan diaries, volume 15 second series, 8 July 1961, MSS Macmillan dep. d. 42. See also Harold Macmillan, *Pointing the Way, 1959–1961*, London: Macmillan, 1972, p. 385.
[54] Telegram from J. C. B. Richmond to the Foreign Office, No. 436, 10 July 1961, FO 371/156850.
[55] Letter from Luce to Stevens, No. 1035/61, 16 July 1961, FO 371/156885.
[56] Telegram from Trevelyan to the Foreign Office, No. 976, 24 July 1961, FO 371/156896.
[57] Minute from Lord Home to the Prime Minister, PM/61/99, 21 July 1961, FO 371/156886.
[58] Minute by Harold Macmillan, 23 July 1961, FO 371/156886; Rahman, *Making of the Gulf War*, p. 253.

emphasized that 'Our immediate aim should be to get an effective Arab League force established in Kuwait as soon as possible to ensure its defence'.[59]

On 20 July, Kuwait was admitted to the Arab League. Two days earlier, the Cabinet Defence Committee had pointed out that 'The continued presence of British troops in Kuwait exposed us to increasing political criticism, particularly from other Arab States, which might in time tend to weaken the Ruler's internal position.'[60] Kuwait's membership of the Arab League opened the possibility of that organization assuming responsibility for defending the Shaikhdom. Trevelyan welcomed this prospect, stressing:

> It seems more than ever from here that if an Arab force is offered which amounts to anything more than a demonstration of the Arab League's inability to provide one, it would be fatal to our position and would play straight into Qasim's hands for us to advise the Shaikh to refuse it. Surely that is just what Qasim is hoping will happen to get him out of his present unfavourable position and to turn most international and all Arab opinion squarely against us.[61]

On 12 August, agreement was reached on the provision of an Arab League Security Force which would assume responsibility for the defence of Kuwait.[62] On completion of the accord, the Ruler requested the withdrawal of British troops,[63] who over the succeeding weeks were replaced by around 3300 troops drawn from the United Arab Republic, Saudi Arabia, the Sudan, Jordan, and Tunisia.[64] Britain was prepared to acquiesce in this development, seeing the League force as a political deterrent as much as a military one.[65] With the exception of a small contingent which stayed behind to assist the Kuwait army in maintaining its equipment, all British forces had departed by 10 October.[66]

At the height of the crisis, Trevelyan had recommended: 'Our public line should be that we are concerned to prevent the rape of Kuwait but not to enforce its perpetual spinsterhood.'[67] The departure of British troops and their replacement by Arab forces symbolized Kuwait's changing position, both regional and international, which had been pre-figured by the

---

[59] Minutes of a meeting of the Cabinet Official Committee on the Middle East, 26 July 1961, OME (61) 2nd meeting, CAB 134/2345.
[60] Cabinet Defence Committee, note of a meeting, 18 July 1961, D (61) 48, CAB 131/26.
[61] Telegram from Trevelyan to the Foreign Office, No. 1024, 3 Aug 1961, DEFE 11/414.
[62] Schofield, *Kuwait and Iraq*, pp. 108–9.
[63] Telegram from Rothnie to the Foreign Office, No. 595, 12 Aug 1961, FO 371/156887.
[64] Assiri, *Kuwait's Foreign Policy*, p. 23.
[65] Telegram from Luce to the Foreign Office, No. 587, 9 Sept 1961, PREM 11/3430.
[66] 'Withdrawal of British forces from Kuwait', Minute by Walmsley, 10 Oct 1961, FO 371/156893.
[67] Telegram from Trevelyan to the Foreign Office, No. 939, 17 July 1961, DEFE 11/413; Ovendale, *Transfer of Power in the Middle East*, p. 234.

termination of formal British protection on 19 June 1961. As an official of the Foreign Office conceded at the beginning of the year: 'Mentally it is difficult, but politically it is necessary, to stop thinking of Kuwait as a "Gulf Shaikhdom", and to treat it as the foreign though friendly Arab power which it is.'[68] Nevertheless, Britain's commitment to the Gulf region remained immutable. Reviewing the events of 1961, Luce concluded:

> it is no exaggeration to say that Britain at this moment stands more deeply committed in the Persian Gulf, both politically and militarily, than at any time since the last war, a situation which is in marked contrast with the great contraction of our political and military commitments elsewhere in the world over the past fifteen years.[69]

Referring to the dangers of Middle East oil production being monopolized by powers hostile to the West, officials of the Treasury and Ministry of Power emphasized that 'the survival of Kuwait as an independent entity, its oil policy not subservient to its more powerful neighbours, constitutes a basic insurance'.[70]

The depth of Britain's commitment to the Gulf in general, and Kuwait in particular, presented Kuwait with a problem. 'At the beginning of 1962', recalled Richmond, 'Kuwait faced the task of proving that she was something more than a collection of oil wells sheltering under a new form of British Imperialism'.[71] In attempting to forge a distinct identity as an independent state, the al-Sabah embarked upon a programme of internal reform and external recognition. While Britain supported the al-Sabah's attempts to broaden the political basis of the regime, Kuwait's growing association with the cause of Arab nationalism raised considerable concern. By 1965, Britain even began to question the value of her existing relationship with Kuwait. Nevertheless, on the death of Shaikh Abdullah at the end of the year, British concerns had yet to prompt a major re-assessment of the Anglo-Kuwaiti relationship. This had to wait for a further three years and was induced principally by domestic British considerations.

II

In the first half of 1961 the strict controls on political activity which had been imposed in the wake of the 1959 disturbances were gradually eased. The renewed Iraqi threat, and the consequent need to attract domestic support in this time of peril, persuaded the al-Sabah to accelerate this

---

[68] Minute by Walmsley, 2 Feb 1961, FO 371/156672.
[69] Letter from Luce to Home, No. 98, 22 Nov 1961, FO 371/156670.
[70] 'Kuwait and Middle East Oil', Note by officials of the Treasury and Ministry of Power attached to Selwyn Lloyd's minute to the Prime Minister, 2 Aug 1961, PREM 11/3452.
[71] Letter from Richmond to Home, No. 2, 2 Jan 1963, FO 371/168726.

process. The first newspapers had appeared in March,[72] and on 12 August a new law was introduced permitting the re-opening of clubs and societies.[73] The most significant development, however, was the decision, also in August, to hold elections for a constituent assembly. These elections, open only to native-born Kuwaitis, were held on 30 December with what the British Embassy described as 'deadening decorum'.[74] The 12 000 voters elected twenty representatives from a total of seventy-four candidates. While acting as a provisional legislature, the assembly's main function was to draft the country's constitution. First meeting on 20 January 1962, the assembly was dissolved after submitting its draft constitution to the Amir, who duly gave his approval on 11 November.

The constitution described Kuwait's political system as an hereditary monarchy under the al-Sabah but placed restrictions on the Amir's powers. While executive authority was vested in the Amir and the Cabinet, which had replaced the Supreme Council, legislative authority was shared by the Amir and the new National Assembly.[75] Consisting of fifty members plus all non-elected Cabinet members, the National Assembly's first elections took place in January 1963. Although parties were officially banned, an opposition grouping, led by Ahmad al-Khatib, soon developed. One of its first forays occurred in April when twelve deputies urged the Government to join unity talks with Egypt, Syria, and Iraq.[76] The vitality of the Assembly was also demonstrated in December 1964 when it opposed the newly constructed cabinet on the grounds that some of its members were involved in business in breach of the constitution.[77] Accepting the Assembly's objections, Abdullah formed a new Cabinet in 1965. Commenting on this turn of events, the British Ambassador in Kuwait, G. N. Jackson, observed: 'The Amir has in fact continued his orderly retreat from absolute power, and refused to allow oligarchy to replace it.'[78] The al-Sabah's reforming activities also extended into the sphere of foreign policy.

One of the principal lessons which the al-Sabah learned from the crisis of 1961 was the need to enhance Kuwait's standing in the Arab world. The low regard in which the Amirate was held was painfully revealed during Shaikh Jabir's tour of Arab capitals in July (see Chapter

---

[72] *Kuwait: Annual Review for 1961* enclosed in Richmond's letter to Home, No. 3, 4 Jan 1962, FO 371/162879.

[73] Letter from M. W. Errock to J. A. Snellgrove, No. 1735/64, 22 March 1964, FO 371/174620.

[74] Letter from British Embassy to the Arabian Department, No. 10123/61, 31 Dec 1961, FO 371/162881.

[75] J. E. Peterson, *The Arab Gulf States: Steps Toward Political Participation*, New York: Praeger, 1988, p. 36.

[76] Jill Crystal, *Oil and Politics in the Gulf: Rulers and Merchants in Kuwait and Qatar*, Cambridge: Cambridge University Press, 1995, p. 86.

[77] Peterson, *The Arab Gulf States*, p. 38.

[78] Letter from G. N. Jackson to P. Gordon Walker, No. 4, 17 Jan 1965, FO 371/179834.

5). Commenting on this experience, A. K. Rothnie (Chargé d'Affaires, Kuwait) recalled:

> it came as something of a shock to Shaikh Jabir al-Ahmad when he found the sister Arab nations less than eager to respond and prone to take the line that there was no reason for them to do much to help a state which had in the past, for all its wealth, done little to help them.[79]

In an effort to rectify this impression and cultivate regional support, an economic delegation from Kuwait visited seven Arab countries (the United Arab Republic, Sudan, Libya, Tunisia, Morocco, Lebanon, and Jordan) in October with a view to studying projects in which Kuwaiti money might be invested. On 17 December, Shaikh Jabir announced that the government intended to establish a special fund, the Kuwait Fund for Arab Economic Development (KFAED).[80] At the beginning of 1962, he unveiled more detailed proposals, including the fixing of the Fund's capital at KD 50 million.[81] Since the Kuwaitis found it impossible to make any saving on current expenditure large enough to finance investment in the Arab world, the KD 50 million had to be taken from the reserves.

Although during the 1950s Britain had jealously guarded Kuwait's investments in London, by the early 1960s she was prepared to acquiesce in their depletion. This decision was taken principally for political, rather than economic reasons. 'As we are all agreed', observed Richmond,

> generous investment by Kuwait in her sister states is an essential complement of her reliance on the Arab League for support in the face of the Iraqi claim, and we can only gain, politically at any rate, if £50 million of the much publicised reserves is withdrawn from London and devoted to the Arabs.[82]

Moreover, the Head of the Foreign Office's Arabian Department, A. R. Walmsley, noted candidly: 'We cannot really do anything whatever to stop the Kuwaitis from taking money out of their London reserves for this (or any other purpose).'[83] In the wake of Qassem's claim to Kuwait, the Cabinet Official Committee stressed that it was 'politically desirable that the Kuwaitis should be discreetly encouraged to increase their investments in Arab League countries'.[84] The pragmatism which characterized Britain's

---

[79] Letter from A. K. Rothnie to Home, No. 78, 8 Nov 1961, FO 371/156894.
[80] Letter from Richmond to Walmsley, No. 11115/62, 4 Jan 1962, FO 371/162906.
[81] Telegram from Richmond to Foreign Office, No. 1, 8 Jan 1962, FO 371/162906. The Fund's capital was raised to KD 100 million in 1963, KD 200 million in 1966, and KD 1 billion in 1974 (Soliman Demir, *The Kuwait Fund and the Political Economy of Arab Regional Development*, New York: Praeger Publishers, 1976, p. 6).
[82] Letter from Richmond to Walmsley, No. 11115/62, 4 Jan 1962, FO 371/162906.
[83] Minute by Walmsley, 13 Feb 1962, FO 371/162906.
[84] Minutes of a meeting of the Cabinet Official Committee on the Middle East, 21 Aug 1961, OME (61) 3rd meeting, CAB 134/2345.

approach to Kuwaiti investments was mirrored in the debates about reform of the Kuwait Investment Board.

In 1960, the Foreign Office had suggested the appointment of a Kuwaiti to the KIB, only to see their proposal founder on the opposition of the Board's chairman, H. T. Kemp (see Chapter 5). A year later fresh impetus for Kuwaiti representation on the Board was provided by the International Bank of Reconstruction and Development (IBRD) which produced a report on Kuwait towards the end of 1961. The IBRD, while praising the work of the Kuwait Investment Board, advised the selection of one or two Kuwaitis, initially in a trainee capacity, to participate in the activities of the Board.[85] This recommendation was strongly endorsed by the Foreign Office which argued:

> we have long felt that exclusive British membership of a Board managing such a large proportion of Kuwait's foreign investments is open to criticism, and that it would be in the interests of Kuwait and the United Kingdom that the Board should be more broadly based.[86]

With similar concerns in mind, the Foreign Office supported the IBRD's other main suggestion, namely the creation in Kuwait of a central investment board, on which the KIB would be represented, to coordinate general investment policy.

The first IBRD recommendation was fulfilled in May 1962 with the appointment of Kuwait's Ambassador in London, Khalifa Ghunaim, to the KIB.[87] At the insistence of the Amir, however, Kemp remained in the chair. Reform of Kuwait's investment institutions was delayed. 'Although the Kuwaitis seem to realise the need for planning and co-ordination', explained Richmond, 'they are attempting to do so much at present with so few experienced Kuwaiti officials that the volume of business gets beyond their control.'[88] By the beginning of 1963, nevertheless, an Advisory Council was established under the chairmanship of Shaikh Jabir. The other members were Lord Piercy (Kuwait Investment Board), Eugene Black (former President of the IBRD), Dr Herman J. Abs (President of the Deutsche Bank), Dr Samuel Schweitzer (Chairman of the Swiss Bank Corporation), Dr Marcus Wallenberg (Swedish Central Bank), and Khalifa Ghunaim. The Council first visited Kuwait in April, producing two main conclusions: the importance of reducing government expenditure on land purchases,[89] and the desirability of allocating to the reserves at least 10 per

---

[85] Extracts from the IBRD Report on Kuwait, 28 Nov 1961, pp. 205–6, FO 371/162905.
[86] Telegram from the Foreign Office to Kuwait, No. 84, 19 Jan 1962, FO 371/162906.
[87] 'Kuwait Investment Board', Note by Loombe, 2 May 1962, FO 371/162908.
[88] Letter from Richmond to Walmsley, No. 11116/62, 30 June 1962, FO 371/162908.
[89] In the first six months of 1961, the government spent £43 million on the purchase of land in Kuwait ('Kuwait: Economic Situation', Note by Loombe, 14 Dec 1961, FO 371/162904).

cent of Kuwait's annual revenue.[90] This second recommendation was to prove difficult to fulfil in the light of the growing demands of other Arab states on Kuwait's financial resources.

The first country to benefit from Kuwait's largesse was Jordan, which received a loan of KD 7 500 000 from the KFAED in April 1962.[91] This was followed in quick succession by a grant of KD 7 million to Sudan.[92] In August, moreover, it was announced that interest re-payments on the loan of £1 million concluded with Jordan in 1960 had been deferred in order to ease the Jordanian government's financial difficulties.[93] In responding to the inquiry of the governor of Aden, Sir Charles Johnston, about the Western Aden Protectorate's eligibility for KFAED assistance, Richmond observed:

> My preliminary view is that the Federation would be near the bottom of any order of priority set up by the Kuwaitis for applicants for access to their Arab Development Fund. Their objective in establishing this fund, to put it bluntly, is to buy friends and influence people. The political support which the Western Aden Protectorate would afford to Kuwait seems likely to be a negative quantity, at any rate for the next few years.[94]

Kuwait's attempts to use its wealth as an instrument of foreign policy can be seen most clearly in relation to Iraq.

'For a year and a half', observed Richmond in early 1963, 'Kuwait has enjoyed, thanks to Qasim, the privilege of having two normally incompatible props to her independence, Arab political and British military support.'[95] The overthrow of Qassem in a bloody revolution in February, however, presented Kuwait with an opportunity to take a more active role in securing its separate existence.

In March 1963, the new Iraqi government of Abdul Salam Arif indicated two possible preconditions for his country's recognition of Kuwait's independence: either the abrogation of the Anglo-Kuwaiti exchange of letters of 1961, or the formation of some sort of association between the two states.[96] Not unnaturally, both proved unacceptable to the Amir. Kuwait's bargaining position was strengthened not only by its election as a member of the United Nations on 14 May, but also by Iraq's precarious financial position. In consequence, Kuwait proposed Iraqi

---

[90] Letter from Richmond to R. S. Crawford, No. 11116/63, 13 April 1963, FO 371/168755.
[91] Telegram from Richmond to the Foreign Office, No. 211, 4 April 1962, FO 371/162907.
[92] Letter from W. P. Cranston to G. L. Hobbs, No. 470, 15 April 1962, FO 371/162907.
[93] Letter from Cranston to M. A. Marshall (Foreign Office), No. 1124/62, 8 Aug 1962, FO 371/162909.
[94] Letter from Richmond to Sir Charles Johnston, No. 11115/62, 11 March 1962, CO 1015/2419 CAA 89/726/03 Part A.
[95] Letter from Richmond to Crawford, No. 1035/63, 7 March 1963, FO 371/168738.
[96] Telegram from Richmond to the Foreign Office, No. 138, 24 March 1963, PREM 11/4359.

recognition of its independence and acceptance of the boundaries as defined in 1932 as a basis for discussions.[97] The Amir also refused to be pressured into an early abrogation of the 1961 exchange of letters. On 4 October, representatives from the Iraqi and Kuwaiti governments signed an agreed minute by which Iraq recognized the 'independence and complete sovereignty of the State of Kuwait within its frontiers as specified in the letter of the Prime Minister of Iraq dated July 21, 1932'.[98] Both countries also agreed to exchange diplomatic representatives. Iraq's conciliatory attitude came at a price, however. On 12 October, Kuwait agreed to grant Iraq an interest-free loan of £30 million to be repaid over a period of twenty-five years.[99]

The apparent strengthening of Kuwait's independent status was welcomed by the British. 'Our own interest in the independence of Kuwait', admitted R. S. Crawford (Assistant Under-Secretary of State, Foreign Office),

> is as great as ever and it is likely to remain so having regard to the increasing volume of oil imports required from the Middle East in the years ahead. Kuwait is the great insurance against the West being damaged by major trouble in other oil-producing countries. Our interest is bound up not only with the steady flow of oil but also in its availability on reasonable terms.[100]

Nevertheless, the price which Kuwait was forced to pay for Iraqi recognition was soon being questioned.

The intention behind the KFAED had been to lend money for specific development projects. The £30 million grant to Iraq, however, was untied, being drawn direct from the reserves rather than the KFAED. Having lent money on these terms to Iraq, the Kuwaitis found themselves exposed to similar requests from other Arab countries. In March 1964, Kuwait agreed to grant a governmental loan of £25 million to Egypt at 4 per cent, repayable over fifteen years.[101] '[N]ow that the Kuwaitis have shown themselves open to UAR and Iraqi blackmail', bemoaned one Foreign Office official, 'there seems no reason why they should not continue to receive further requests for aid.'[102] These sentiments proved prophetic. Between March and August 1965, a batch of new loans was concluded with Egypt, Algeria, Morocco, Lebanon, and Sudan, prompting one Foreign Office official to describe Kuwait as the 'milch-cow of the Arab world'.[103] Kuwait's

---

[97] Letter from Errock to Home, No. 76, 3 July 1963, FO 371/168739.
[98] Telegram from Sir Roger Allen to the Foreign Office, No. 1037, 5 Oct 1963, FO 371/168740.
[99] Letter from Jackson to Home, No. 112, 16 Oct 1963, FO 371/168741.
[100] 'Iraq–Kuwait Agreement', Minute by Crawford, 1 Oct 1963, FO 371/168741.
[101] Telegram from Jackson to the Foreign Office, No. 69, 11 March 1964, FO 371/174605.
[102] Minute by Snellgrove, 9 Sept 1964, FO 371/174605.
[103] Minute by M. S. Berthoud, 16 Sept 1965, FO 371/179846.

assiduous efforts to win support in the Arab world through financial contributions were mirrored in the diplomatic sphere.

'Kuwait's foreign policy', opined the Foreign Office at the beginning of 1965, 'is based on the twin pillars of Britain's defence guarantee . . . and Egyptian diplomatic support'.[104] These two apparently incompatible props to Kuwaiti independence placed the Amir and his government in an ambiguous position, neatly summed up by Britain's Ambassador in Kuwait, G. N. Jackson: 'The pattern of relations with Her Majesty's Government seemed the exact reverse, or mirror image, of those with the United Arab Republic: private effusiveness with public frigidity and even attack.'[105] Indeed, when speaking to members of Britain's diplomatic establishment in the Gulf, the Amir expressed not only the warmth of his feelings towards Britain but also his firm intention to maintain the Anglo-Kuwaiti exchange of letters.[106] In private, he even confessed that his family 'put their trust in God and the British'.[107] In public, however, a very different stance was adopted.

Referring to Kuwait in 1964, Jackson observed: 'As a rich man in a poor world it must perforce live dangerously.'[108] In an attempt to lessen the danger, the Kuwaitis felt the need to associate themselves with popular Arab causes. In consequence, Kuwait became something of a haven for groups opposed to British-backed regimes in the Arabian peninsula. Bahraini exiles, rebels from Oman, and leading members of the South Arabian National Liberation Front all sheltered in Kuwait.[109] Press reports, strongly denied by the Amir, also appeared claiming that Kuwait had contributed £80 000 to the Arab League Fund for the Liberation of South Arabia.[110] Reports that the Kuwait office in Dubai was being used for Arab League purposes did nothing to ally British suspicions.[111] To make matters worse, hostility towards Britain manifested itself in the Kuwait National Assembly, the suppression of riots in Bahrain in March 1965 being deplored as 'Imperialist operations'. Press attacks were also commonplace,

---

[104] 'The Situation in Kuwait', Foreign Office Brief, 11 Feb 1965, FO 371/179834.

[105] Letter from Jackson to Gordon Walker, No. 1, 7 Jan 1965, FO 371/179833.

[106] Minute by Walmsley, 4 Jan 1963, FO 371/168784; Telegram from Jackson to the Foreign Office, No. 471, 6 Oct 1963, FO 371/168740; Letter from Luce to Crawford, No. 1042/64, 13 April 1964, FO 371/174595.

[107] Minute by Allen, 27 May 1965, FO 371/179834.

[108] Letter from Jackson to Gordon Walker, No. 75, 11 Nov 1964, FO 371/174595.

[109] 'Anglo-Kuwait Relations', Minute by T. F. Brenchley, 26 March 1965, FO 371/179839.

[110] Letter from A. T. Lamb to M. S. Weir, No. 1695/65G, 10 April 1965, FO 371/179741. The Foreign Office was particularly concerned at the reported existence of a National Liberation Front Office in Kuwait. A. T. Lamb (Consul, Kuwait) was asked to inform the Kuwaitis that 'any support from them for the N.L.F. is all the more illogical, to say the least, in that Kuwait is the main beneficiary from the Aden base which the N.L.F. are out to destroy'. (Letter from Weir to Lamb, BM 1041/365, 19 Jan 1965, CO 1055/75 ADN 58/7/021.)

[111] Telegram from the Foreign Office to Kuwait, No. 383, 8 June 1965, FO 371/179839.

particularly from Egyptian-controlled newspapers such as *Al Talia*.[112] While criticism of Britain in the National Assembly and the press was by no means orchestrated by the government of Kuwait, little was done to curb it. When Jackson urged the Amir to take action, the latter replied that this would merely create a 'ready-made theme for anti-imperialist propaganda'.[113] In seeking to explain such attitudes, Jackson wrote:

> Caught between dependence on both the United Arab Republic and ourselves, the Sabah are trying to be all things to all men. The practice of double talk, from being a subterfuge, has been elevated to the status of a policy, of the wisdom of which they profess to be convinced.[114]

Despite the al-Sabah's private expressions of fidelity, Kuwait's growing association with the causes of Arab nationalism led some in British circles to suggest a reassessment of Anglo-Kuwaiti relations.

'It seems to us here', expostulated Luce in March 1965,

> that the time has come to make strong representations to the Amir of Kuwait about the extent to which his country is being used for purposes which are a serious threat not only to the stability of the Gulf regimes and to the interests of H.M.G. but also to those of Kuwait itself.[115]

A few months later, the Political Resident identified 'certain advantages' in shedding the military commitment to Kuwait, making particular reference to Britain's domestic economic and financial difficulties.[116] British doubts were also expressed about both the seriousness of the Iraqi threat and the likelihood of Kuwait ever actually invoking the terms of the exchange of letters again. With such considerations in mind, an official of the Foreign Office concluded: 'we are paying a premium of 100% for indifferent cover against an improbable risk'.[117] On the other side of the debate, a number of objections were raised to a fundamental alteration in Anglo-Kuwaiti relations.

While Jackson lamented the al-Sabah's tendency to 'pay protection money to the housebreakers while publicly criticising the police', he was not in favour of a redrawing of the relationship with Kuwait.[118] 'Any other regime that we should be likely to get could be much worse,' he stressed, 'and, quite apart from considerations of oil, could cause wide political repercussions all over the Persian Gulf and beyond.' Although conceding that Britain could purchase oil either from a successor regime or elsewhere, Jackson noted that it would be 'hardly at the same price'. The Ambassador

---

[112] Letter from Luce to Crawford, 15 March 1965, FO 371/179741.
[113] Letter from Jackson to Crawford, No. 1011/65G, 8 April 1965, FO 371/179741.
[114] Letter from Jackson to Michael Stewart, No. 32, 30 May 1965, FO 371/179839.
[115] Letter from Luce to Crawford, 15 March 1965, FO 371/179741.
[116] Letter from Luce to Brenchley, No. 1072, 31 May 1965, FO 371/179839.
[117] 'A Heresy', Minute by D. C. P. Gracie, 13 July 1964, FO 371/174610.
[118] Letter from Jackson to Stewart, No. 32, 30 May 1965, FO 371/179839.

also opined that both Shaikh Abdullah, and his chosen successor, Shaikh Sabah Salim, would seek to retain the exchange of letters.

Jackson's views proved persuasive. 'If we put our threats into effect and abrogated the 1961 Exchanges of Letters as a result of the Kuwaitis' "bad behaviour" and failure to meet our terms,' emphasized the Foreign Office, 'it seems clear that we would incur the Kuwaitis' lasting enmity; that they would turn to the U.A.R. and that we would lose all the present benefits which our close association with Kuwait brings.'[119] The Cabinet Official Committee on Defence and Oversea Policy came to a similar conclusion towards the end of October 1965.[120]

Assessing Britain's commitment to Kuwait in the context of a review of Britain's defence spending in the Middle East, the committee stressed:

> Politically Kuwait's independence, especially from Iraq, is important for the stability of the Gulf and the continuance of good relations between the United Kingdom on the one hand and Iran and Saudi Arabia on the other; both the latter would consider that their position had been very seriously weakened by an extremist takeover of Kuwait with its immense resources and wealth.

From the economic point of view, the Committee was keen to emphasize that

> Kuwait has special importance because of its immense oil resources in which B.P. has a fifty per cent share, and because of its position as an independent producing country. So long as these retain their value, as they seem certain to do into the seventies, the basis for Her Majesty's Government's support of Kuwait will remain.

The most serious threat to Kuwait's independence was perceived to be from an internal coup assisted by Iraq. Mindful of the likelihood of Britain's complete withdrawal from the military base in Aden, the committee urged that 'it is vital for the deterrence of Iraq that our forces and facilities in the Gulf should be built up, and seen to be built up, to the level necessary to deal with the threat of a coup in Kuwait'. The committee also comforted itself with the thought that 'as long as the present Amir is alive there should be no difficulty about maintaining the main lines of Anglo-Kuwaiti co-operation'. While prompting a flurry of speculation, the death of the Amir on 24 November 1965 did not precipitate any immediate alteration in Anglo-Kuwaiti relations, Shaikh Sabah pledging himself to the British connection soon after his accession.[121] Indeed, it was not until July 1968 that Shaikh Jabir, the new Prime Minister and heir-apparent,

---

[119] Draft Foreign Office despatch to Kuwait, 22 Oct 1965, FO 371/179839.
[120] The following is based on 'Defence Review Study Middle East: Persian Gulf and South Arabia', Note by the Secretaries, 27 Oct 1965, Annex A: United Kingdom Commitments in the Persian Gulf, OPD (O) (65) 66, CAB 148/45.
[121] Telegram from Jackson to the Foreign Office, No. 53, 13 Dec 1965, FO 371/179839.

Dependence and Independence, 1961–5

declared that Kuwait would not tolerate any foreign presence in the area, British or otherwise.[122] The termination of the exchange of letters, however, was not to take place until 1971. Despite the portentous glow which surrounded Jabir's announcement, the impetus for the abrogation of the Anglo-Kuwaiti defensive alliance came from Britain.

Soon after Labour's return to office in October 1964, the new Prime Minister, Harold Wilson, promised to maintain Britain's 'east of Suez' role.[123] This commitment was soon given substance in the Defence White Paper of February 1965 which described the British contribution to maintaining peace and stability as 'paramount in many areas East of Suez'.[124] Referring specifically to the Persian Gulf, the Foreign Secretary, Michael Stewart, remarked:

> In our absence there would be a security vacuum which would be likely to do grave harm to political stability throughout the area and to the production and transportation of oil, as well as encourage a renewal of Soviet southward pressure.[125]

The harsh economic realities which faced Wilson's administrations, however, soon necessitated far-reaching re-assessments of Britain's global commitments.

Yawning balance of payments deficits, coupled with constant pressure on the pound, were to characterize the early years of Wilson's period in power.[126] As 1965 wore on, the Treasury managed to establish the principle not only that the defence budget should be fixed at £2000 million, but also that 'Britain's strategic coat should in future be cut according to her financial cloth'.[127] In the opinion of John Darwin, the Treasury's victory resulted in 'the most far-reaching change in Britain's world position to occur since the withdrawal from India twenty years before'.[128] The process began with the Defence White Paper of 1966 which relayed the government's decision not to replace Britain's aging fleet of aircraft carriers, the backbone of her east-of-Suez presence.[129] The Defence White Paper also envisaged the abandonment of the British base at Aden when South Arabia became independent in 1967 or 1968.[130] Military assistance to Kuwait,

---

[122] J. B. Kelly, *Arabia, the Gulf and the West*, London: Weidenfeld and Nicolson, 1980, p. 172.
[123] Phillip Darby, *British Defence Policy East of Suez, 1947–1968*, London: Oxford University Press, 1973, p. 284.
[124] *Statement on the Defence Estimates 1965*, London: HMSO, Feb 1965, p. 9, Cmd. 2592.
[125] 'The Middle East', Memorandum by the Secretary of State for Foreign Affairs, 24 March 1965, C. (65) 49, CAB 129/120 Part 2.
[126] Alec Cairncross, *The British Economy since 1945*, Oxford: Blackwell, 1992, p. 151.
[127] John Darwin, *Britain and Decolonisation: The Retreat from Empire in the Post-War World*, Basingstoke: Macmillan, 1988, p. 291.
[128] Ibid.
[129] *Statement on the Defence Estimates 1966. Part I: The Defence Review*, London: HMSO, Feb 1966, p. 10, Cmd. 2901.
[130] Ibid., p. 8.

moreover, was to be limited to air cover, with ground troops being made available only if the Amir provided sufficient notice to enable them to be brought in from Britain or the Far East.[131] The Defence Secretary, Denis Healey, questioned even this reduced commitment, suggesting the restriction of British assistance to air support alone.[132] Anglo-Kuwaiti relations came under renewed pressure following the 1967 Arab–Israeli conflict, the Six-Day War.

Israel's remarkably swift victory not only stunned its enemies, but also fuelled rumours that it had received outside assistance. Suspicion, not surprisingly, fell on Britain and the United States, resulting in an embargo on exports to these two countries by the oil-producing states of the Arab world. While the British Foreign Secretary, George Brown, confidently predicted that Saudi Arabia, Libya, and the Persian Gulf Shaikhdoms would endeavour to restore normal relations with the West, he admitted that 'Kuwait is less reliable owing to the regime's predelication [sic] for nationalist gestures.'[133] Brown was also reported as being 'not happy about the present situation in which the Kuwaitis feel free to discriminate against British interests while we remain committed to their defence'.[134] Although in August the Khartoum Conference of Arab powers agreed to lift the oil embargo, more economic gloom undermined still further Britain's position in the Persian Gulf.

At the beginning of November 1967, the British government assured nervous Gulf rulers that Britain's imminent departure from Aden did not presage an abandonment of her responsibilities to them.[135] However, the devaluation of the pound on 18 November, and subsequent need to reduce government expenditure, exposed the hollowness of Britain's reassurances of only a few days earlier. After bitter Cabinet in-fighting, the Prime Minister announced on 16 January 1968 that British forces would be withdrawn from the Gulf by the end of 1971.[136] It was against this background that Shaikh Jabir announced the abrogation of the exchange of letters and the effective ending of Britain's special position in Kuwait. When the al-Sabah again looked for external support following the Iraqi invasion of 1990, it was the United States, rather than Britain, which acted as guarantor of Kuwaiti independence.

[131] 'Kuwait', Minute by T. F. Brenchley, 23 May 1966, FO 371/185420.

[132] 'Military Assistance to Kuwait', Minute from Denis Healey to the Foreign Secretary, MO/3/7/3, 30 Sept 1966, FO 371/185420.

[133] Annex to 'Arab Attitudes and British Economic Interests in the Middle East', Memorandum by the Secretary of State for Foreign Affairs, 7 July 1967, CAB 129/132 C (67) 123.

[134] Letter from D. M. Day (Assistant Private Secretary to the Secretary of State for Foreign Affairs) to R. M. Hastie-Smith (Assistant Private Secretary to the Secretary of State for Defence), 14 Aug 1967, DEFE 11/548.

[135] Kelly, *Arabia, the Gulf and the West*, pp. 47–8.

[136] Glen Balfour-Paul, *The End of Empire in the Middle East: Britain's Relinquishment of Power in her Last Three Arab Dependencies*, Cambridge: Cambridge University Press, 1994, p. 125.

Conclusion

As a starting point, I take it that our policy in Kuwait is to ensure the uninterrupted and increasing flow of oil to the Western world. All other considerations must yield place to this fundamental necessity.[1]

Our position in Kuwait depends on our relations of confidence with the ruling family.[2]

In July 1958, at the height of the Middle East crisis following the Iraqi Revolution, Harold Macmillan wrote: 'Kuwait, with its massive oil production, is the key to the economic life of Britain'.[3] Indeed, any decline in Kuwait's strategic importance to Britain following Indian independence in 1947 was more than compensated for by the spectacular post-war growth in oil production. By the early 1950s, it was estimated that Kuwait's reserves amounted to 16 per cent of the world's total.[4] In 1953, Kuwait alone provided 58 per cent of Britain's oil needs.[5] The Shaikhdom's value to Britain was measured not only by the quantity of oil exports, but also by the terms under which that oil was purchased. Britain's ability to obtain Kuwait oil for sterling allowed her to conserve scarce post-war dollar reserves. Oil from Kuwait, moreover, mitigated the disruption to Britain's supplies from Iran following the nationalization of the Anglo-Iranian Oil Company in 1951.

---

[1] Letter from Aubrey Halford to Sir Bernard Burrows, No. 1034/6/57, 14 Nov 1957, FO 371/126905.
[2] Telegram from the Foreign Office to Bahrain, No. 1459, 8 Aug 1958, FO 371/132786.
[3] Macmillan diaries, volume 5 second series, 18 July 1958, MSS Macmillan dep. d. 32. See also Harold Macmillan, *Riding the Storm, 1956–1959*, London: Macmillan, 1971, p. 523.
[4] William Roger Louis, 'Musaddiq and the Dilemmas of British Imperialism', in James A. Bill and William Roger Louis (eds), *Musaddiq, Iranian Nationalism and Oil*, London: I. B. Tauris, 1988, p. 247.
[5] Mustafa M. Alani, *Operation Vantage: British Military Intervention in Kuwait 1961*, Surbiton: LAAM, 1990, p. 36.

The Ruler's willingness to invest his money in sterling also contributed towards the stability of the sterling area. As a Foreign Office official commented in 1961: 'the preservation of arrangements under which we secure oil from Kuwait and are assured that Kuwait's investment policy is helpful from the sterling area point of view are the linchpin of the whole structure of our position in the Gulf'.[6] In these circumstances, the maintenance of Kuwait as an independent oil-producer became the overriding concern of British policy. Soon after Abdul Karim Qassem's revival of Iraqi claims to Kuwait, a Foreign Office official remarked:

> our fundamental interest in Kuwait (and in the rest of the Gulf) is the continued independence of Kuwait (and the other states). That is to say that they should continue to have an independent oil policy of their own and their policy should not fall under the control of any Power which is, or is likely to become, seriously hostile to us.[7]

It was with these concerns in mind that Britain despatched military forces to Kuwait in the summer of 1961. When the Foreign Secretary, Lord Home, asserted on 3 July that 'Our concern is to see that the independence of Kuwait is secured',[8] he was speaking no less than the truth. Three days later, Britain submitted a draft resolution to the United Nations Security Council calling upon all states to respect Kuwait's independence and territorial integrity.[9]

The survival of the al-Sabah was also perceived as important in the preservation of the British stake in Kuwait. 'Our best chance of protecting our economic interests', declared the Foreign Office in September 1961, 'lies in the preservation of an independent Kuwait, under the present regime if possible, and the continuance of co-operation between Her Majesty's Government and the Kuwait Government.'[10] Unlike the Hashemite monarchy in Iraq, upon which Britain had also placed great reliance, the al-Sabah proved inveterate survivors. Their endurance can be accounted for in a number of ways.

Shaikh Abdullah's determination to channel oil revenues into development projects and create a modern welfare state clearly increased the numbers who had a stake in the survival of the regime. By the close of the 1950s, over 27 000 boys and nearly 18 000 girls were in school.[11] The opening of the first state hospital in 1949 marked the start of a programme

---

[6] Minute by R. S. Crawford, 6 March 1961, FO 371/156834.
[7] Minute by A. R. Walmsley, 5 July 1961, FO 371/156883.
[8] *Parliamentary Debates, Lords*, Vol. 232, 3 July 1961, col. 1199.
[9] *Foreign Relations of the United States, 1961-1963. Volume 17: Near East, 1961–1962*, Washington DC: United States Government Printing Office, 1994, p. 179.
[10] 'Kuwait', Report by Officials, Sept 1961, C (61) 140, CAB 129/106.
[11] Jill Crystal, *Oil and Politics in the Gulf: Rulers and Merchants in Kuwait and Qatar*, Cambridge: Cambridge University Press, 1995, p. 78.

to provide comprehensive health care. '[T]he Kuwaitis', remarked H. G. Jakins in 1951, 'seem bent on creating a health service which will be a model for the Gulf'.[12] Referring to the results of Shaikh Abdullah's policies, Rosemarie Said Zahlan has noted: 'The ruler had provided his people with a welfare state, the extent of which was unknown even in the most advanced European countries.'[13] Oil revenues allowed the state to make such lavish provisions without levying any taxes. Attractive and abundant employment opportunities were also provided, so much so that by 1955 55.6 per cent of the labour force was employed by the government.[14] The British Ambassador, G. N. Jackson, went so far as to describe the civil service as a 'system of indoor relief for Kuwaitis'.[15] M. R. Asmar, moreover, has demonstrated that this channelling of Kuwaitis into non-productive, bureaucratic sectors was made possible by the large pool of migrant workers from which the state could draw for the rest of the economy.[16] In a similar vein, Muhammad Rumaihi has observed: 'the motive force of the society is not production but the distribution of revenue by the state; actual production of oil is carried out entirely by foreigners, the local population playing a virtually insignificant role in the productive process'.[17] Support for this interpretation is given by Jackson's observation in 1964 that 'if a mysterious plague killed off every Kuwaiti tomorrow the economy would continue very much as it does at present'.[18]

The distributive policies of Shaikh Abdullah helped to insulate the al-Sabah from any serious challenge to their privileged position. As the Political Agent, Aubrey Halford, put it in 1959: 'If the Kuwaiti bandwagon were not a comfortable vehicle for all its passengers, its top-heaviness might have brought it off the road by now.'[19] Three years earlier, a Foreign Office official had noted: 'Kuwait is prosperous and most of the Kuwaitis are too busy making money to cultivate political passions.'[20] However, a number of considerations, besides the distributive policies of the al-Sabah, can be

---

[12] Ibid.
[13] Rosemarie Said Zahlan, *The Making of the Modern Gulf States: Kuwait, Bahrain, Qatar, the United Arab Emirates and Oman*, London: Unwin Hyman, 1989, p. 36.
[14] Jaqueline S. Ismael, *Kuwait: Dependency and Class in a Rentier State*, Gainesville, Florida: University Press of Florida, 1993, p. 106.
[15] Letter from G. N. Jackson to R. A. Butler, No. 129, 24 Dec 1963, FO 371/174584. By 1963, over half current government expenditure was absorbed by the civil service (Letter from M. W. Errock to Lord Home, No. 85 (E), 17 July 1963, FO 371/168751).
[16] M. R. Asmar, 'The State and Politics of Migrant Labour in Kuwait', PhD. thesis, University of Leeds, 1990, pp. 226-7.
[17] Muhammad Rumaihi, *Beyond Oil: Unity and Development in the Gulf*, London: Al Saqi Books, 1986, p. 138.
[18] Letter from Jackson to P. Gordon Walker, No. 75, 11 Nov 1964, FO 371/174595.
[19] Letter from Halford to Sir George Middleton, No. 6, 11 Feb 1959, FO 371/140081.
[20] Minute by C. T. E. Ewart-Biggs, 18 April 1956, FO 371/120550. See also Sir Rupert Hay, *The Persian Gulf States*, Washington, DC: The Middle East Institute, 1959, pp. 104–5.

adduced to explain the survival of the ruling family, the first of which relates to their symbolic value.

Commenting on Shaikh Abdullah a year after Kuwait had achieved full independence, the British Ambassador in Kuwait, J. C. B. Richmond, recorded: 'he provides the focus and the symbol of the political existence of Kuwait and it is difficult to imagine this separate existence continuing without a Sabah ruler'.[21] Richmond went on to state that 'the Amir provides an ideal image of what a Kuwaiti would wish to become, old, wise, conciliatory and rich, and above all with no taint of non-Kuwaiti blood'. Indeed, Shaikh Abdullah provided a powerful stabilizing force amid the stresses and strains which accompanied Kuwait's rapid modernization from the early 1950s. His unimpeachable character,[22] however, did not shield the al-Sabah completely from public obloquy, the rapacity and selfishness of certain members of the family attracting widespread local condemnation.[23] Nevertheless, Kuwaitis, who by 1961 formed barely more than 50 per cent of the total population of 321 621,[24] were conscious of the continuing value of the al-Sabah.

'The Sabah', opined Richmond in 1962, 'have in their favour that they are Kuwaiti to the bone and that they are clearly and visibly the principal safeguard for other born Kuwaitis of the latter's undoubtedly privileged position.'[25] The ruling family also demonstrated a willingness to protect the elite status enjoyed by native-born Kuwaitis. In December 1959, the Naturalization Decree limited Kuwaiti citizenship to those residents, and their heirs, who had resided in the state continuously since 1920.[26] An amendment published in 1960 permitted Arab nationals with ten years residence to become citizens. Nevertheless, the total number of naturalizations was not to exceed fifty in any one year. This amendment was described by the Political Agency in Kuwait as 'reactionary' and indicating

---

[21] Letter from J. C. B. Richmond to Lord Home, No. 40, 6 June 1962, FO 371/162882.

[22] Following a visit to Kuwait in January 1962, Margaret Luce, wife of the Political Resident, wrote of Shaikh Abdullah: 'he is genuinely unimpressed by money, only faintly amused at suddenly having found himself one of the richest men in the world, and he has been absolutely firm about not squandering the new wealth' (Margaret Luce, *From Aden to the Gulf: Personal Diaries, 1956–1966*, Salisbury: Michael Russell, 1987, p. 138).

[23] Letter from Sir Rupert Hay to A. D. M. Ross, 18 Oct 1952, FO 371/98333; Letter from Halford to Burrows, No. 1, 5 Jan 1958, FO 371/132757.

[24] Richard Gott, 'The Kuwait Incident', in D. C. Watt (ed.), *Survey of International Affairs 1961*, London: Oxford University Press, 1965, p. 523, n. 2. In 1960, Richmond had remarked on the Kuwaitis' determination to 'remain a privileged minority in a growing community in which their numbers and to which their contribution grow less and less' (Nigel John Ashton, *Eisenhower, Macmillan and the Problem of Nasser: Anglo-American Relations and Arab Nationalism, 1955–59*, Basingstoke: Macmillan, 1996, p. 222).

[25] Letter from Richmond to Home No. 40, 6 June 1962, FO 371/162882.

[26] Kamal Osman Salih, 'Kuwait: Political Consequences of Modernization, 1750–1986', *Middle Eastern Studies*, 27, 1 (1991): 50.

Conclusion 139

that Kuwaitis had realized that it 'may be more comfortable and profitable not to be pan-Arab'.[27] The al-Sabah's capacity for self-regulation and reform also enhanced their ability to survive challenges to their authority.

Criticism of the al-Sabah, during celebrations in 1959 to mark the first anniversary of the United Arab Republic, stung the ruling family into a flurry of reforming activity, the most notable example of which was the displacement of the malfeasant Shaikh Fahad. 'The shock of February 1', noted Halford, 'brought everyone to his senses. The Family as a whole realised how its very existence had been imperilled by the indiscretions of a few of its members'.[28] Reflecting the new mood, the Kuwait Agency's diary for April–May 1959 commented:

> The Ruling Family as a whole seems to be determined to put itself beyond reproach in the role of benevolent autocrats. Legislation is being churned out at a bewildering speed; no shaikh expects to be allowed to absent himself from his post this summer;[29] and extravagance and corruption are to be rooted out. Shaikh Fahad, for all his qualities, was too vulnerable on all these counts and seemed an obvious victim.[30]

Halford, moreover, observed that

> The Ruling family are going through a phase of earnest desire to put their house in order the better to resist attack from all corners, whether Communist fomented and helped from Iraq and elsewhere abroad or reformist subversion at home.[31]

Such reforming endeavours prompted an official of the Foreign Office to minute: 'I cannot think of any other Ruling family in the Arabian Peninsula which would be capable of such comparatively far sighted measures with regard to their own position in the State.'[32] The determination to expunge the more conspicuous examples of corruption at the time of Shaikh Fahad's demise in 1959 can be compared with the circumstances surrounding Shaikh Abdullah Mubarak's displacement two years later.

---

[27] Letter from the Political Agency, Kuwait, to the Political Residency, Bahrain, No. 1609/10, 17 Feb 1960, FO 371/149101.

[28] Letter from Halford to R. A. Beaumont, No. 10112/59, 25 June 1959, FO 371/140286.

[29] At the beginning of 1958, Halford noted: 'the Shaikhs are tending to spend more and more time on their holidays abroad and do not seem to be taking their responsibilities as Presidents of the Government Departments and, therefore, as Ministers of State, as seriously as they should. At the same time they show little or no sign of being able, or willing, to delegate responsibility to junior officials during their absences. The result is, therefore, that development tends to stagnate and little progress can be made on those matters which are of general interest and benefit to the people of Kuwait as a whole' (Letter from Halford to Burrows, No. 1, 5 Jan 1958, FO 371/132757).

[30] *Confidential Annex to Kuwait Diary No. 5*, covering the period 28 April–25 May 1959, FO 371/140067.

[31] Telegram from Halford to the Foreign Office, No. 316, 17 May 1959, FO 371/140083.

[32] Minute by W. J. Adams, 19 May 1959, FO 371/140083.

Conclusion

In March 1960, the Assistant Political Agent, D. J. McCarthy, reported that Abdullah Mubarak's extravagance was the subject of growing obloquy.[33] A year later, McCarthy's superior, J. C. B. Richmond, likened Abdullah Mubarak to 'an elector of the Holy Roman Empire who having given up hopes of eventual election as emperor retires to his dukedom to plan the taking of the Empire by force'.[34] Clearly suspicious of Abdullah Mubarak's intentions, the Supreme Council set about clipping his wings. An opportunity was provided by a visit from representatives of the International Bank of Reconstruction and Development (IBRD) in the early months of 1961. The resulting report emphasized the need to establish proper budgeting and accounting systems.[35] This recommendation was especially appropriate to Abdullah Mubarak's departments, which provided no accounts for their expenditure. Following detailed and outspoken criticism of his activities and administrative methods in the Supreme Council, Abdullah Mubarak resigned his offices.[36] Soon after, the Ruler's son, Shaikh Sa'ad, was appointed President of the police and public security department.[37] In addition to their preparedness to put their own house in order, the al-Sabah's survival can be ascribed to the fact that the military has not become a major factor in the political process.

In 1949, General Husni al-Zaim seized power in Syria. Although Zaim's period in power was short-lived, his actions established a precedent which was widely followed in the Arab world. During the 1950s, small groups of army officers ousted the existing regimes in Egypt, Iraq, and the Sudan.[38] Only in Jordan and the Yemen did attempted military coups fail. By 1960, the majority of Arabs were living under regimes founded and led by soldiers.[39] In Kuwait, the al-Sabah took care to keep the military firmly under its control. In the 1950s, a small but well-equipped army under the command of members of the ruling family was created.[40] At the time of the Iraqi Revolution, Shaikh Abdullah Mubarak discounted the possibility of subversion within the Kuwait army, stressing that it was a small force

---

[33] Letter from D. J. McCarthy to Walmsley, No. 13836/60, 31 March 1960, FO 371/149056.
[34] Letter from Richmond to Beaumont, No. 10112/61, 12 March 1961, FO 371/156825.
[35] 'Internal Situation in Kuwait', Minute by Beaumont, 12 May 1961, FO 371/156825.
[36] Letter from Richmond to Walmsley, No. 10112/61, 11 June 1961, FO 371/156825.
[37] Letter from Richmond to Walmsley, No. 10112/61, 18 June 1961, FO 371/156825.
[38] Eliezer Be'eri, 'The Waning of the Military Coup in Arab Politics', *Middle Eastern Studies*, 18, 1 (1982): 69.
[39] For accounts of the role of the military in Arab countries, see Eliezer Be'eri, *Army Officers in Arab Politics and Society*, New York: Praeger, 1970; George Haddad, *Revolutions and the Military in the Middle East: The Arab States*, 2 parts, New York: Robert Speller and Sons, 1971 and 1973; P. J. Vatikiotis, *The Egyptian Army in Politics*, Westport, Connetticut: Greenwood Press, 1975 (first published by Indiana University Press, 1961).
[40] 'The Kuwait Army', Memorandum by J. L. Christie, 27 Feb 1960, enclosed in Richmond's letter to Middleton, No. 5, 7 March 1960, DEFE 11/409. See also Roger Owen, *State, Power and Politics in the Making of the Modern Middle East*, London: Routledge, 1992, p. 210.

concentrated in his hands.[41] The only concern was that Abdullah Mubarak might, at some future date, attempt to use armed force in order to pursue his claim to the succession.[42] His displacement in 1961, however, foreclosed this threat. His replacement at the head of the army, Major-General Mubarak al-Abdullah, was conspicuously loyal and, being from a minor branch of the al-Sabah family, had no pretensions to the throne.

In the aftermath of Qassem's renewed claims to Kuwait, Britain discussed the possibility of increasing the size of the army to a brigade group with a company of nearly 50 tanks.[43] Harold Macmillan, however, was decidedly sceptical about this proposal. Apart from doubting whether the Kuwaitis were sufficiently numerous to organize a force of this size, the Prime Minister opined: 'I doubt if it would be wise to entrust them with large quantities of modern arms; after all the tanks which we sold to Iraq were soon used to overturn the Hashemites'.[44] In 1964, Shaikh Jabir (Minister of Finance), Shaikh Sa'ad (Minister of the Interior), Shaikh Mohammad (Minister of Defence), and the Prime Minister, Shaikh Sabah, agreed that too large an army would pose a danger to the family. 'With Nasser as their example,' noted Shaikh Mohammad, 'every young officer in the Arab world imagined himself as a future President of the Republic.'[45] By keeping Kuwait's armed forces relatively small, nevertheless, the al-Sabah exposed Kuwait to the dangers of external attack. In these circumstances the protection of outside powers assumed particular importance.

While the rapid growth of Britain's oil interests in the Gulf states, and particularly Kuwait, provided a new and powerful incentive for maintaining their independence, the new-found wealth also made them more attractive prizes for their larger neighbours. Referring to the Gulf states in May 1956, the Foreign Secretary, Selwyn Lloyd, noted: 'we have on our side the consciousness, in the Rulers if not in the more volatile of their subjects, that they owe the independent existence of their States to our protection'.[46] In explaining the tacit support given to Britain at the time of the Suez crisis, an official of the Foreign Office recorded: 'The Sabah family realise that their position in Kuwait depends in the last resort on the maintenance of the existing relationship with HMG.'[47] Writing three years

---

[41] Telegram from A. K. Rothnie to the Foreign Office, No. 334, 17 July 1958, FO 371/132761.
[42] 'The Supply of Arms for the Forces of Shaikh Abdullah Al-Mubarak at Kuwait', Minute by D. H. M. Riches, 7 June 1956, FO 371/120623.
[43] Minute from Harold Watkinson (Minister of Defence) to the Foreign Secretary, 5 July 1961, FO 371/156883.
[44] Minute from Harold Macmillan to the Foreign Secretary, No. M 221/61, 6 July 1961, FO 371/156883.
[45] Letter from Jackson to T. F. Brenchley, No. 1205/64G, 28 May 1964, FO 371/174595.
[46] 'Persian Gulf', Note by the Secretary of State for Foreign Affairs, 14 May 1956, CP (56) 122, CAB 129/81.
[47] Minute by J. C. Moberly, 28 Nov 1956, FO 371/120684.

later, the former Political Resident, Sir Rupert Hay, noted: 'Both the Rulers and their people at present realize that they owe their independence to British protection, but for which they would by this time have been absorbed by their more powerful neighbours.'[48] The willingness of Shaikh Abdullah in 1961 to replace the 1899 Agreement with an exchange of letters under which Britain committed herself to offering assistance, if so requested, demonstrated the continued importance placed on British military protection.

The al-Sabah's ultimate dependence on Britain for defence did not mean that the ruling family entered a suffocatingly close relationship with the protecting power. Aware of the growing strength of Arab nationalism, the al-Sabah were careful to avoid becoming too closely associated with imperial Britain. Although British experts were employed in the Kuwait government, they remained in an advisory role and enjoyed no formal executive powers. Indeed, the al-Sabah fiercely protected their internal autonomy. Writing in 1956, Selwyn Lloyd stressed: 'In Kuwait the Ruler and his family are jealous of their prerogatives in internal affairs and resent anything that looks like interference on our part.'[49] Reviewing Shaikh Abdullah's reign shortly after his death in November 1965, the British Ambassador in Kuwait, G. N. Jackson, noted: 'His friendly feelings for Britain were the more valuable for not being advertised and because they implied no dangerous dependence, blind partiality or unbecoming subservience.'[50] 'In his relations with Britain', concluded Jackson, 'Abdulla Salim appeared to have drawn wisely the lesson from Iraq and Jordan that for an Arab, since 1948, to have the reputation of being "a friend of Britain" brings advantage neither to the man concerned nor to Britain herself.'

---

[48] Hay, *Persian Gulf States*, p. 69.
[49] 'Persian Gulf', Note by the Secretary of State for Foreign Affairs, 14 May 1956, CP (56) 122, CAB 129/81. See also 'An Analysis of the Position and Problems of the United Kingdom Government in the States of the Persian Gulf', Commonwealth Relations Office Memorandum, 6 June 1956, DO 35/10065.
[50] Letter from Jackson to Michael Stewart, No. 56, 5 Dec 1965, FO 371/179854.

Appendix 1: Oil Production and Revenue, 1946–65

Year	Oil Production (millions of barrels)	Revenue (KD thousands)
1946	5.9	200
1947	16.2	no data
1948	46.5	3425
1949	89.9	2950
1950	125.7	3100
1951	204.9	7500
1952	273.4	34850
1953	314.6	60161
1954	349.8	69302
1955	402.8	100498
1956	405.5	103921
1957	424.8	110161
1958	522.4	149734
1959	525.9	146843
1960	619.2	168605
1961	633.3	164702
1962	714.6	188814
1963	765.2	(1963–4) 198772
1964	842.2	(1964–5) 258400
1965	861.5	(1965–6) 279180

Source: Y. S. F. al-Sabah, *The Oil Economy of Kuwait*, London: Kegan Paul International, 1980, pp. 47, 52.

Appendix 2: Political Agents, Kuwait

Jakins, Herbert George (b. 1897)
Acting Consul-General, Alexandria, 1948; transferred to Bahrain 1949; acted as Political Resident, Persian Gulf and Political Agent, Bahrain; Political Agent, Kuwait, 1949–51.

Pelly, Cornelius James (b. 1908)
CMG (1952), OBE (1944); Consul, Bushire, 1945; Political Agent at Bahrain, 1947; Political Agent, Kuwait, 1951–5; Acting Political Resident, Bahrain, 1952.

Bell, Gawain Westray (1909–95)
KCMG (1957); CBE (1955); MBE mil. (1942); served with HM Forces, 1941–5; member of the Sudan Political Service, 1931–41 and 1945–55; Political Agent, Kuwait, 1955–7.

Halford, Aubrey Seymour (b. 1914)
CMG (1958); entered the Foreign Office, 1937; Deputy Secretary-General, Council of Europe, 1949; Counsellor, Tokyo, 1953; acting Chargé d'Affaires, Seoul, 1954; Counsellor and Consul-General, Benghazi, 1955; Political Agent, Kuwait, 1957–9.

Richmond, John Christopher Blake (1909–90)
CMG (1959), KCMG (1963); Oriental Counsellor, Baghdad, 1947; acted as Chargé d'Affaires, Baghdad, 1948; transferred to the Foreign Office, 1951; Counsellor and Consul-General, Amman, 1953; acted as Chargé d'Affaires, 1953 and 1954; Consul-General, Houston, 1955; transferred to Cairo, 1959; Political Agent, Kuwait, 1959–61; Consul-General, Kuwait, 1961; Ambassador, Kuwait, 1961–3.

Appendix 3: Political Residents, Persian Gulf

Hay, William Rupert (1893–1962)
KCMG (1952), KICE (1947); entered Political Department, Government of India, 1920; Deputy Secretary External Affairs Department, Government of India, 1936–40; Resident Waziristan, 1940–1; Resident, Persian Gulf, 1941–2; Revenue and Judicial Commissioner, Baluchistan, 1942–3; Agent to the Governor-General, Resident, and Chief Commissioner, Baluchistan, 1943–6; Political Resident, Persian Gulf, 1946–53.

Burrows, Bernard Alexander Brocas (b. 1910)
KCMG (1958), CMG (1950); appointed as 3rd Secretary to the Foreign Office, 1934; transferred to Cairo, 1937; Head of the Eastern Department, Foreign Office, 1947; transferred to Washington as Counsellor, 1950; Political Resident, Persian Gulf, 1953–8.

Middleton, George Humphrey (b. 1910)
KCMG (1955), CMG (1950); Head of Personnel Department, Foreign Office, 1949; transferred to Tehran as Counsellor, 1951; acted as Chargé d'Affaires, 1951 and from 28 Jan 1952 until the rupture of relations on 31 Oct 1952; seconded to the Commonwealth Relations Office and appointed Deputy United Kingdom High Commissioner, India, 1953; Ambassador, Beirut, 1956; Political Resident, Persian Gulf, 1958–61.

Luce, William Henry Tucker (1907–77)
GBE (1961), KCMG (1957); served in the Sudan service, 1930–56; Governor and Commander-in-Chief, Aden, 1956–60; Political Resident, Persian Gulf, 1961–6; Personal Representative of the Foreign and Commonwealth Office Secretary for the Persian Gulf, 1970–2.

Appendix 4: British Politicians

Eden, R. Anthony (1897–1977)
1st Earl of Avon (1961), KG (1954); MP, 1923–57; Secretary of State for Foreign Affairs, 1935–8, for Dominion Affairs, 1939–40, for War, 1940, for Foreign Affairs, 1940–5; Deputy Leader of the Opposition, 1945–51; Secretary of State for Foreign Affairs and Deputy Prime Minister, 1951–5; Prime Minister, 1955–7.

Heath, Edward (b. 1916)
KG (1992), MBE (1946), PC (1945); MP, 1950 to the present; Government Chief Whip, 1955–9; Minister of Labour, 1959–60; Lord Privy Seal with Foreign Office responsibilities, 1960–3; Secretary of State for Industry, Trade, Regional Development and President of the Board of Trade, 1963–4; Leader of the Opposition, 1965–70; Prime Minister, 1970–4; Leader of the Opposition, 1974–5.

Home, Alexander Frederick Douglas- (1903–95)
14th Earl of Home (1951–63), Baron, (1974); MP, 1931–45, 1950–1, 1963–74; Secretary of State for Commonwealth Relations, 1955–60; Secretary of State for Foreign Affairs, 1960–3; Prime Minister, 1963–4; Leader of the Opposition, 1964–5; Secretary of State for Commonwealth Affairs, 1970–4.

Macmillan, M. Harold (1894–1986)
1st Earl of Stockton (1984); MP, 1924–9, 1931–45, 1945–64; Secretary of State for Foreign Affairs, 1955; Chancellor of the Exchequer, 1955–7; Prime Minister, 1957–63.

Selwyn Lloyd, John Selwyn Brooke (1904–78)
Baron (1976); MP, 1945–70; MP and Speaker of the House of Commons, 1971–7; Minister of State, Foreign Office, 1951–4; Minister of Supply, 1954–5; Minister of Defence, 1955; Secretary of State for Foreign Affairs, 1955–60; Chancellor of the Exchequer, 1960–2; Lord Privy Seal, Leader of the House of Commons, 1963–4.

Appendix 5: Rulers of Kuwait

Shaikh Ahmad (1885–1950)
Son of Shaikh Jabir (r. 1915–17) and nephew of Shaikh Salim (r. 1917–21); visited Britain, 1919; assumed power on 24 March 1921; signed oil concession agreement with the Kuwait Oil Company, 23 Dec 1934; faced widespread internal opposition to his rule, 1938–9.

Shaikh Abdullah (1895–1965)
Son of Shaikh Salim (r. 1917–21) and cousin of Shaikh Ahmad (r. 1921–50); temporary Ruler following the death of his father; president of the Kuwait *Majlis*, 1938–9; headed the finance department during the 1940s; Ruler of Kuwait, 1950–65.

Shaikh Sabah (1913–77)
Son of Shaikh Salim (r. 1917–21) and half-brother of Shaikh Abdullah (r. 1950–65); head of the police department until 1959; head of the health department, 1959–61; Minister of Foreign Affairs and Deputy Prime Minister, 1962; appointed Heir-Apparent, Oct 1962; Prime Minister, 1963–5; Ruler of Kuwait, 1965–77.

Shaikh Jabir (1926–)
Son of Shaikh Ahmad (r. 1921–50) and nephew of Shaikh Abdullah (r. 1950–65); head of public security, Ahmadi, 1949–59; President of the finance department from 1959; Minister of Finance and Economy, 1962–3; Deputy Prime Minister and Minister of Finance and Industry, 1963–5; Minister of Commerce, 1965; Prime Minister, 1965–77; Ruler of Kuwait, 1977 to the present.

Appendix 6: Al-Sabah Family Tree

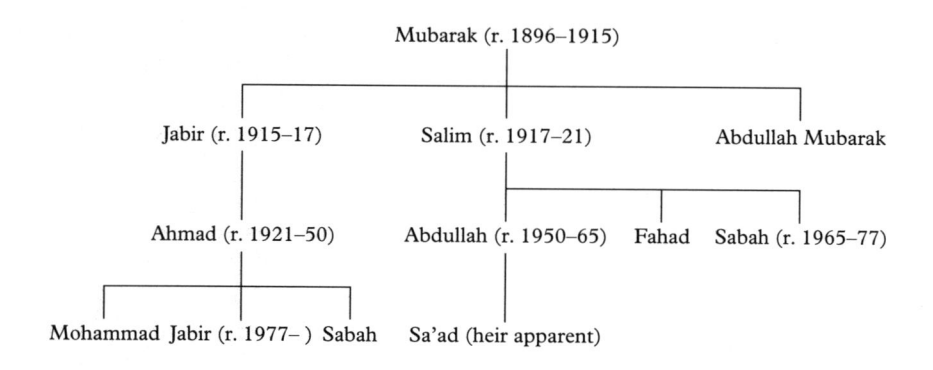

```
                        Mubarak (r. 1896–1915)
        ┌───────────────────────┼───────────────────────┐
   Jabir (r. 1915–17)      Salim (r. 1917–21)       Abdullah Mubarak
        │              ┌─────────┼─────────┬─────────────┐
   Ahmad (r. 1921–50)  Abdullah (r. 1950–65)  Fahad  Sabah (r. 1965–77)
     ┌──┴──┐                    │
Mohammad Jabir (r. 1977– ) Sabah   Sa'ad (heir apparent)
```

Bibliography

Unpublished Sources

Official Documents

Public Record Office, London

Cabinet Office
CAB 128   Cabinet Minutes
CAB 129   Cabinet Memoranda
CAB 130   Ad-Hoc Committees: General and Miscellaneous Series
CAB 131   Defence Committee
CAB 134   Cabinet Committees: General Series from 1945
CAB 148   Defence and Oversea Policy Committee and Sub-Committee: Minutes and Papers, 1964–70

Colonial Office
CO 1015   Aden: Original Correspondence
CO 1055   Aden: Original Correspondence

Ministry of Defence
DEFE 7   Registered Files: General Series
DEFE 11   Chiefs of Staff Committee: Registered Files

Commonwealth Relations Office
DO 35   Original Correspondence: General

Foreign Office
FO 371   Political Departments: General Departments
FO 1016   Embassy and Consular Archives: Persian Gulf Residencies and Agencies

Ministry of Fuel and Power
POWE 33   Petroleum: Correspondence and Papers

Prime Minister's Department
PREM 11   Prime Minister's Office: Correspondence and Papers, 1951–64

Treasury
T 231   Exchange Control Division: Files
T 236   Overseas Finance Division: Files

India Office Library and Records, London

R/15/1   Political Residency: Bushire, 1763–1947
R/15/5   Political Agency: Kuwait, 1904–1947

Bank of England, London

OV 72   Persian Gulf
OV 73   Middle East
EC 5   Exchange Control Act

Company Records

BP Archive, University of Warwick

Records of the Kuwait Oil Company

Private Papers

Bodleian Library, Oxford

MSS Macmillan dep. d. 32   Macmillan diaries, volume 5 second series
MSS Macmillan dep. d. 42   Macmillan diaries, volume 15 second series

Middle East Centre, St Antony's College, Oxford

Papers of H. R. P. Dickson
Papers of Sir Rupert Hay

Churchill Archives Centre, Cambridge

HSTD 2/2   Papers of W. F. Hasted: Letters relating to development in Kuwait, 1952–4.

Published Official Papers

Exchange of Notes regarding Relations between the United Kingdom of Great Britain and Northern Ireland and the State of Kuwait, 19 June 1961, London: HMSO, 1961, Cmd. 1409.
Foreign Relations of the United States, 1958–1960. Volume 11: Lebanon and Jordan, Washington, DC: United States Government Printing Office, 1992.
Foreign Relations of the United States, 1958–1960. Volume 12: Near East Region; Iraq, Iran, Arabian Peninsula, Washington, DC: United States Government Printing Office, 1993.
Foreign Relations of the United States, 1961–1963. Volume 17: Near East, 1961–1962, Washington, DC: United States Government Printing Office, 1994.

Bibliography

Parliamentary Debates, Commons, Volume 642 (1960–1).
Parliamentary Debates, Lords, Volume 232 (1960–1).
Statement on the Defence Estimates 1965, London: HMSO, Feb 1965, Cmd. 2592.
Statement on the Defence Estimates 1966. Part I: The Defence Review, London: HMSO, Feb 1966, Cmd. 2901.

Books and Articles

Abir, Mordechai, *Saudi Arabia in the Oil Era: Regimes and Elites; Conflict and Collaboration*, London: Croom Helm, 1988.
Abu-Hakima, Ahmad Mustafa, *History of Eastern Arabia 1750–1800: The Rise and Development of Bahrain and Kuwait*, Beirut: Khayats, 1965.
Abu-Hakima, Ahmad Mustafa, *The Modern History of Kuwait, 1750–1965*, London: Luzac and Company, 1983.
Ahmed, A. Ahmed, 'Kuwait Public Commercial Investment in Arab Countries', *Middle Eastern Studies*, 31, 2 (1995): 293–306.
Alani, Mustafa M., *Operation Vantage: British Military Intervention in Kuwait 1961*, Surbiton: LAAM, 1990.
Alghanim, Salwa, *The Reign of Mubarak al-Sabah: Shaikh of Kuwait 1896–1915*, London: I. B. Tauris, 1998.
Anderson, Ewan W. and Rahidian, Khalil H., *Iraq and the Continuing Middle East Crisis*, London: Pinter Publishers, 1991.
Anderson, Irvine H., *Aramco, the United States and Saudi Arabia: A Study of the Dynamics of Foreign Oil Policy, 1933–1950*, Princeton, NJ: Princeton University Press, 1981.
Anderson, Irvine H., 'The American Oil Industry and the Fifty-Fifty Agreement of 1950', in James A. Bill and William Roger Louis (eds), *Musaddiq, Iranian Nationalism and Oil*, London: I. B. Tauris, 1988, pp. 143–63.
Aruri, Naseer H., *Jordan: A Study in Political Development, 1921–1965*, The Hague: Martinus Nijhoff, 1972.
Ashton, Nigel John, *Eisenhower, Macmillan and the Problem of Nasser: Anglo-American Relations and Arab Nationalism, 1955–59*, Basingstoke: Macmillan, 1996.
Ashton, Nigel John, 'A Microcosm of Decline: British Loss of Nerve and Military Intervention in Jordan and Kuwait, 1958 and 1961', *The Historical Journal*, 40, 4 (1997): 1069–83.
Ashton, Nigel, 'Britain and the Kuwaiti Crisis, 1961', *Diplomacy and Statecraft*, 9, 1 (1998): 163–81.
Assiri, Abdul-Reda, *Kuwait's Foreign Policy: City-State in World Politics*, Boulder, Colorado: Westview Press, 1990.
Balfour-Paul, Glen, *The End of Empire in the Middle East: Britain's Relinquishment of Power in her Last Three Arab Dependencies*, Cambridge: Cambridge University Press, 1994.
Bamberg, J. H., *The History of the British Petroleum Company: Volume 2: The Anglo-Iranian Years, 1928–1954*, Cambridge: Cambridge University Press, 1994.

al-Baharna, Husain M., *The Arabian Gulf States: Their Legal and Political Status and Their International Problems*, second edition, Beirut: Librairie Du Liban, 1975.
Bar-On, Mordechai, 'David Ben-Gurion and the Sèvres Collusion', in William Roger Louis and Roger Owen (eds), *Suez 1956: The Crisis and its Consequences*, Oxford: Clarendon Press, 1991, pp. 145–60.
Be'eri, Eliezer, *Army Officers in Arab Politics and Society*, New York: Praeger, 1970.
Be'eri, Eliezer, 'The Waning of the Military Coup in Arab Politics', *Middle Eastern Studies*, 18, 1 (1982): 69–81.
Bell, Sir Gawain, *Shadows on the Sand*, London: C. Hurst and Company, 1983.
Bulloch, John, *The Gulf: A Portrait of Kuwait, Qatar, Bahrain, and the UAE*, London: Century Publishing, 1984.
Burrows, Bernard, *Footnotes in the Sand: The Gulf in Transition, 1953–1958*, Salisbury: Michael Russell, 1990.
Busch, Briton Cooper, *Britain and the Persian Gulf, 1894–1914*, Berkeley and Los Angeles: University of California Press, 1967.
Busch, Briton Cooper, 'Britain and the Status of Kuwayt, 1896–1899', *Middle East Journal*, 21, 2 (1967): 187–98.
Cable, James, *Intervention at Abadan: Plan Buccaneer*, Basingstoke: Macmillan, 1991.
Cain, P. J. and Hopkins, A. G., *British Imperialism: Crisis and Deconstruction, 1914–1990*, London: Longman, 1993.
Cairncross, Alec, *The British Economy since 1945*, Oxford: Blackwell, 1992.
Carlton, David, *Anthony Eden: A Biography*, London: Allen Lane, 1981.
Carlton, David, *Britain and the Suez Crisis*, Oxford: Basil Blackwell, 1988.
Chisholm, A. H. T., *The First Kuwait Oil Concession Agreement: A Record of the Negotiations, 1911–1934*, London: Frank Cass, 1975.
Cohen, Michael, *Palestine and the Great Powers, 1945–1948*, Princeton, NJ: Princeton University Press, 1982.
Cohen, Michael J., *Palestine to Israel: From Mandate to Independence*, London: Frank Cass, 1988.
Cohen, Michael, 'A Note on the Mansion House Speech, May 1941', *Asian and African Studies*, 11, 3 (1977): 375–86.
Crystal, Jill, *Kuwait: The Transformation of an Oil State*, Boulder, Colorado: Westview, 1992.
Crystal, Jill, *Oil and Politics in the Gulf: Rulers and Merchants in Kuwait and Qatar*, Cambridge: Cambridge University Press, 1995.
Crystal, Jill, 'Abdullah al-Salim al-Sabah', in Bernard Reich (ed.), *Political Leaders of the Contemporary Middle East and North Africa*, New York: Greenwood Press, 1990, pp. 8–14.
Dann, Uriel, *Iraq Under Qassem: A Political History, 1958–1963*, New York: Praeger, 1969.
Dann, Uriel, *King Hussein and the Challenge of Arab Radicalism: Jordan, 1955–1967*, New York: Oxford University Press, 1989.
Darby, Phillip, *British Defence Policy East of Suez, 1947–1968*, London: Oxford University Press, 1973.
Darwin, John, *Britain and Decolonisation: The Retreat from Empire in the Post-War World*, Basingstoke: Macmillan, 1988.

Darwin, John, *The End of the British Empire: The Historical Debate*, Oxford: Blackwell, 1991.
Dawisha, A. I., *Egypt in the Arab World: The Elements of Foreign Policy*, London: Macmillan, 1976.
Dekmejian, R. Hrair, *Egypt under Nasser: A Study in Political Dynamics*, London: University of London Press, 1972.
Demir, Soliman, *The Kuwait Fund and the Political Economy of Arab Regional Development*, New York: Praeger Publishers, 1976.
Devereux, David R., *The Formulation of British Defence Policy Towards the Middle East, 1948–56*, London: Macmillan, 1990.
al-Ebraheem, Hassan A., *Kuwait: A Political Study*, Kuwait: Kuwait University Press, 1975.
Elliot, Matthew, *'Independent Iraq': The Monarchy and British Influence, 1941–58*, London: Tauris Academic Studies, 1996.
Elliot, Matthew, 'The Death of King Ghazi: Iraqi Politics, Britain and Kuwait in 1939', *Contemporary British History*, 10, 3 (1996): 63–81.
Elm, Mostafa, *Oil, Power and Principle: Iran's Oil Nationalization and its Aftermath*, Syracuse, NY: Syracuse University Press, 1992.
El-Rayyes, Riad N., 'Arab Nationalism and the Gulf', in B. R. Pridham (ed.), *The Arab Gulf and the Arab World*, London: Croom Helm, 1988, pp. 67–94.
Eppel, Michael, 'Iraqi Politics and Regional Policies, 1945–9', *Middle Eastern Studies*, 28, 1 (1992): 108–19.
Farouk-Sluglett, Marion and Sluglett, Peter, 'The Social Classes and the Origins of the Revolution', in Robert A. Fernea and William Roger Louis (eds), *The Iraqi Revolution of 1958: The Old Social Classes Revisited*, London: I. B. Tauris, 1991, pp. 118–41.
Finnie, David H., *Shifting Lines in the Sand: Kuwait's Elusive Frontier with Iraq*, London: I. B. Tauris, 1992.
Fitzgerald, C. P., *The Birth of Communist China*, Harmondsworth: Penguin Books, 1964.
Fullick, Roy and Powell, Geoffrey, *Suez: The Double War*, London: Leo Cooper, 1990.
Gangal, S. C., 'India and the Commonwealth', in M. S. Rajan (ed.), *India, Foreign Relations during the Nehru Era*, Bombay: Asia Publishing House, 1976, pp. 77–102.
Gott, Richard, 'The Kuwait Incident', in D. C. Watt (ed.), *Survey of International Affairs 1961*, London: Oxford University Press, 1965, pp. 519–45.
Haddad, George, *Revolutions and the Military in the Middle East: The Arab States*, 2 parts, New York: Robert Speller and Sons, 1971 and 1973.
Hahn, Peter L., *The United States, Great Britain, and Egypt, 1945–1956: Strategy and Diplomacy in the Early Cold War*, Chapel Hill, NC: The University of North Carolina Press, 1991.
Halliday, Fred, *Arabia Without Sultans*, Harmondsworth: Penguin Books, 1979.
Halliday, Fred, 'The Gulf Between Two Revolutions: 1958–1979', in Tim Niblock (ed.), *Social and Economic Development in the Arab Gulf*, London: Croom Helm, 1980, pp. 210–38.
Hay, Sir Rupert, *The Persian Gulf States*, Washington, DC: The Middle East Institute, 1959.

Holden, David, and Johns, Richard, *The House of Saud*, London: Sidgwick and Jackson, 1981.
Holland, R. F., *European Decolonization: An Introductory Survey*, Basingstoke: Macmillan, 1985.
Hollier, Anita, 'The BP Archive', *Contemporary Record*, 7, 3 (1993): 654–62.
Hopwood, Derek, *Egypt: Politics and Society, 1945–90*, third edition, London: HarperCollins, 1991.
Iskandar, Marwan, *The Cloud Over Kuwait*, New York: Vantage Press, 1991.
Ismael, Jacqueline S., *Kuwait: Dependency and Class in a Rentier State*, Gainesville, Florida: University Press of Florida, 1993.
Jasse, Richard L., 'The Baghdad Pact: Cold War or Colonialism?', *Middle Eastern Studies*, 27, 1 (1991): 140–56.
Joyce, Miriam, *Kuwait, 1945–1996: An Anglo-American Perspective*, London: Frank Cass, 1998.
Joyce, Miriam, 'Preserving the Sheikhdom: London, Washington, Iraq and Kuwait, 1958–1961', *Middle Eastern Studies*, 31, 2 (1995): 281–92.
Katouzian, Homa, 'Oil Boycott and the Political Economy: Musaddiq and the Strategy of Non-oil Economics', in James A. Bill and William Roger Louis (eds), *Musaddiq, Iranian Nationalism and Oil*, London: I. B. Tauris, 1988, pp. 203–27.
Kelidar, A. R., 'The Arabian Peninsula in Arab and Power Politics', in Derek Hopwood (ed.), *The Arabian Peninsula: Society and Politics*, London: George Allen and Unwin, 1972, pp. 145–59.
Kelly, J. B., *Arabia, the Gulf and the West*, London: Weidenfeld and Nicolson, 1980.
Kerr, Malcolm H., *The Arab Cold War: Gamal 'Abd al-Nasir and His Rivals, 1958–1970*, London: Oxford University Press, 1971.
Khadduri, Majid, *Independent Iraq, 1932–1958: A Study in Iraqi Politics*, second edition, London: Oxford University Press, 1960,
Khadduri, Majid, *Republican Iraq: A Study in Iraqi Politics since the Revolution of 1958*, London: Oxford University Press, 1969.
Khadduri, Majid, 'Iraq's Claim to the Sovereignty of Kuwayt', *New York University Journal of International Law and Politics*, 23 (1990): 5–34.
Khalidi, Rashid, 'Consequences of the Suez Crisis in the Arab World', in William Roger Louis and Roger Owen (eds), *Suez 1956: The Crisis and its Consequences*, Oxford: Clarendon, 1991, pp. 377–92.
Khalidi, Rashid, 'The Impact of the Iraqi Revolution on the Arab World', in Robert A. Fernea and William Roger Louis (eds), *The Iraqi Revolution of 1958: The Old Social Classes Revisited*, London: I. B. Tauris, 1991, pp. 106–18.
Khouja, M. W. and Sadler, P. G., *The Economy of Kuwait: Development and Role in International Finance*, London: Macmillan 1979.
Kingston, Paul W. T., *Britain and the Politics of Modernization in the Middle East, 1945–1958*, Cambridge: Cambridge University Press, 1996.
Krozewski, Gerold, 'Sterling, the "Minor" Territories, and the End of Formal Empire, 1939–1958', *The Economic History Review*, 46, 2 (1993): 239–65.
Krozewski, Gerold, 'Finance and Empire: The Dilemma Facing Great Britain in the 1950s', *The International History Review*, 18, 1 (1996): 48–69.
Kyle, Keith, *Suez*, London: Weidenfeld and Nicolson, 1991.

Kyle, Keith, 'Suez and the Waldegrave Initiative', *Contemporary Record*, 9, 1 (1995): 378–93.
Lacouture, Jean and Simonne, *Egypt in Transition*, London: Methuen, 1958.
Lapping, Brian, *End of Empire*, London: Guild Publishing, 1985.
Lenczowski, George, *Oil and State in the Middle East*, New York: Cornell University Press, 1960.
Little, Douglas, 'A Puppet in Search of a Puppeteer? The United States, King Hussein, and Jordan, 1953–1970', *The International History Review*, 17, 3 (1995): 512–44.
Little, Douglas, 'His Finest Hour? Eisenhower, Lebanon and the 1958 Middle East Crisis', *Diplomatic History*, 20, 1 (1996): 27–54.
Lloyd, Selwyn, *Suez 1956: A Personal Account*, London: Jonathan Cape, 1978.
Longrigg, Stephen Hemsley, *Oil in the Middle East: Its Discovery and Development*, second edition, London: Oxford University Press, 1961.
Lorimer, J. G., *Gazetteer of the Persian Gulf, Oman and Central Arabia*, Vol. 1, Part 1B, Westmead, Farnborough: Gregg International Publishers Limited, 1970 (first published Calcutta, 1915).
Louis, William Roger, *The British Empire in the Middle East, 1945–1951: Arab Nationalism, the United States, and Postwar Imperialism*, Oxford: Clarendon, 1984.
Louis, William Roger, 'Musaddiq and the Dilemmas of British Imperialism', in James A. Bill and William Roger Louis (eds), *Musaddiq, Iranian Nationalism and Oil*, London: I. B. Tauris, 1988, pp. 228–60.
Louis, William Roger, 'The British and the Origins of the Iraqi Revolution', in Robert A. Fernea and William Roger Louis (eds), *The Iraqi Revolution of 1958: The Old Social Classes Revisited*, London: I. B. Tauris, 1991, pp. 31–61.
Louis, William Roger, 'The Tragedy of the Anglo-Egyptian Settlement of 1954', in William Roger Louis and Roger Owen (eds), *Suez 1956: The Crisis and its Consequences*, Oxford: Clarendon, 1991, pp. 43–71.
Louis, William Roger and Robinson, Ronald, 'The Imperialism of Decolonization', *Journal of Imperial and Commonwealth History*, 22, 3 (1994): 462–511.
Love, Kennett, *Suez: The Twice-Fought War*, London: Longman, 1970.
Lucas, W. Scott, *Divided We Stand: Britain, the United States and the Suez Crisis*, London: Hodder and Stoughton, 1991.
Lucas, W. Scott, 'The Path to Suez: Britain and the Struggle for the Middle East, 1953–56', in Anne Deighton (ed.), *Britain and the First Cold War*, Basingstoke: Macmillan, 1990, pp. 253–72.
Lucas, W. Scott, 'Redefining the Suez "Collusion"', *Middle Eastern Studies*, 26, 1 (1990): 88–112.
Luce, Margaret, *From Aden to the Gulf: Personal Diaries, 1956–1966*, Salisbury: Michael Russell, 1987.
Macmillan, Harold, *Riding the Storm, 1956–1959*, London: Macmillan, 1971.
Macmillan, Harold, *Pointing the Way, 1959–1961*, London: Macmillan, 1972.
Maddy-Weitzman, Bruce, 'Jordan and Iraq: Efforts at Intra-Hashimite Unity', *Middle Eastern Studies*, 26, 1 (1990): 65–75.
Mansfield, Peter, *The Arabs*, London: Penguin Books, 1985.
Mansfield, Peter, *Kuwait: Vanguard of the Gulf*, London: Hutchinson, 1990.
Marlowe, John, *Arab Nationalism and British Imperialism: A Study in Power Politics*, London: The Cresset Press, 1961.

Marlowe, John, *The Persian Gulf in the Twentieth Century*, London: The Cresset Press, 1962.
Marr, Phebe, *The Modern History of Iraq*, Boulder, Colorado: Westview Press, 1985.
Mendelson, Maurice and Hulton, Susan, 'Iraq's Claim to Sovereignty over Kuwait', in Richard Schofield (ed.), *Territorial Foundations of the Gulf States*, London: UCL Press, 1994, pp. 117–52.
Morris, Benny, *The Birth of the Palestine Refugee Problem, 1947–1949*, Cambridge: Cambridge University Press, 1987.
al-Mughni, Haya, *Women in Kuwait: The Politics of Gender*, London: Saqi Books, 1993.
Morsy, Laila Amin, 'Britain's Wartime Policy in Egypt, 1940–42', *Middle Eastern Studies*, 25, 1 (1989): 64–94.
Newton, C. C. S., 'Sterling Crisis of 1947 and the British Response to the Marshall Plan', *The Economic History Review*, 37, 3 (1984): 391–408.
Oren, Michael B., 'A Winter of Discontent: Britain's Crisis in Jordan, December 1955–March 1956', *International Journal of Middle East Studies*, 22 (1990):171–84.
Ovendale, Ritchie, *The Origins of the Arab–Israeli Wars*, London: Longman, 1984.
Ovendale, Ritchie, *Britain, the United States and the Transfer of Power in the Middle East, 1945–1962*, London: Leicester University Press, 1996.
Ovendale, Ritchie, 'Great Britain and the Anglo-American Invasion of Jordan and Lebanon in 1958', *The International History Review*, 16, 2 (1994): 284–303.
Owen, Roger, *State, Power and Politics in the Making of the Modern Middle East*, London: Routledge, 1992.
Penrose, Edith and E. F., *Iraq: International Relations and National Development*, London: Ernest Benn, 1978.
Petersen, Tore Tingvold, 'Anglo-American Rivalry in the Middle East: The Struggle for the Buraimi Oasis, 1952–1957', *The International History Review*, 14, 1 (1992): 71–91
Peterson, J. E., *The Arab Gulf States: Steps Toward Political Participation*, New York: Praeger, 1988.
Podeh, Elie, *The Quest for Hegemony in the Arab World: The Struggle over the Baghdad Pact*, Leiden: E. J. Brill, 1995.
Podeh, Elie, 'The Struggle over Arab Hegemony after the Suez Crisis', *Middle Eastern Studies*, 29, 1 (1993): 91–110.
Podeh, Elie, 'Ending an Age-Old Rivalry: The *Rapprochement* between the Hashemites and the Saudis, 1956–1958', in Asher Susser and Aryeh Shmuelevitz (eds), *The Hashemites in the Modern Arab World: Essays in Honour of the Late Professor Uriel Dann*, London: Frank Cass, 1995, pp. 85–108.
Podeh, Elie, 'The Drift towards Neutrality: Egyptian Foreign Policy during the Early Nasserist Era, 1952–55', *Middle Eastern Studies*, 32, 1 (1996): 159–78.
Porter, A. N., and Stockwell, A. J., *British Imperial Policy and Decolonization, 1938–1964*, 2 vols, Basingstoke: Macmillan, 1987 and 1989.
Pridham, B. R. (ed.), *The Arab Gulf and the West*, London: Croom Helm, 1985.
Raad, Zeid, 'A Nightmare Avoided: Jordan and Suez 1956', *Israel Affairs*, 1, 2 (1994): 288–308.

Rahman, H. *The Making of the Gulf War: Origins of Kuwait's Long-Standing Territorial Dispute with Iraq*, Reading: Ithaca Press, 1997.

Rahman, Habibur, 'Kuwaiti Ownership of Warba and Bubiyan', *Middle Eastern Studies*, 29, 2 (1993): 292–306.

Rathmell, Andrew, *Secret War in the Middle East: The Covert Struggle for Syria, 1949–1961*, London: Tauris Academic Studies, 1995.

Richmond, J. C. B., *Egypt 1798–1953: Her Advance towards a Modern Identity*, London: Methuen, 1977.

Rumaihi, Muhammad, *Beyond Oil: Unity and Development in the Gulf*, London: Al Saqi Books, 1986.

Rush, Alan, *Al-Sabah: History and Genealogy of Kuwait's Ruling Family, 1752–1987*, London: Ithaca Press, 1987.

al-Sabah, Y. S. F., *The Oil Economy of Kuwait*, London: Kegan Paul International, 1980.

Safran, Nadav, *Saudi Arabia: The Ceaseless Quest for Security*, Ithaca, NY: Cornell University Press, 1988.

Salibi, Kamal S., *The Modern History of Lebanon*, London: Weidenfeld and Nicolson, 1965.

Salibi, Kamal, *The Modern History of Jordan*, London: I. B. Tauris, 1993.

Salih, Kamal Osman, 'Kuwait: Political Consequences of Modernization, 1750–1986', *Middle Eastern Studies*, 27, 1 (1991): 46–66.

Salih, Kamal Osman, 'The 1938 Kuwait Legislative Council', *Middle Eastern Studies*, 28, 1 (1992): 66–100.

Satloff, Robert B., *From Abdullah to Hussein: Jordan in Transition*, New York: Oxford University Press, 1994.

Schenk, Catherine R., *Britain and the Sterling Area: From Devaluation to Convertibility in the 1950s*, London: Routledge, 1994.

Schenk, Catherine R., 'Closing the Hong Kong Gap: The Hong Kong Free Dollar Market in the 1950s', *The Economic History Review*, 47, 2 (1994): 335–53.

Schenk, Catherine R., 'Finance and Empire: Confusions and Complexities: A Note', *The International History Review*, 18, 4 (1996): 869–72.

Schofield, Richard, *Kuwait and Iraq: Historical Claims and Territorial Disputes*, second edition, London: Royal Institute of International Affairs, 1993.

Schofield, Richard (ed.), *Territorial Foundations of the Gulf States*, London: UCL Press, 1994.

Schofield, Richard, 'The Kuwaiti Islands of Warbah and Bubiyan, and Iraqi Access to the Gulf', in Richard Schofield (ed.), *Territorial Foundations of the Gulf States*, London: UCL Press, 1994, pp. 153–75.

Seale, Patrick, *The Struggle for Syria: A Study of Post-War Arab Politics, 1945–1958*, new edition, London: I. B. Tauris, 1986.

Shwadran, Benjamin, *The Middle East, Oil and the Great Powers*, third edition, Jerusalem: Israel Universities Press, 1973.

Shwadran, Benjamin, 'The Kuwait Incident', *Middle Eastern Affairs*, 13, 1 (1962): 2–13.

Silverfarb, Daniel, *Britain's Informal Empire in the Middle East: A Case Study of Iraq, 1929–1941*, New York: Oxford University Press, 1986.

Silverfarb, Daniel, *The Twilight of British Ascendancy in the Middle East: A Case Study of Iraq, 1941–1950*, Basingstoke: Macmillan, 1994.

Silverfarb, Daniel, 'The Revision of Iraq's Oil Concession, 1949–52', *Middle Eastern Studies*, 32, 1 (1996): 69–95.
Smith, Simon C., 'British Records on Kuwait', *European Review of History*, 2, 2 (1995): 273–4.
Smith, Simon C., 'Rulers and Residents: British Relations with the Aden Protectorate, 1937–59', *Middle Eastern Studies*, 31, 3 (1995): 509–23.
Snell-Mendoza, Morice, 'In Defence of Oil: Britain's Response to the Iraqi Threat towards Kuwait, 1961', *Contemporary British History*, 10, 3 (1996): 39–62.
Strange, Susan, *Sterling and British Policy: A Political Study of an International Currency in Decline*, Oxford: Oxford University Press, 1971.
al-Tajir, Mahdi Abdulla, *Bahrain 1920–1945: Britain, the Shaikh and the Administration*, London: Croom Helm, 1987.
Tal, Lawrence, 'Britain and the Jordan Crisis of 1958', *Middle Eastern Studies*, 31, 1 (1995): 39–57.
Terry, Janice J., *The Wafd, 1919–1952: Cornerstone of Egyptian Political Power*, London: Third World Centre for Research and Publishing, 1982.
The GCC *Border Disputes Seminar: With Special Reference to Iraq and Kuwait*, London: Gulf Centre for Strategic Studies, 1992.
Tibawi, A. L., *A History of Modern Syria including Lebanon and Palestine*, London: Macmillan, 1969.
Tomlinson, B. R., 'Indo-British Relations in the Post-Colonial Era: The Sterling Balances Negotiations, 1947–49', *Journal of Imperial and Commonwealth History*, 13, 3 (1985): 142–62.
Townsend, John, 'Some Reflections on the Life and Career of Sir Percy Cox', *Asian Affairs*, 24, 3 (1993): 259–72.
Trevelyan, Humphrey, *The Middle East in Revolution*, London: Macmillan, 1970.
Tuson, Penelope, *The Records of the British Political Residency and Agencies in the Persian Gulf*, London: India Office Library and Records, 1979.
Tzahor, Zeev, 'Holocaust Survivors as a Political Factor', *Middle Eastern Studies*, 24, 4 (1988): 432–44.
Vatikiotis, P. J., *The Egyptian Army in Politics*, Westport, Connecticut: Greenwood Press, 1975 (first published by Indiana University Press, 1961).
Vatikiotis, P. J., *Nasser and His Generation*, New York: St Martin's, 1978.
Vatikiotis, P. J., *The History of Modern Egypt: From Muhammad Ali to Mubarak*, fourth edition, London: Weidenfeld and Nicolson, 1991.
Vaïsse, Maurice, 'France and the Suez Crisis', in William Roger Louis and Roger Owen (eds), *Suez 1956: The Crisis and its Consequences*, Oxford: Clarendon Press, 1991, pp. 131–43.
Warburg, Gabriel, 'Lampson's Ultimatum to Faruq, 4 February 1942', *Middle Eastern Studies*, 11, 1 (1975): 24–32.
Warner, Geoffrey, 'Review Article: The United States and the Suez Crisis', *International Affairs*, 67, 2 (1991): 303–17.
Wilkinson, John C., *Arabia's Frontiers: The Story of Britain's Boundary Drawing in the Desert*, London: I. B. Tauris, 1991.
Winstone, H. V. F. and Freeth, Zahra, *Kuwait: Prospect and Reality*, London: George Allen and Unwin, 1972.
Wyatt, David K., *Thailand: A Short History*, New Haven, Connecticut: Yale University Press, 1984.

Yapp, M. E., *The Making of the Modern Near East, 1792–1923*, London: Longman, 1987.
Yapp, M. E., *The Near East since the First World War*, London: Longman, 1989.
Yapp, Malcolm, 'The Nineteenth and Twentieth Centuries', and 'British Policy in the Persian Gulf', in Alvin J. Cottrell (ed.), *The Persian Gulf States: A General Survey*, Baltimore: Johns Hopkins University Press, 1980, pp. 41–100.
Zahlan, Rosemarie Said, *The Making of the Modern Gulf States: Kuwait, Bahrain, Qatar, the United Arab Emirates, and Oman*, London: Unwin Hyman, 1989.
Zahlan, Rosemarie Said, 'Hegemony, Dependence and Development in the Gulf', in Tim Niblock (ed.), *Social and Economic Development in the Arab Gulf*, London: Croom Helm, 1980, pp. 61–79.

Theses

Asmar, M. R., 'The State and Politics of Migrant Labour in Kuwait', PhD. thesis, University of Leeds, 1990.
Gargash, A. M., 'Political Participation in Kuwait and the Arab Emirates: 1938–1979', PhD. thesis, University of Cambridge, 1989.
Hashim, Saeed Khalil, 'The Influence of Iraq on the Nationalist Movements of Kuwait and Bahrain, 1920–1961', PhD. thesis, University of Exeter, 1984.
al-Mdairis, Falah, 'The Arab Nationalist Movement in Kuwait from its Origins to 1970', PhD. thesis, University of Oxford, 1987.

Index

Abd al-Ilah, 83, 89, 90, 112
Abdullah, King of Jordan, 82–3
Abdullah, Shaikh (r. 1950–65), 110 n. 71, 147 (biog.), 147
  abdication, 39, 42
  and Arab League, 66, 93, 94, 94 n. 118, 96, 122
  and Arab nationalism, 67
  and Arab Union, 85, 86, 94
  and Arab world, 79, 107, 110, 122, 123, 130, 142
  and British Advisers 21–5, 46, 48
  and British business, 54
  claims to succession, 20–1
  and constitution, 125
  and date gardens, 47–8
  death, 124, 142
  and development board, 27, 42
  and extra-territoriality, 101–02
  and Kemp, H. T., 34, 39, 43
  and Kuwait Oil Company, 31–2, 34–5, 55–6
  and *Majlis*, 10, 12, 13
  and Nasser, 93
  and popularity, 23
  and Qassem, Abdul Karim, 116, 117
  redistribution of wealth, 136–7
  relations with Britain, 68, 92, 94, 95–6, 96–7, 111, 114, 119, 122, 130, 131, 132, 142
  relations with Iraq, 86, 128–9
  Ruler of Kuwait, 21
  and Shaikh Abdullah Mubarak, 20–1, 24, 29, 42
  and Shaikh Ahmad, 6, 9, 17
  and Shaikh Fahad, 24, 41, 99
  and sterling area, 39, 43, 74, 136
  and Suez crisis, 70–1
  symbolic role, 138
Abdullah Jabir, Shaikh, 69
Abdullah Mubarak, Shaikh, 69, 91, 92
  and Britain, relations with, 28–9, 71, 102
  character, 25
  and development board, 28
  and the military, 140–1
  resignation, 140

  and Shaikh Abdullah, 20–1, 24, 29, 42
  and Shaikh Fahad, 98
  succession, claims to, 20–1
  and Suez crisis, 71
Abu Dhabi, 80
Aden, 130 n. 110, 132, 133, 134
Aden Protectorate, 75, 75 n. 107, 128
Advisory Council, 127
Ahmad, Shaikh (r. 1921–50), 147 (biog.)
  and American Independent Oil Company, 31
  and British Advisers, 11, 16–17, 18–19, 30
  and Cable and Wireless, 54
  character of, 7, 11
  and 1921 Council, 10 n. 53
  death, 20
  and Iraq, 7, 8, 9, 117
  and *Majlis*, 10–13
  political philosophy, 9
  and Qatar, 19 n. 27
  and Shaikh Abdullah, 6, 9, 17
Alani, Mustafa, 120–1, 122
Algeria, 63, 69, 129
American Independent Oil Company (AMINOIL), 31, 33, 35
Aniza, 3
Anglo-Egyptian treaty (1936), 61, 111
Anglo-Iranian Oil Company
  changes name, 6 n. 26
  income tax, claims relief on, 34, 56–7, 56 n. 138
  nationalization and effects of, 32, 34 n. 125, 37, 67, 135
Anglo-Persian Oil Company, 6
Arabian-American Oil Company (ARAMCO), 32, 55–6
Arabian Oil Company, 109, 110, 110 n. 71
Arab League, 57, 66, 67, 92–3, 94, 96, 97, 118, 123
Arab nationalism, 1, 2, 66, 67, 68, 81–2, 100, 110, 122, 124, 131, 142
Arab Union, 83, 84, 85, 86, 87, 90, 91, 94, 116
Arif, Abdul Salam, 128
Ashton, Nigel John, 29, 65, 83 n. 25, 121

Asmar, M. R., 137
Aswan dam, 62
Aulad Salim, 13, 17, 18, 24, 41

Baath Party, 81, 82
Baghdad Pact, 62, 74, 75, 83, 89, 90
al-Baharna, Husain M., 117
Bahrain, 14, 16, 17, 26, 29, 46, 92, 130
Bani Utub, 3
al-Barrack, Muhammad, 9, 10
al-Barzani, Mulla Mustafa, 118 n. 26
Beaumont, R. A., 102, 112
Belgrave, Charles, 16, 29
Bell, G. W., 58, 68, 70, 71, 144 (biog.)
  and British interests in Kuwait, 50
  and Crichton, 77–8
  and Political Resident, 49 n. 84
  and Shaikh Abdullah Mubarak, 42
  and Suez crisis, 72, 73, 77
Ben-Gurion, David, 63–4
'Big Five', the, 51, 53, 54, 55
Board of Trade, 44
British advisers, 11, 16, 17–20, 21–3, 39, 142
  senior adviser, 40, 45–6, 49–50
  see also, Crichton, G. C. L.; Hasted, W. F.; Roper, H. L.
British companies, 51 n. 95
  see also Anglo-Iranian Oil Company
Anglo-Persian Oil Company; 'Big Five', the; British Petroleum; Cable and Wireless; Kuwait Oil Company; Shell Oil
British Petroleum, 56, 56 n. 137, 132
Brown, George, 134
Bubiyan, 6, 7, 87
Bulloch, John, 118, 120
Buraimi oasis, 80
Burgan, 6, 46
Burrows, B. A. B., 18, 49, 67, 68–9, 80, 81, 86, 93, 95, 145 (biog.)
  and federation of Gulf States, 74–5
  instructions, 44–5
  and senior adviser, 48
  and Suez crisis, 72–3
Butler, R. A., 8, 46
Butler, Victor, 52

Cable and Wireless, 54–55
Caccia, Sir Harold, 56
Cain, P. J., 105–06
Carlton, David, 65
Challe, Maurice, 63
Chamoun, Camille, 91
China, 101 n. 5

Churchill, Winston, 46, 62
Clubs, 70, 97, 125
Cobbold, C. F., 77
Colonial Office, 43
Commonwealth, the British, 118
Conference of Maritime Nations, 69
Constituent assembly, 125
Council, see *Majlis*
Cox, Sir Percy, 5–6
Cranston, W. P., 107, 108
Crawford, R. S., 112, 129
Crichton, G. C. L., 25–7, 29, 34, 45
  and development board, 27–8, 42
  and Hasted, 52–3
  resignation, 77
  and senior adviser, views on, 40
  and Shaikh Fahad, 43
Crystal, Jill, 2, 24
Currie, Sir Phillip, 4,
Curzon, Lord, 5

Darwin, John, 61, 65, 133
Defence White Papers, 133
Devaluation, 134
Dickson, H. R. P., 15,
Dulles, Allen, 91
Dulles, John Foster
  and Kuwait, 92 n. 92,
  and Lebanon, 91
  and Suez crisis, 64, 69
Duncan, Enoch Sevier, 41

East of Suez, 133
Eden, Anthony, 146 (biog.)
  and Arab unity, 92–3
  and Canal Zone, 61
  collusion, 63–4, 63 n. 35
  and Iraqi-Jordanian axis, 83
  and Nasser, 62, 63
  resignation, 65
  and Shaikhdoms, Persian Gulf, 38
Egypt
  and Britain, 58, 59, 61–2, 73, 111, 112
  and Israel, 61
  and Kuwait, 67, 68, 68 n. 69, 93, 129, 130
  and Saudi Arabia, 62, 89
  and Suez war, 64, 81
  union with Syria, 82
Eisenhower, Dwight D., 63, 92
Erskine, General, 61
Ewart-Biggs, C. T. E., 54
Exchange Control, 75–6, 76 n. 112, 104–05
Extra-territoriality, 101 n. 5, 101–03, 103 n. 19

Index

Fahad Salim, Shaikh, 91
  and Britain, 41, 98–9
  and Cable and Wireless, 55
  character, 41
  corruption, 41, 98, 139
  and Crichton, 43
  death, 99
  and development board, 43
  and Hasted, W. F., 42, 43, 52
  resignation, 99
  and Shaikh Abdullah, 24, 41, 99
  and Shaikh Abdullah Mubarak, 98
  and Suez crisis, 71
Farouk, King, 59, 59 n. 8, 61
Feisal, King I, 111
Feisal, King II, 84, 86, 90, 97
Foreign Office
  and Arab League, 93
  and Arab unity, 98 n. 137, 100
  and British Advisers, appointment of, 21, 40
  and British companies, 52, 55
  and development board/development, 27–8, 29, 50–1
  and executive council, 40
  and Kuwait Investment Board, 108, 127
  and Kuwait Oil Company Concession, 33
  and occupation of Kuwait, 71–2, 71 n. 89
  and Persian Gulf, 14, 75, 100
  political agreements, 109
  and sterling area, 33
  and surplus revenues, Kuwaiti, 38
Fowle, T. C., 9–10, 11, 12, 14
France, 63–4, 69
Furlonge, G. W., 38

Gaitskill, Hugh, 64
Garabet, Salim, 41
Gaury, G. S. de, 8, 9, 12, 14, 16
Gentlemanly capitalism, 105–06
Gethin, J. A. F., 23, 29
Ghazi, King, 8, 13 n. 72
Ghunaim, Khalifa, 127
Glubb, Sir John, 62, 83
Godley, Sir Arthur, 4,
Greenway, Sir Charles, 6
Gulf Oil Corporation, 6, 33, 34

Habash, George, 70
Haines, C. H., 103
Halford, Aubrey, 86, 93, 95, 101, 109–10, 137, 144 (biog.)
  and al-Sabah, 81, 99, 100, 139, 139 n. 29
Halliday, Fred, 36, 66

Hashemites, 2, 87, 88, 89, 136, 141
Hasted, W. F., 27, 27 n. 83, 52 n. 106, 54 n. 126
  and Crichton, 52–3
  demoted, 52
  and development, 50, 51
  doubts about, 45
  resignation, 54
  and Shaikh Fahad, 42, 43, 52
Hay, Sir Rupert, 14, 66, 142, 145 (biog.)
  and British Advisers, 17, 18, 19–20, 21–2, 23, 40, 42
  and Fahad, Shaikh, 41
  and federation of Gulf States, 74 n. 106
  and nationalization of Anglo-Iranian Oil, 68
  political developments, 40, 57
  and succession, views on, 21
  and surplus revenue, Kuwaiti, 38
  and welfare state, 50
Hayter, Sir William, 94
Healey, Denis, 134
Heath, Sir Edward, 112–13, 146 (biog.)
Heikel, Mohammed, 81
Hickinbotham, Sir Tom, 75 n. 107.
Home, Lord, 113, 119, 120, 122, 136, 146 (biog.)
Hood, Lord, 92
Hopkins, A. G., 105–06
Hoyer Millar, F. R., 119
Hulton, Susan, 117
Hussein, King, 62–3, 82, 82 n. 21, 83, 84, 89, 91, 108

Ibn Saud, Abdul Aziz, 5, 6, 80
India, 2, 103–04, 133, 135
Informal empire, 115
International Bank of Reconstruction and Development, 127, 140
Iraq, 5, 6, 9, 13, 136
  and Baghdad Pact, 62
  and Britain, 59, 65, 73, 111–12, 113
  and Egypt, 88, 125
  and instability, 87
  and Jordan, 82–3, 84, 89
  and Kuwait, 8, 47, 84, 85–6, 87, 93, 108, 115–18, 128–9, 132
  Revolution (1958), 29, 90, 91, 116, 135
  and Saudi Arabia, 88–9
  and Suez crisis, 88
  and Syria, 82
Iraq Petroleum Company, 32
Iskandar, Marwan, 120
Ismailia, 61
Israel, 59, 60–1, 63 n. 35, 63–4, 72, 73, 134

Jabir, Shaikh (r. 1915–17), 6
Jabir, al-Ahmad Shaikh (r. 1977–), 98, 147 (biog.)
  and Advisory Council, 127
  Arab countries, tour of, 108, 122, 125–6
  and Britain, 132, 134
  British jurisdiction, 102
  and currency reform, 104
  and investment, 107
  and the military, 141
  President, finance department, 99
Jabri, Majadin, 52, 53
Jabr, Salih, 112
Jackson, G. N., 130, 131, 137, 142
Ja'far, Izzat, 11, 21
Jakins, H. G., 20, 137, 144 (biog.)
  and British Advisers, 21, 24
  compares Kuwait and Bahrain, 26
  and Crichton, 26, 27
  and nationalization of Anglo-Iranian Oil, 67
  Political Agent, Kuwait, 21
Johnston, C. H., 84, 128
Jordan, 59, 62, 65, 73, 91, 108, 113, 113 n. 88, 123, 126, 128
  and Baghdad Pact, 83, 89
  and Iraq, 82–3, 84, 89
Jordan, L. T., 39

Kemball, Arnold, 3
Kemp, H. T., 19
  and British Advisers, 23, 24, 25
  functions of, 19 n. 22
  and investment, 39, 43
  and Kuwait Investment Board, 44, 108, 127
  and Shaikh Abdullah, 34, 39, 43
  and Southwell, C. A. P. , 56
Kennet, Lord, 44
Khadduri, Majid, 118
Khalidi, Rashid, 88
Khartoum Conference, 134
al-Khatib, Ahmad, 69, 70, 97, 125
Knox, S. G., 4
Korean War, 30
Krozewski, Gerold, 106
Kurdistan, 118 n. 26
Kuwait
  and Arab League, 123
  and Arab world, 58, 66–7, 78, 79, 80, 81, 85 n. 43, 94–5, 96, 104–05, 115, 121, 122, 124, 125–6, 129–30
  currency reform, 103–05
  elections, 125
  military intervention, British, 71 n. 89, 71–2, 92, 114, 120

and Nasser, 69, 73
nationalism, Kuwaiti, 50, 101, 103
occupation, proposed British, 64, 93
and Ottoman empire, 3–4, 5, 31 n. 105, 46–7, 117
relations with Britain, 4, 5, 7, 7–8, 44–6, 49–50, 51–2, 53–4, 65, 69, 70, 73, 75, 77, 78, 79, 80, 81, 93, 95–6, 102, 105, 109, 110, 112–14, 115, 120, 122, 123–4, 130–4, 136
relations with Egypt, 67, 68, 68 n. 69, 129, 130
relations with Iraq, 7–8, 47, 80, 84, 85–6, 87, 93, 108, 115–18, 128–9, 132
relations with Kuwait Oil Company, 55
relations with Saudi Arabia, 5, 68, 80
and sterling area, 31, 36, 74, 76–7, 106
sterling balances, 106–07
and United Arab Republic, 85, 85 n. 43, 97
and United Nations, 128
welfare state, 50, 137
Kuwait Fund for Arab Economic Development (KFAED), 108, 126, 126 n. 81, 128, 129
Kuwait gap, 75–7
Kuwait Investment Board (KIB), 44, 108–09, 127
Kuwait oil, 6
  and expansion, 30, 37–8, 143
  importance to Britain, 75, 113, 124, 129, 131, 132, 135, 136
Kuwait Oil Company (KOC), 110
  and British Advisers, 22–3
  concession, 6
  concession revision, 16, 31–5, 55–7
  formation, 6
  increases production, 37
  and *Majlis*, 11, 14
  political agreement, 109
  relations with Kuwait, 55
  suspension of operations, 14

Lampson, Sir Miles, 59, 59 n. 8
Lansdowne, Lord, 5
Lapping, Brian, 65
Lausaunne, Treaty of, 8, 117
Lebanon, 59, 91, 126, 129
Libya, 65, 126, 134
Lloyd, Selwyn, 146 (biog.)
  and Arab League, 93
  British jurisdiction, 102
  and coup, possible, 91

and Gulf States, 64, 68, 75, 141
Kuwaiti independence, 95–6, 110–11
and Nuri Said, 87, 88
and the al-Sabah, 142
and senior adviser, 46
and Suez crisis, 63 n. 36, 64–5
Loombe, C. E., 38, 38 n. 17, 51, 53, 103, 104
Luce, Margaret, 138 n. 22
Luce, Sir William, 122, 124, 131, 145 (biog.)
Lutfi, Ashraf, 102

McCarthy, D. J., 101, 140
Macmillan, Harold, 91, 92, 114, 122, 135, 141, 146 (biog.)
Maher, Ali, 59
Majlis, 3, 10–14, 16, 69
Makins, Sir Roger, 38–9, 43
Mansfield, Peter, 91
Marlowe, John, 66
Maud, Sir John, 48
Mendelson, Maurice, 117
Middleton, Sir George, 85 n. 43, 145 (biog.)
Migrant labour, 137
Mohammad, Shaikh, 141
More James Carmichael, 6
Morocco, 126, 129
Mubarak al-Abdullah, General, 141
Mubarak (the Great), Shaikh, 4, 5, 20, 117
Mulla Salleh, Abdullah, 15, 26–7, 27 n. 76, 39
Mulla Salleh, Khan Bahadur, 11, 12
al-Munayyis, Muhammad, 13
Musaddiq, Muhammad, 37, 67
Muscat, 17, 18

al-Nabulsi, Suleiman, 89
Nahas Pasha, 41, 61
Najd, 5, 6
Nasser, Gamal Abdel, 57, 61, 73, 83
and Eden, Anthony, 62–3
and King Saud, 89
philosophy, 68, 81–2
and Shaikh Abdullah, 93
strikes, calls for, 69
and United Arab Republic, 82, 82 n. 18
National Assembly, 125, 130
National Culture Club, 69, 70
National Liberation Front, 130, 130 n. 110

Naturalization Decree, 138
Neguib, Muhammad, 61
Nehru, Jawaharlal, 64
Neutral Zone, 5, 33, 80, 109, 110 n. 71

Oil, *see* American Independent Oil Company; Anglo-Iranian Oil Company; Anglo-Persian Oil Company; Arabian-American Oil Company; Arabian Oil Company; British Petroleum; Iraq Petroleum Company; Kuwait oil; Kuwait Oil Company; Oil nationalism; Qatar Petroleum Company; Shell Oil
Oil nationalism, 66
Oman, 130
Ovendale, Ritchie, 29

Palestine, 59, 60
Palestinians, 60, 60 n. 15 n. 16
Parkes, R. W., 89
Parry, E., 19, 19 n. 24, 43
Patterson, Sir Maurice, 8
Pelly, C. J., 20, 29, 66, 144 (biog.)
and British companies, 51, 53, 54
and senior adviser, 49–50
and Shaikh Abdullah, 34, 39, 42, 43
and Shaikh Abdullah Mubarak, 42
and Shaikh Fahad, 41
Persian Gulf, 1–2, 66, 73–5, 74 n. 106, 80, 124, 133, 134
Piercy, Lord, 44, 127
Pirie-Gordon, C. M., 43–4
Plant, Phillip, 20, 20 n. 32, 24
Political Agent, 4–5, 15, 19
upgrading of, 48–9
Political Residency, 14
Political Resident, 5, 49 n. 84
Porter, A. N., 65
Portsmouth, treaty of, 111–12
Prior, C. G., 16

Qassem, Abdul Karim, 90, 91, 116–20, 118 n. 26, 121, 123, 128, 136, 141
al-Qatami, Jasim, 97
Qatar, 19–20, 24, 64, 72, 74
Qatar Petroleum Company, 19
Qusour, 12

Rapp, Sir Thomas, 45–6
Reilly, N. M. P., 35

Rendel, G. W., 7
Riches, D. H. M., 67, 93, 115–16
Richmond, J. C. B., 102–03, 104–05, 107, 110, 112, 127, 138 n. 24, 140, 144 (biog.)
  and Kuwait Fund for Arab Economic Development, 126, 128
  and al-Sabah, 35, 138
Rifai, Samir, 83, 85
Roper, H. L., 25
Rose, C. M., 29, 42, 50, 51, 52, 53, 66
Rothnie, A. K., 101, 126
Rowan, Sir Leslie, 76
Rumaihi, Muhammad, 137
Rusk, Dean, 120

Sa'ad, Shaikh, 140, 141
al-Sabah
  and Britain, 2, 36–7, 49, 65, 78, 79, 92, 100, 102, 121, 130, 131, 135, 136, 141–2
  challenges to, 97–8
  extravagance/corruption, 39, 42, 98, 138, 139, 140
  foreign exchange, requests for, 35
  intra-family relations, 6, 8–9, 11, 13–14, 19 n. 27, 39–40, 71, 98–9
  and the military, 140–1
  and Qassem, Abdul Karim, 116
  and reform, 98–9, 124–5, 139
  survival of, 1, 2–3, 71, 78, 98–9, 136–42
  symbolic role, 138
  see also under individual Shaikhs
Sabah al-Ahmad, Shaikh, 98
Sabah Salim, Shaikh, 71, 71 n. 85, 132, 141, 147 (biog.)
Sadat, Anwar, 67
Said, Ahmad, 97
al-Said, Nuri, 32, 39, 84, 86 n. 52, 87, 88, 90, 94, 117
Salim, Shaikh (r. 1917–21), 6, 7, 10 n. 53
San Remo Conference, 60, 111
Saud, King, 89, 110 n. 71
Saudi Arabia, 5, 32, 55–6, 59, 62, 68, 80, 88–90, 110 n. 71, 120, 123, 134
Serpell, D. R., 39
Shell Oil, 109
Shi'ahs, 12
Shuckburgh, C. A. E., 92, 93
Shwadran, Benjamin, 118
Siam, 101 n. 5
Silverfarb, Daniel, 111

Six-Day War, 134
Snell-Mendoza, Morice, 121
South Arabia, 130, 133
Southwell, C. A. P., 34, 35, 48, 56
Soviet Union, 65
Sterling Area, 30–1, 31 n. 101, 33, 36, 43, 44–5, 74, 75–7, 105–06, 136
Sterling Balances, 37, 105–06
Stevens, Sir Roger, 73–4, 75
Stewart, Michael, 133
Stockwell, A. J., 65
Strang, Sir William, 38
Sudan, 61, 111, 123, 126, 128, 129
Suez crisis, 29, 58, 61–5, 67, 68, 75, 76, 119, 120
Supreme Council, 98, 114, 125, 140
al-Suwaidi, Taufiq, 8, 85, 117
Syria, 59, 62, 64–5, 81, 89, 125, 140
  union with Egypt, 82, 82 n. 18

Templer, Sir Gerald, 83
Thorneycroft, Peter, 77
Touqan, Suleiman, 83
Transjordan, *see* Jordan
Trevelyan, Sir Humphrey, 116, 116 n. 10, 121–2, 123
Troutbeck, John, 17–18, 61, 87–8
Tunisia, 123, 126
Turkey, 3, 8, 62, 117

UNESCO, 110
United Arab Republic, 82, 82 n. 18, 83, 90, 97, 123, 126
United States of America, 48
  consul, 41, 41 n. 37
  co-operation with Britain, 119–20
  and Kuwait, 91, 120, 134
  and Lebanon, 91
  loan to Britain, 31 n. 101
  Marshall Aid, 30
  and Persian Gulf, 92
  and Saudi Arabia, 59, 120
  Six-Day War, 134
  Suez crisis, 62, 64
  and Syria, 81

Wafd, 59, 61
Walmsley, A. R., 103, 126
Warba, 6, 7, 87

Weightman, Hugh, 11, 15
Whishaw, C. P., 44
Wilson, Harold, 133
Woods-Ballard, B., 18
Wright, Sir Michael, 74, 75, 82, 84, 86, 87, 88, 90

Yemen, 62, 140

Zahlan, Rosemarie Said, 137
al-Zaim, Husni, 140
Zionism, 60